IMAGES
of America

HIGHLAND COUNTY

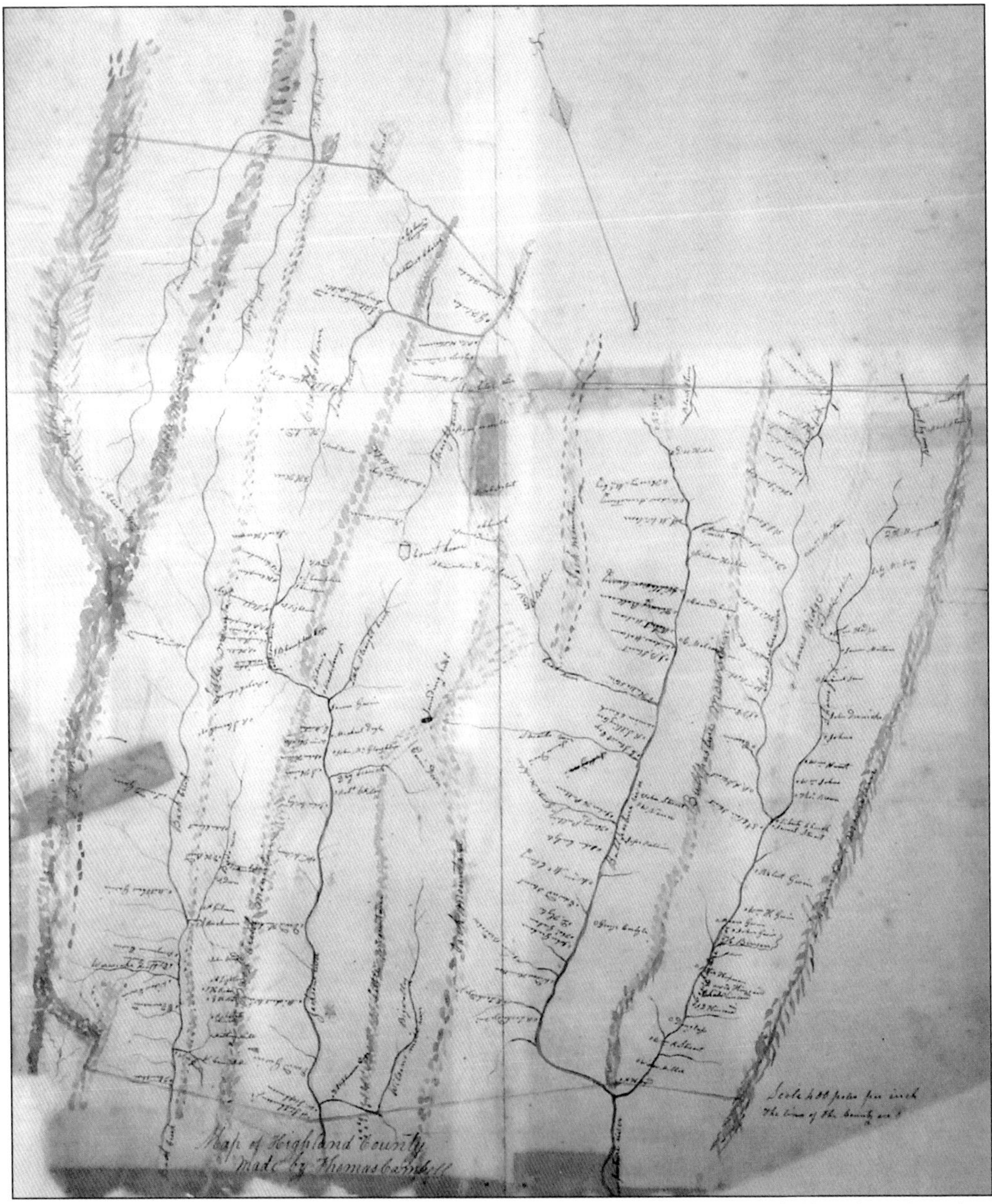

Upon the creation of Highland County, Virginia, in 1847, Thomas Campbell authored its first map. In October of that year, Campbell, as county surveyor, drew out the boundaries of the new district. This map hung for years in a back corner of the courthouse. The Highland County Historical Society had the map restored and returned to the courthouse. (Courtesy of the Highland County Historical Society.)

ON THE COVER: L. W. Shoulder and Company was one of two store buildings in Doe Hill. Known as the Jones Store for many years, the building is still visible on entering the town from the south on Route 654. The signs on the storefront advertise school supplies and shoes, among other items. (Courtesy of the *Recorder*.)

IMAGES
of America

HIGHLAND COUNTY

Chris Scott

ARCADIA
PUBLISHING

ISBN 978-0-7385-5331-3

Published by Arcadia Publishing
Charleston, South Carolina

Printed in the United States of America

Library of Congress Catalog Card Number: 2007934443

For all general information contact Arcadia Publishing at:
Telephone 843-853-2070
Fax 843-853-0044
E-mail sales@arcadiapublishing.com
For customer service and orders:
Toll-Free 1-888-313-2665

Visit us on the Internet at www.arcadiapublishing.com

To Heather and Ruth, my heart and my soul. Without you there is no book, and no joy in life. I love you both more than I ever thought possible.

To the people of Highland County: the born-heres, the come-heres, the left-heres, the coming-heres, the insiders, the outsiders, the new, the old, the pillars, and the additions. To us all. We are Highland County, and this is our story.

CONTENTS

Acknowledgments

One person alone did not create this book. Many have contributed, though their names might not be on the cover. Folks opened up their albums and told me stories, memories of past events, and the legends of a county.

I need to thank many individuals for their donations of photographs. Lyle and Georgianne Maloy Hull were very willing to share. Georgianne has done considerable family genealogical research and is very active in passing everything on that she's learned. Libby Woods Hefner and Janet Mullenax have both collected a treasure trove of family photographs and stories. They make these histories come alive.

Robin and Nancy Vance were the first to step forward with their collection of family photographs and were incredibly helpful chasing down stories. Sarah Samples, Nancy Mullenax Hedges, and Kyle and Karla Obaugh opened up their collections to me and were willing to loan out some one-of-a-kind items. I am grateful.

Kent Botkin is a voracious collector of Highland County memorabilia. His passion has led him to put together a breathtaking collection of photographs, postcards, artwork, and more. He proved to be an asset of immeasurable importance. Thank you.

Highland County is blessed to have some tremendously helpful organizations. The Highland Center, particularly Betty Mitchell, provided useful help. Anne Adams and the *Recorder* newspaper were incredibly supportive.

Crysta Stanton, Lorraine White, and the entire Highland Historical Society are on a mission. They have committed themselves to preserving Highland County's past. The Highland County Museum and Heritage Center is a benefit to our community. In addition, the Family History Research Library is an excellent resource for investigation and study. The society has provided desk space, advice, listening ears, contacts, editing, and so much more. Lorraine spent hours editing and fact checking. Bless you.

Finally, I need to acknowledge my wife, Heather, and sing her praises from these mountaintops. Thank you for your support not only in the writing of this book, but in everything. I love you.

INTRODUCTION

How do you tell the story of a county? Where do you begin? What do you include? Is the entire story of a place and a people contained in dates and names? Is *story* the same thing as *history*? I started this book planning to tell the entire history of Highland County, Virginia, through photographs. Quickly I realized that there was no way to do that in this space. This book is not and cannot be an exhaustive telling of the history of Highland County. Rather, this is a telling of the story of Highland County. It is an attempt to provide snapshots of the area, both literal and figurative. These are the incidents and moments of daily life that do not often make it into traditional history texts.

We all tell history from our own vantage points. We pick different stories to emphasize and inconvenient facts to bury. History looks different from where each of us stands. When I started to collect the photographs and stories, I found it fascinating to spend time with people. I heard wonderful tales; even those with no photographs painted vivid pictures for me. So many people stepped forward to tell me a story or episode that I *had* to include. Many times I heard the phrase, "You simply cannot tell the history of Highland County without talking about . . ." And I know some people will look upon the finished product and discount the whole work because there are not enough images from their end of the county, because there are not enough of their lineage or too many of someone else's, or for any number of reasons.

Nevertheless, this story is the story of a county. Whether one was born here, has come here, or has in fact never been here, it is a common narrative. Stories of life and love and work and family are common themes no matter where one resides.

Highland County has a rich heritage. In his 1911 work *History of Highland County Virginia*, Oren F. Morton begins his examination of the region with a description of the physical geography. He lists the longitude and latitude of the county, pointing out that the district covers the northern end of the Appalachian Mountains with Shenandoah Mountain on the east and the Allegheny Front on the west. For Morton's purposes, that was a perfect place to begin. And he certainly has a point. The mountains that surround the county have affected the region and its people. We are affected by the remoteness they inflict and the barriers they erect.

This is a county set apart by physical boundaries. One arrives by crossing Virginia's mountains. The remoteness impacted the way the economy and social structure evolved. People relied on themselves and watched out for neighbors. People traded and bartered and grew what they needed.

There are five valleys that make up this region: the Alleghany Valley, the Blue Grass Valley, the Monterey Valley, the Bull Pasture Valley, and the Cow Pasture Valley. Also, 10 streams originate in Highland County and then develop into much larger and better-known rivers. In fact, a Hightown barn was constructed so that rain falling on the roof either washed down one side and fed into the James River or ran off the other, becoming the Potomac River. This farm is known, for obvious reasons, as Dividing Waters Farm. According to legend, the three "pasture" rivers were named by hunters who killed a buffalo calf at the first stream, calling it the Calfpasture River; a cow at the second, naming it the Cowpasture River; and a bull at the third, christening it the Bullpasture River.

Both German and Scotch-Irish first came to this region in 1745, about 30 years after the major flight of Scotch-Irish from Ulster, Ireland. The Scotch-Irish leaving Ulster were mainly Protestant immigrants from Northern Ireland. This year also dates to just over 30 years after German immigrants began to make homes in America in earnest.

Highland County's official birth date is March 19, 1847, when the bill to create the district out of pieces of Bath and Pendleton Counties passed the Virginia legislature. Designated the county seat, Bell's Place, a small town of only a couple of buildings, was later renamed Monterey in tribute to Pres. Zachary Taylor's victory in the Mexican-American War. Bell's Place was "a patch of woods and laurel thickets on the saddle between the two straight creeks." Getting its name from the height of its mountains, Highland County lays claim to be one of the highest average elevations east of the Mississippi River.

Despite its remote location, Highland did not escape the grip of war. Young people from the county have participated in each of this country's wars. When the Civil War exploded, more than 500 men enlisted in the effort. Most of those young men signed up for their native Confederate army, though some did go north and fight for the preservation of the Union. Bloodshed came to the region when Gen. Thomas "Stonewall" Jackson fought and won the first victory in his famous Valley Campaign on Sitlington Hill overlooking McDowell on May 8, 1862. McDowell Presbyterian Church was used as a hospital during the battle, which claimed almost 800 casualties. This event is reenacted every other year at the McDowell Battlefield Days.

One of the very first silent movies to be filmed on location was shot in rural Highland County, in the Blue Grass Valley. *Tol'able David* was released to wide acclaim in 1921, winning a "medal of honor." Still shown annually in the county during the Maple Festival, it is considered a classic.

The population of Highland County has varied in number over the years. Varying from approximately 4,000 when the county was formed in 1847 to the high of 5,647 in 1900, the population stands at roughly half of that 1900 number in the 2000 census. This fosters a well-connected community. Neighbors are not faceless people, but rather good friends, classmates, and possibly relatives.

One of the southernmost counties in the nation to make Maple syrup on any appreciable scale, Highland County has hosted a large Maple Festival every March since 1958. The festivities attract many thousands of visitors during the two weekends. Maple syrup has proven an economic and culinary mainstay for the county.

History and story are two aspects of any community. Our pasts need to be explored to help determine where we choose to go in the future. The telling of these histories should be a communal project. Communities together should decide what makes up their joint DNA. We need to celebrate both the facts and the stories of a place. The photographs displayed herein attempt to do that.

Very few of these photographs were professionally done. Most are simply everyday people chronicling everyday events that, in the process, become something extraordinary.

One

GETTING THERE
CARS AND ROADS

When settlers first arrived in the area to be known as Highland County, there were no real roads. Trails existed over the mountains, but wagon roads were not carved out until much later. On one occasion, a pastor moving into the area was forced to bring only what a pack mule could carry, leaving all his furniture behind. Gradually, though, roads started to wind through the county. Their creation was driven by commerce and necessity, as early roads in Highland County were toll roads, with a fee for use.

Road improvements are inexorably tied to the development of Highland County. The Staunton-Parkersburg Turnpike was completed in the 1840s with Claudius Crozet as chief builder. Construction began at each end and met in the middle in 1847. In fact, it can be argued that Highland County was formed because of the road. The Bell family quickly divided its land into town lots for sale, and Bell's Place was born. A French native and recipient of the Legion of Merit from Napoleon personally, Crozet taught engineering at West Point before becoming principal engineer and surveyor for Virginia.

The Staunton-Parkersburg thoroughfare opened up the county to the outside world like never before. Improved and paved in the early part of the 1930s, the turnpike, officially known as Virginia State Route 250, continues to serve as a vital conduit for goods and people into and out of the county. Highlanders with cars and trucks were able to capitalize on the newly improved roads by carrying livestock, crops, dry goods, and more over the mountains, widening their commercial base.

For many years, taking a trip over these roads was a special event or rare business opportunity; today travel both within and outside Highland is an everyday occurrence, with many residents going over the mountains daily to work or school. Transitioning from an oddity and luxury to an assumed necessity, cars have changed and developed along with society as a whole. In addition to the automobile industry, a failed attempt was made to bring railroads into Monterey in the early 1900s.

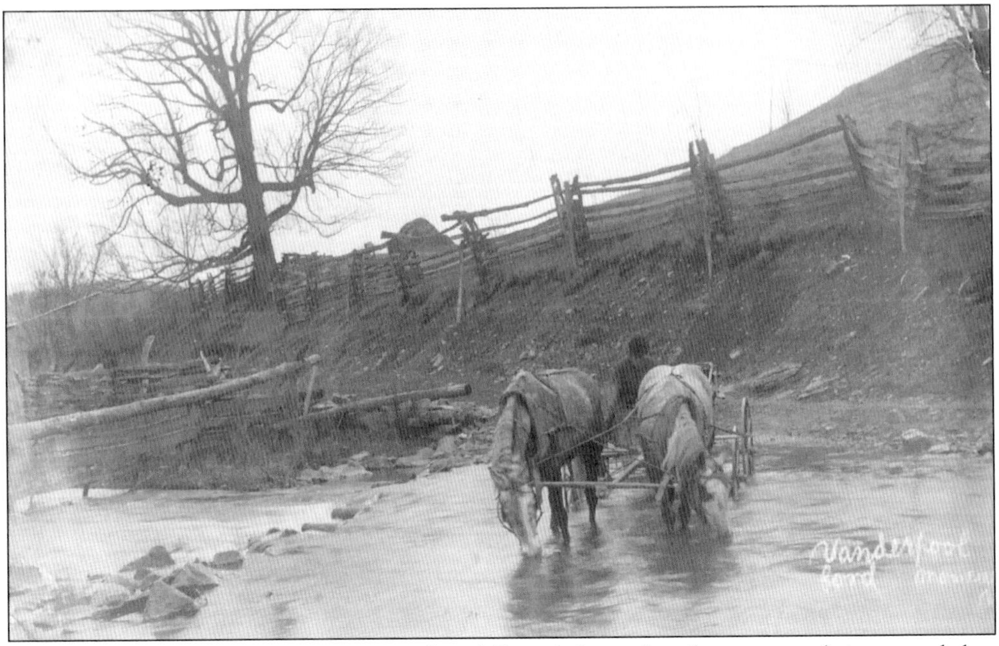

Early roads in Highland County quite often followed the paths of streams and rivers, and that meant an occasional crossing. This ford in Vanderpool is located south of Monterey on Route 220. Dutch explorer John Vanderpool discovered the gap that was later named for him. Taken in 1913, this photograph shows transportation prior to both modern roads and automobile traffic. (Courtesy of Kent Botkin.)

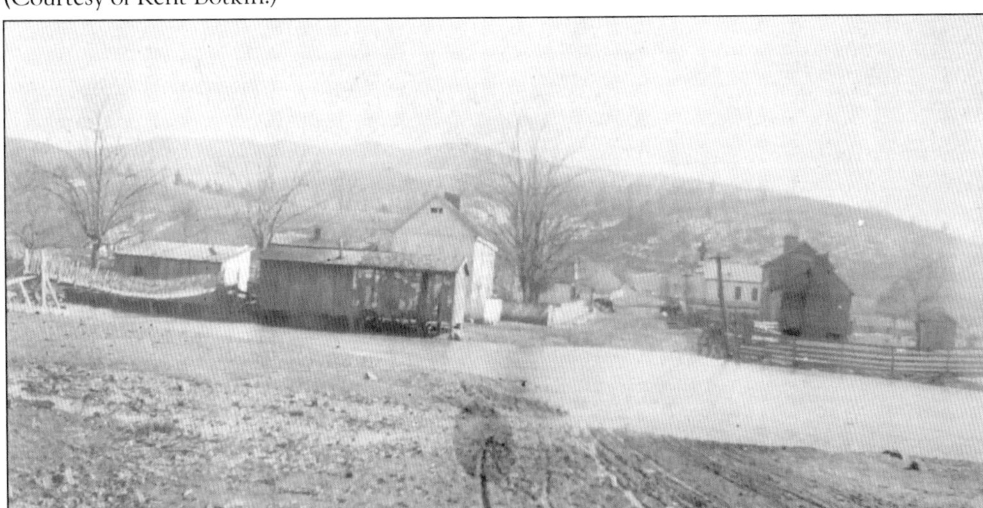

Headwaters, as the name implies, sits at the headwaters of the Potomac River. Shown here in 1900, before the construction of the bridge over Shaw's Fork, the existing road was already widely used. Headwaters Presbyterian Church, constructed by Lank Simmons this same year, is the white clapboard structure ahead on the right. (Courtesy of Kent Botkin.)

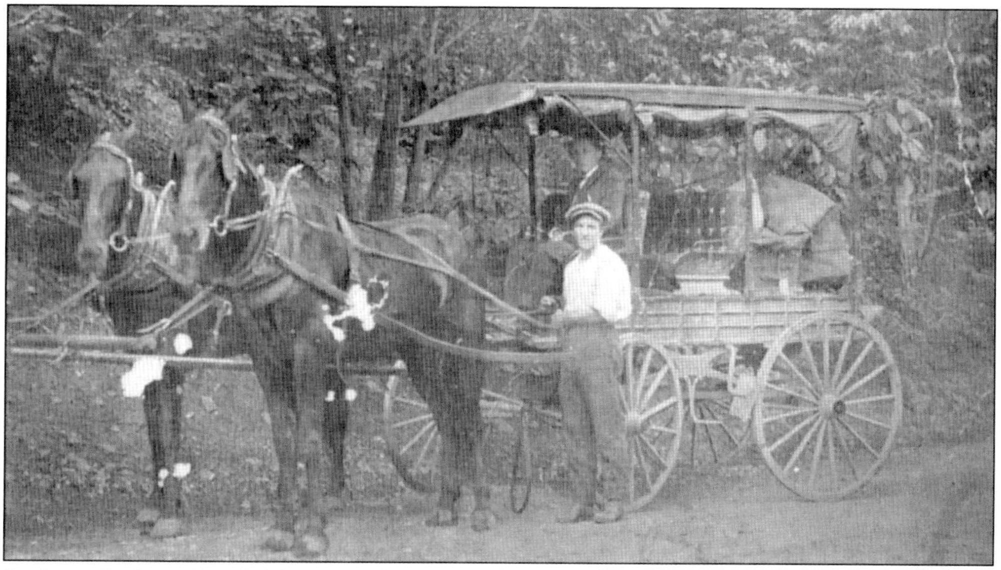

In the early days of mail delivery in the county, letters and packages were carried from Staunton to Monterey in this horse-drawn hack. Owing to the remoteness of the county, mail delivery was an extremely valued service. The first post office, called Bullpasture, opened in Highland in 1830. It later became known as Clover Creek. (Courtesy of Kent Botkin.)

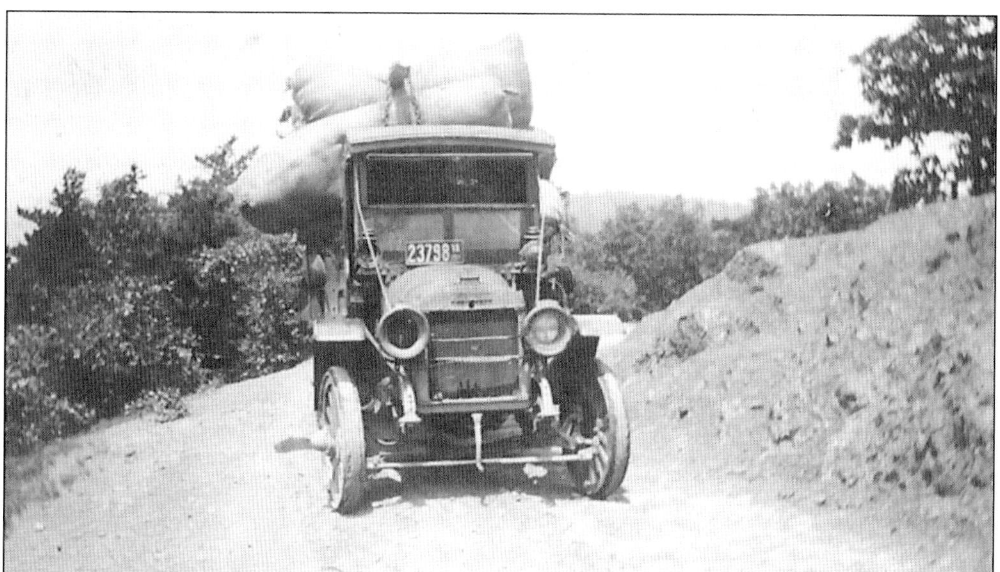

Trucks helped to make commerce easier by increasing the amount that could be taken to market and lessening the time it took to get there. This truck travels up Shenandoah Mountain with a load of wool in 1919, before the surfacing and widening of Route 250. (Courtesy of Kent Botkin.)

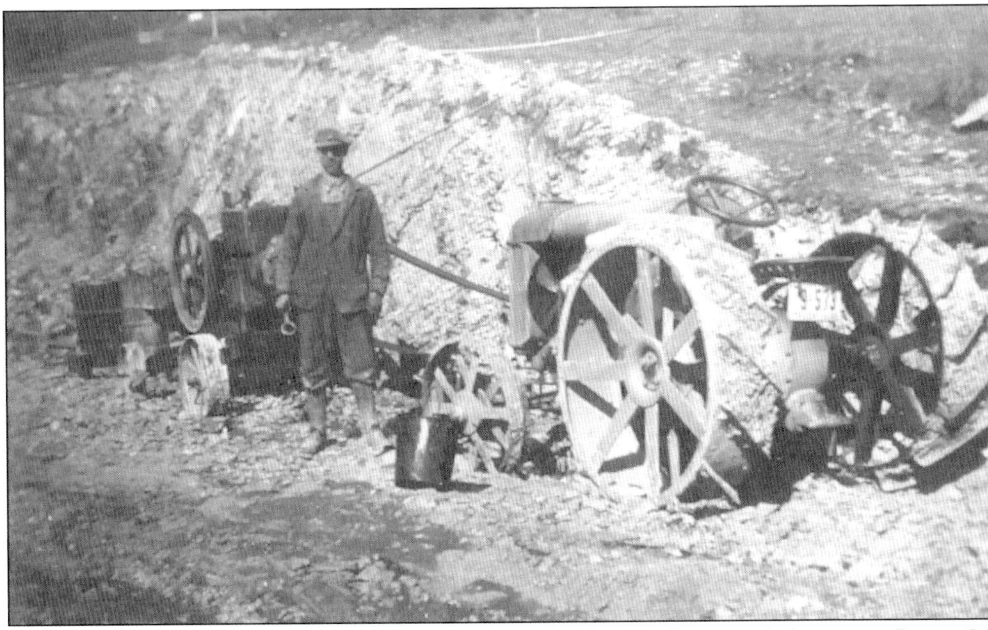

Martin Botkin, a road crew supervisor, stands next to his machinery while paving Route 84. Botkin supervised several convict crews that worked from sunup to sundown on this road-building project. Dr. Fox from Monterey was brought into witness convict beating to ensure safety. Botkin was born on March 23, 1887, near Palo Alto and died on April 21, 1959, in Staunton, Virginia. (Courtesy of Kent Botkin.)

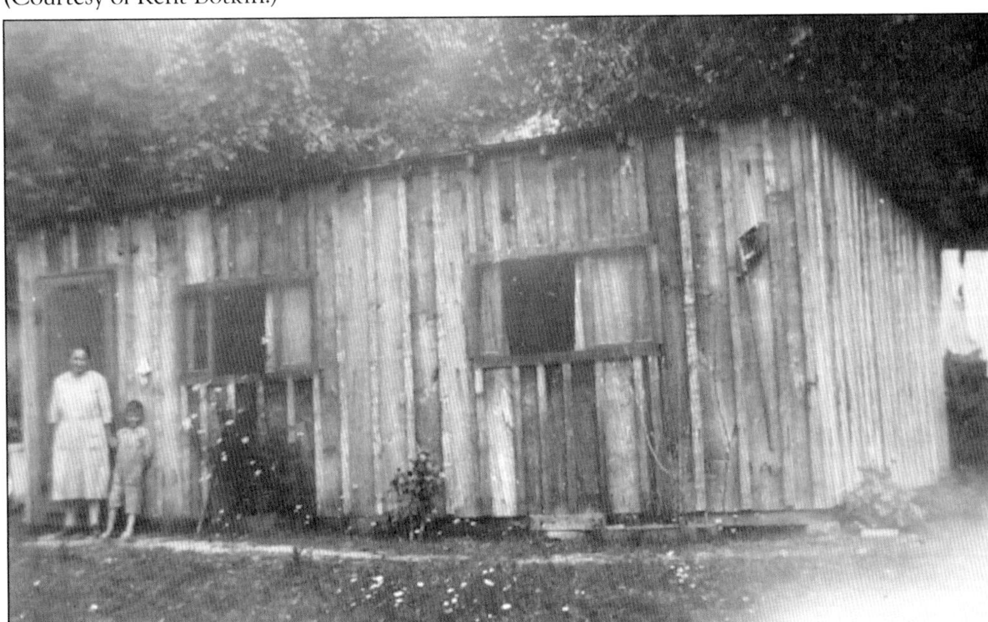

Martin's wife, Jane Botkin (left), stands with the couple's five-year-old son, Ray (right), in front of their portable home in the Mill Gap area. The home was easily dismantled to allow the family to travel with Martin. As the roads moved ahead, so did the shanty. Convict crews built many of the roads in the county. The family still owns a twig rocker crafted by a convict as a gift for Ray. (Courtesy of Kent Botkin.)

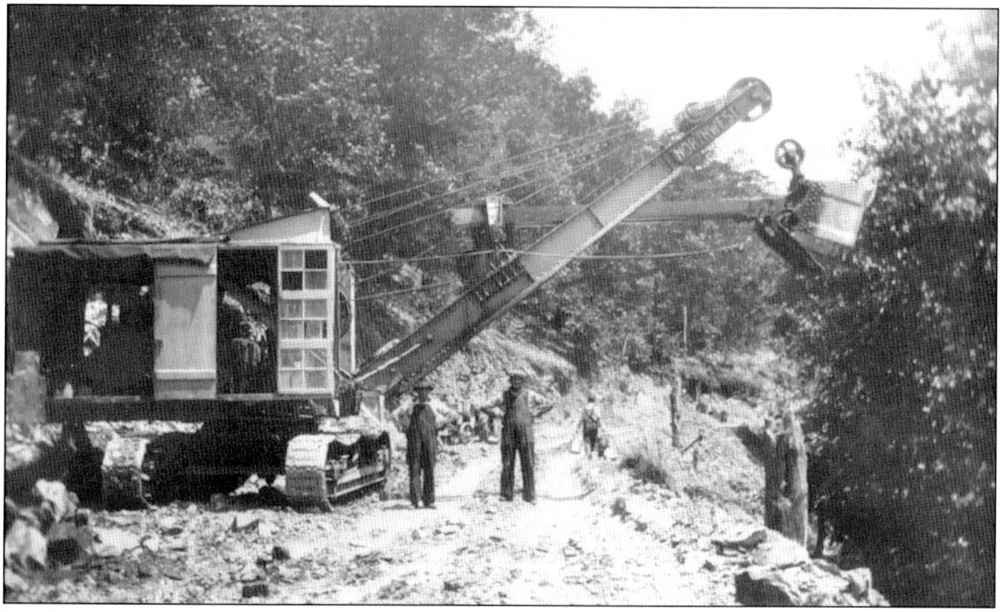

Road construction has always been demanding work, but paving Highland County's roads proved to be even more so. Two unidentified workers pose on Bullpasture Mountain while surfacing Route 250, also known as the Staunton-Parkersburg Turnpike. A young boy walks away into the background, carrying what appears to be a lunch pail for the workers. (Courtesy of Kent Botkin.)

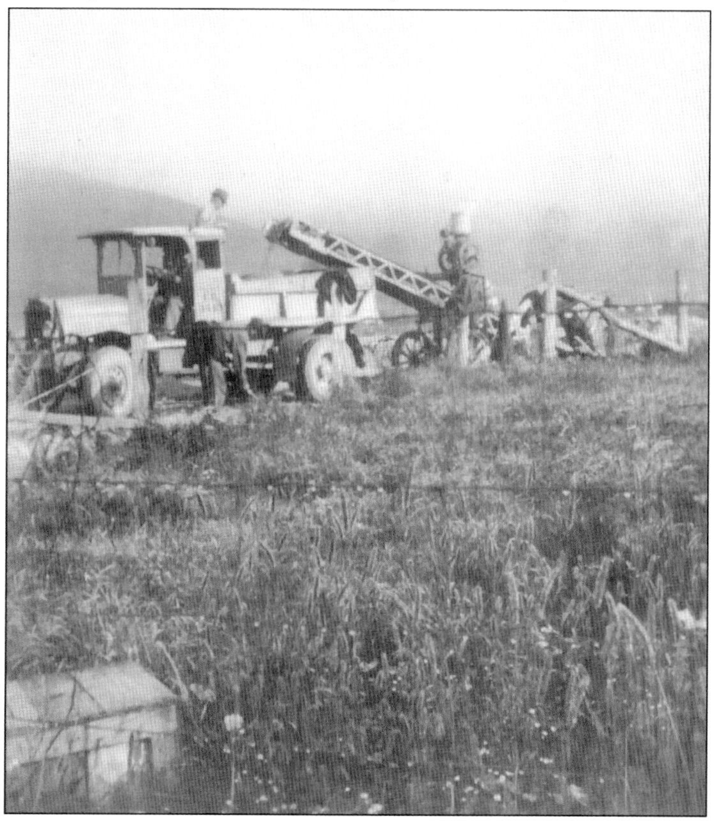

The highway department brought road modernization in the 1920s and 1930s. Road crews graded and surfaced many roads in the county during this time, including this section of Route 84 in the Mill Gap area, seen in the late 1920s. Crews used a system of trucks, conveyor belts, and physical labor. (Courtesy of Libby Woods Hefner.)

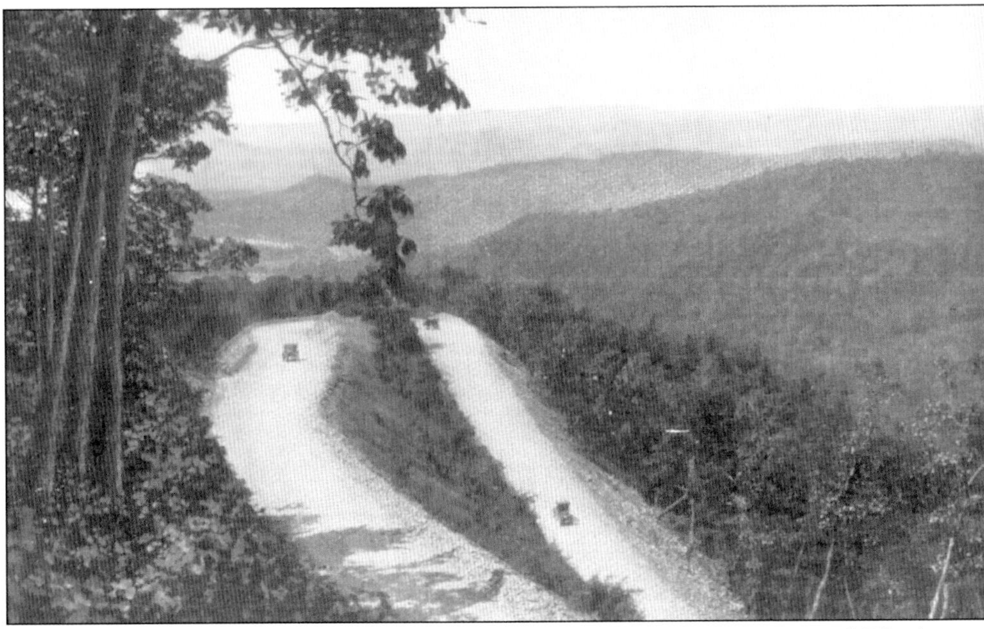

To cover the steep grades on the roads in Highland County, some turns are required. This hairpin turn on the west side of Shenandoah Mountain follows the more natural incline of the mountain. Capturing a busy traffic moment for the time period, this view was taken before the paving of the Staunton-Parkersburg Turnpike. This photograph was featured in *National Geographic* magazine. (Courtesy of Lyle and Georgianne Maloy Hull.)

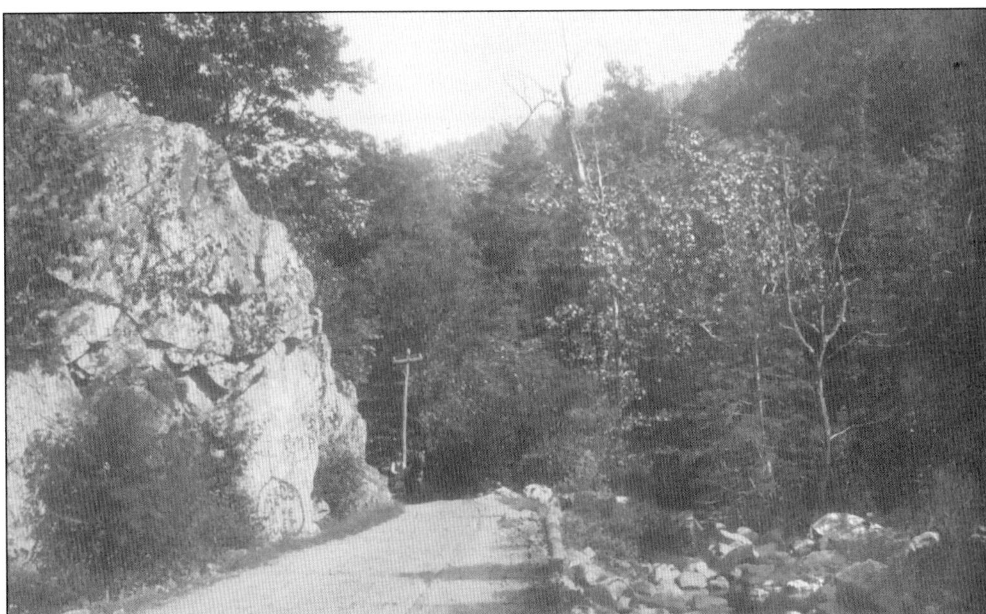

In 1909, bored residents painted graffiti on an outcropping of rock. Just west of McDowell on Route 250 (the Staunton-Parkersburg Turnpike), Standing Rock is another popular photographic subject. This rock cutout has been depicted on numerous postcards mailed all over the world. (Courtesy of Kent Botkin.)

In a style reminiscent of Bonnie and Clyde, two young people from Mill Gap pose in front of a prized luxury possession. Dewey Richardson and Ethel Mullenax Rexrode stand by Dewey's automobile. (Courtesy of Janet Mullenax.)

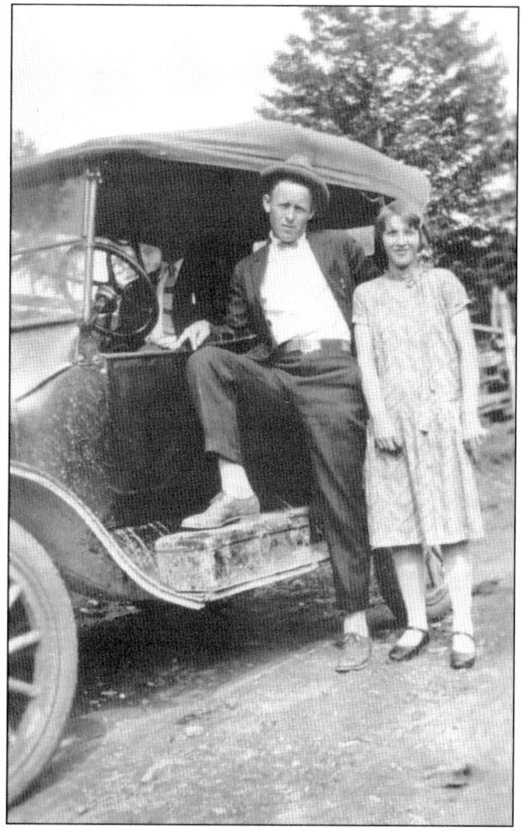

The purchase of a new automobile was a social event in Highland County. Here Howard Colaw shows off his car to friends. Pictured from left to right are Glen Hammer, Geneva High, Opal High, Howard Colaw, Opal High (cousin to the first Opal High), Eva High, and Winnie Hevener. (Courtesy of Janet Mullenax.)

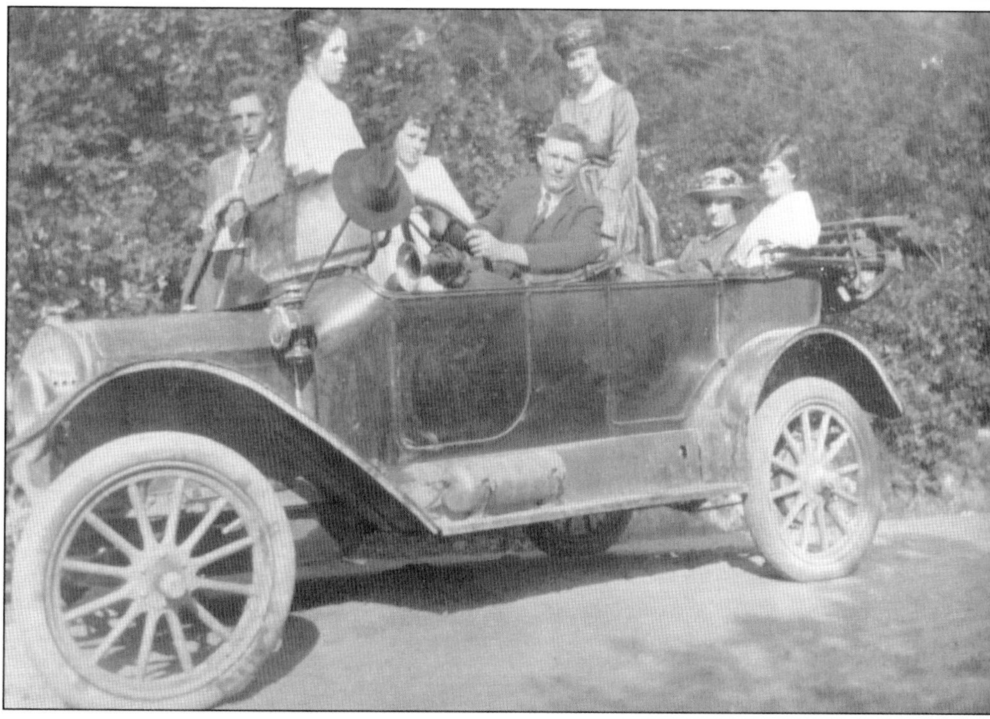

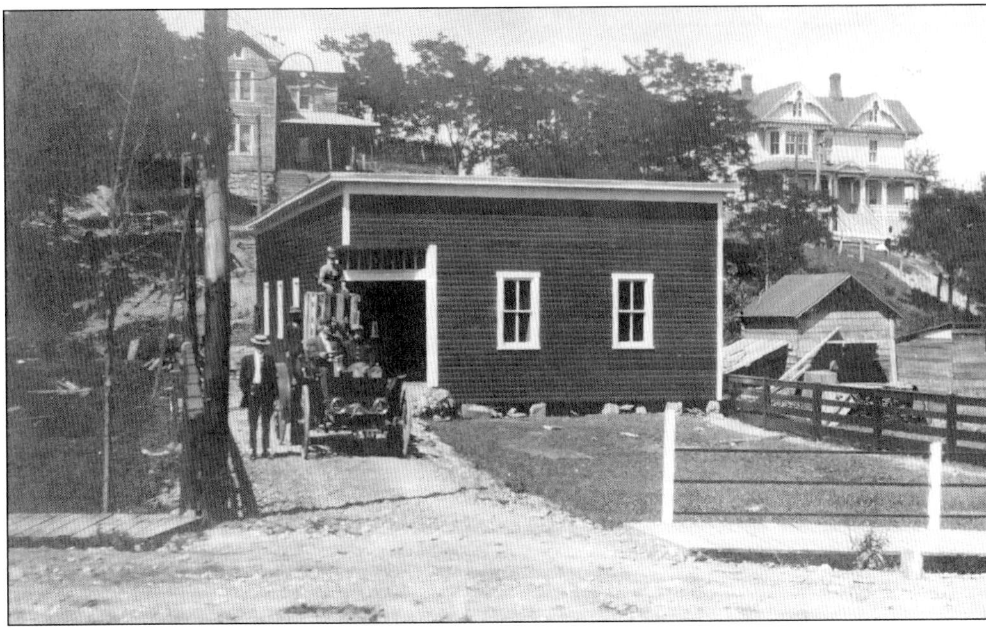

With each technological step, other needs are inadvertently created. The advent of the automobile opened up a new career field for the enterprising individual in Highland County. William F. Kyle started his garage in Monterey in 1913. Later Kyle added an automobile dealership. The banner promotes the 1916 Dort at a price of $650. The Dort was only produced for nine years, from 1914 to 1925. Apparently Kyle was an early seller, as this was only two years after the automobile line was introduced. The proud men standing around in their white shirts are unidentified. This building (below) later housed Hammer Chevrolet. Kyle owned a few other businesses in Monterey, including the Monterey Water, Light, and Plumbing Company. (Courtesy of the *Recorder*.)

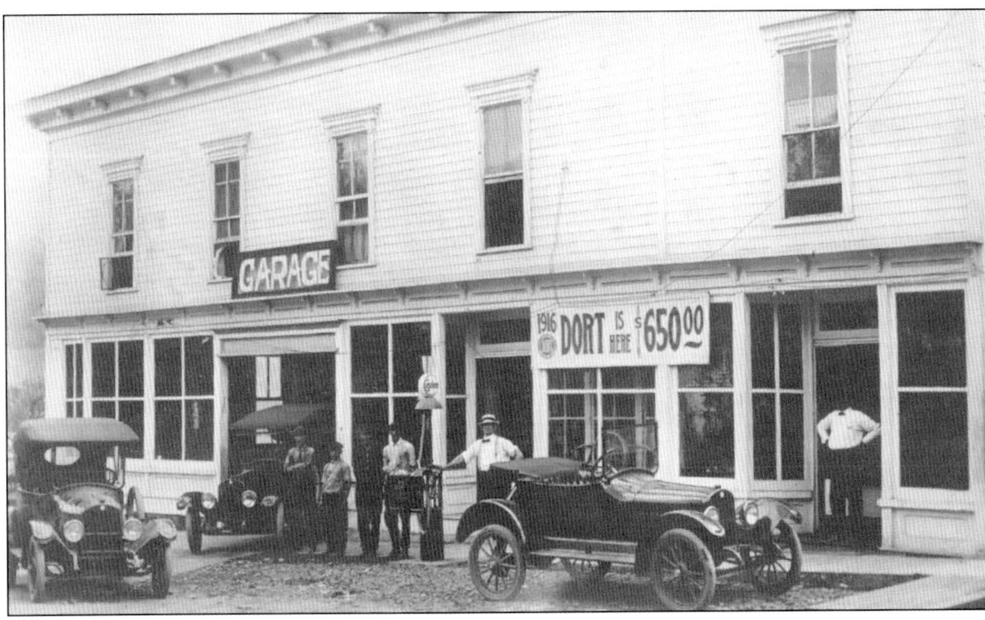

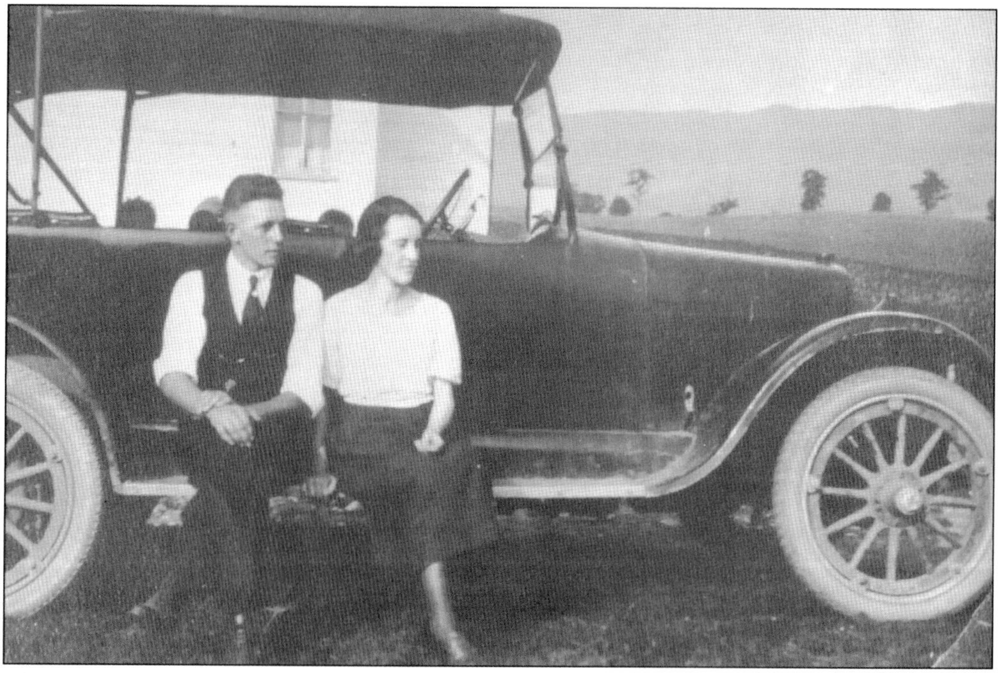

Chaperones and automobiles were components of many Highland County dates in the early part of the 20th century. In this photograph, taken at the Highland County Poor Farm before their marriage, Glen Hammer and Monna Mullenax Hammer pose while Monna's siblings peek over the far side. After the couple wed, Glen opened Hammer Chevrolet in Monterey and served as sheriff for 24 years. (Courtesy of Janet Mullenax.)

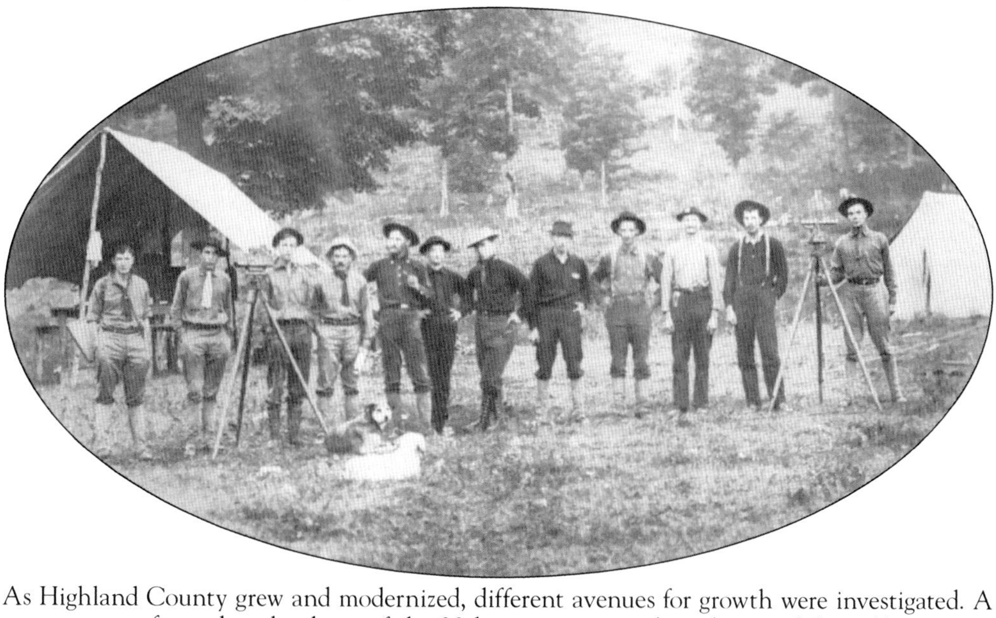

As Highland County grew and modernized, different avenues for growth were investigated. A company was formed at the dawn of the 20th century to explore the possibility of bringing a railroad to the county. Metzger's Corps of Engineers pose with their surveying equipment on Sunday, September 20, 1906. The idea of the railroad was abandoned soon after this photograph was taken. (Courtesy of Kent Botkin.)

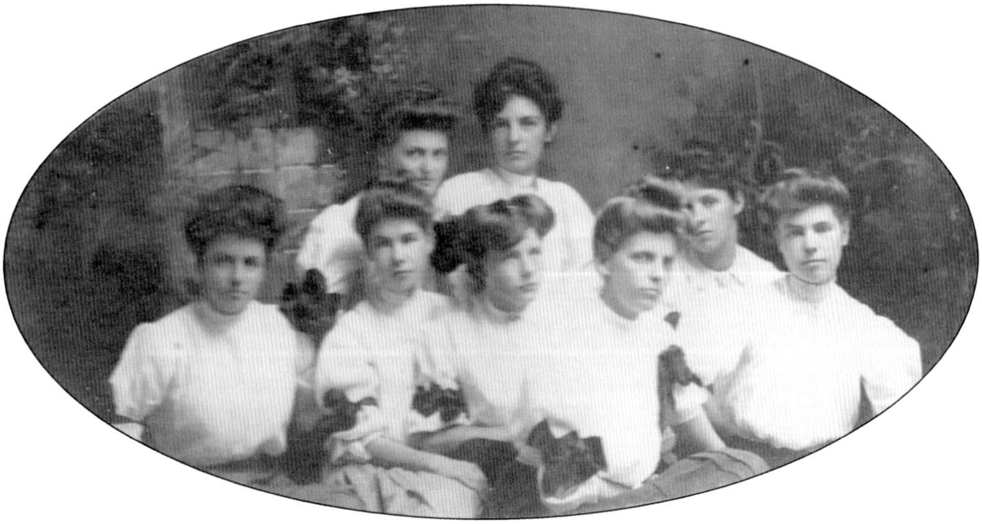

Then as now, a good man is hard to find—and a visiting man is not to be passed up. Unidentified women show their sense of humor in this set of before and after photographs from 1905. In the above photograph, they are poised and looking confidently into the future. In the below photograph, they pretend to have received word that the proposed railroad has fallen through and the engineers surveying for the railroad would be leaving town. (Courtesy of the *Recorder*.)

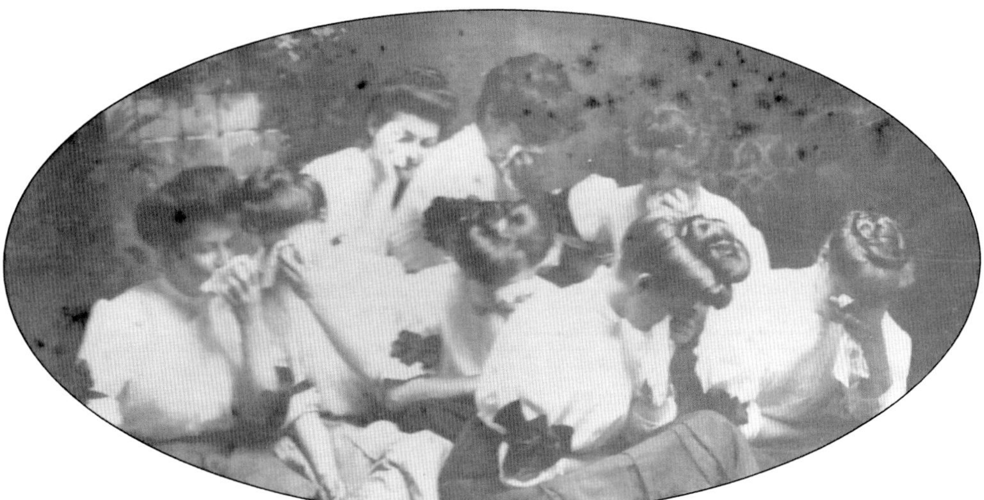

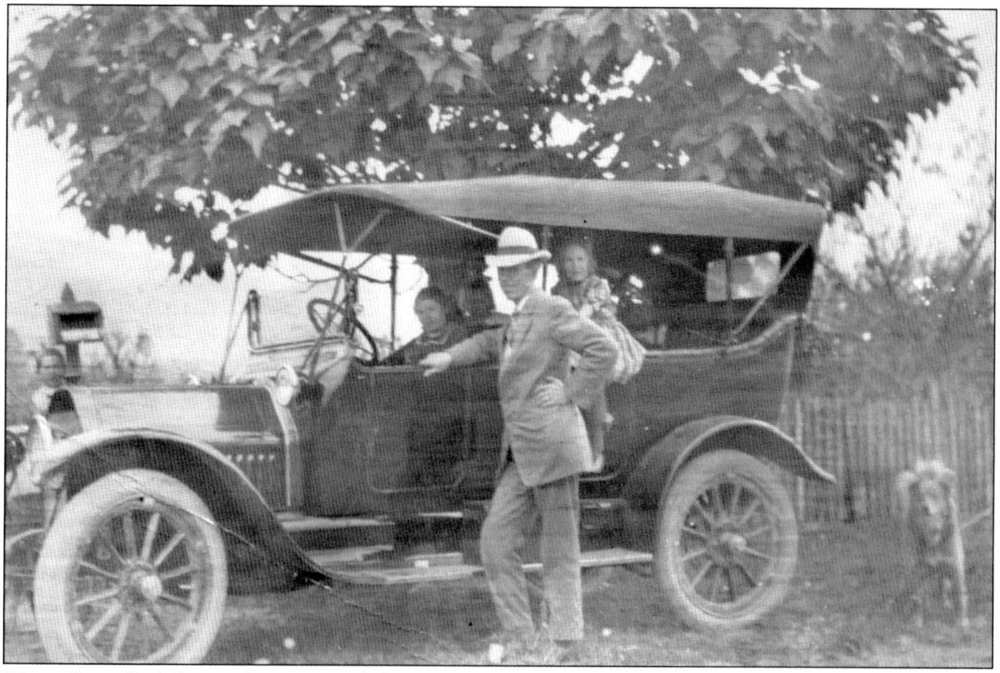

Harry Lunsford (center) poses with his car. Many automobiles, such as this one, were shipped by rail to Durbin, West Virginia, retrieved, and brought to Highland. A prominent member of the Highland County community, Lunsford ran stores in Hightown and Monterey before his appointment as a county trial judge by Judge Joseph A. Glasgow in 1924. (Courtesy of Robin and Nancy Vance.)

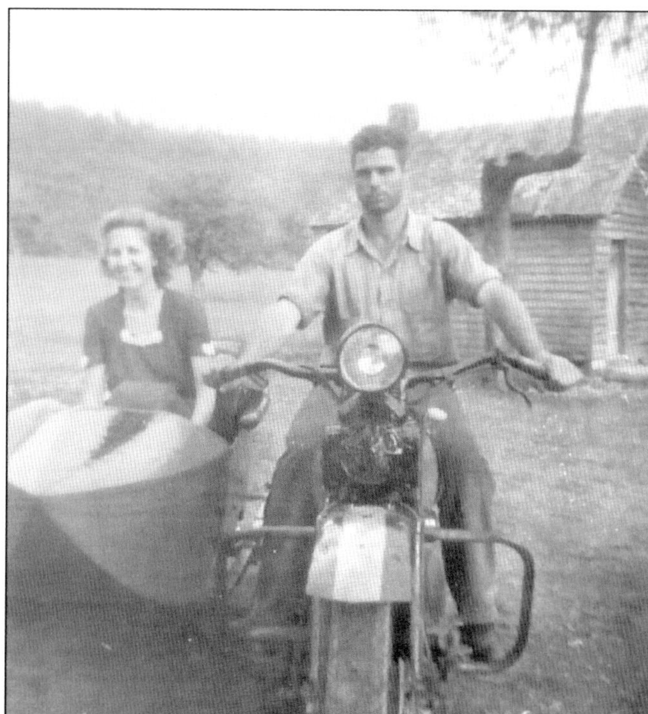

Transportation in Highland County means getting there any way one can. Motorcycles have been popular in rural America for many years due to their maneuverability, low entry cost to purchase, and small operating expense. Here Irene Vance and "Buge" Neil go for a ride. (Courtesy of Robin and Nancy Vance.)

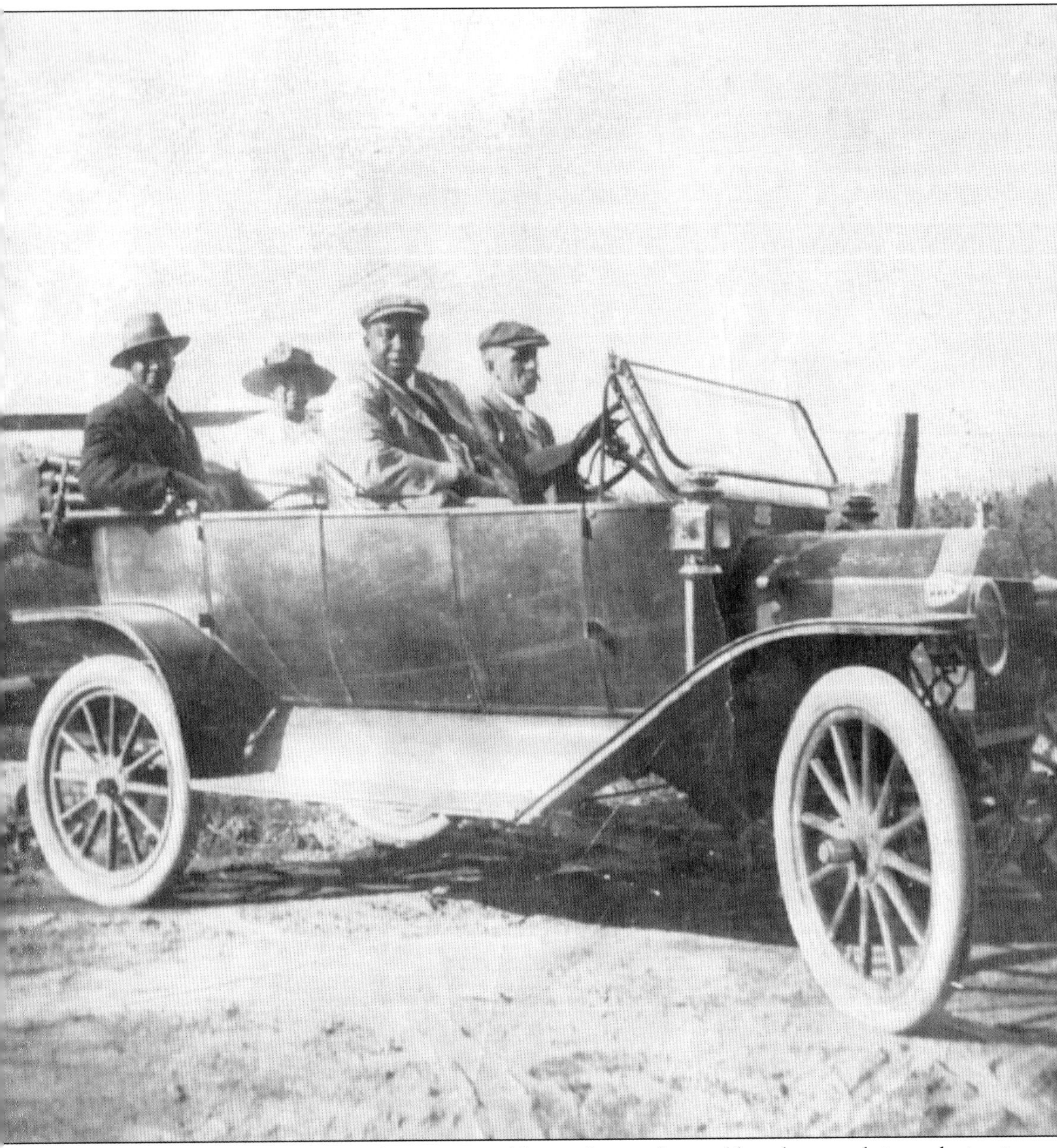

This 1913 Model T Ford, with its convertible top down, changed hands several times during its stint in Highland County. Charles Smith (third from left) was at least the third owner of the vehicle. Though he owned it for many years, he did not actually drive it, as he never learned to operate an automobile. Smith kept the vehicle in a specially made barn at his home in Anthony's Burg, outside of McDowell. Whenever he wanted to go to town, he would have others drive him. Smith purchased the Ford from William Henry Swadley, owner of Swadley's Garage in McDowell (who had also never driven the car), with money made from selling ginseng. Swadley bought the vehicle from Forrest Hepler of Millboro. Smith's heirs eventually sold the car to Graham "Peachie" Hicklin for the then-reasonable price of $7. Hicklin owned the car for many years, driving it to the 1939 World's Fair in New York, before eventually reselling the Ford to a collector who restored it. (Courtesy of Kent Botkin.)

Two

Seeing Highland's Landmarks
Places, Views, and Events

An early-1900s tourist flyer made the claim that Highland County offered "no mosquitoes, tramps or fevers" and was the "home of the buckwheat cake and maple syrup, fat cattle and blue grass." From scenes of unspoiled mountain ridges and charming country streets to quiet past battlefields, Highland County is an area ripe for postcards.

The county has a history of tourism. In 1860, the town of Sugar Tree Grove was renamed McDowell in honor of Gov. James McDowell, Virginia's governor from 1843 to 1846, who frequently vacationed in the area. Legendary inventor Thomas Edison, along with Henry Ford, Harvey Firestone, and others, visited Bolar Springs in August 1918. They are only a few of a long line of tourists, both prominent and common, to explore the majestic views of Highland County.

A little-known area, Anthony's Burg was created immediately following the Civil War, when Robert Sitlington gave a large section of land to a group of former slaves for the development of a community. The name comes from Hebert Anthony, the gentleman placed in charge.

Known by its nickname, "Virginia's Little Switzerland," Highland County boasts the highest average elevation of any county east of the Mississippi River. The area's mountains, with a highest elevation of 4,291 above sea level at Sounding Knob, are very much a scenic wonder. Wander down a country road or a town street, and everything looks as if it were arranged by a movie company. Homes and stores remain from the early days of the county. A historically significant battlefield still sits calmly, largely untouched by modern hands.

Landmark moments often help define a community. Highland County has had its share of just such moments. Monterey experienced a major fire in 1947 that turned the county courthouse to an empty shell. War came to Highland in 1862, when North met South in a bloody clash. These are the events and places of a county.

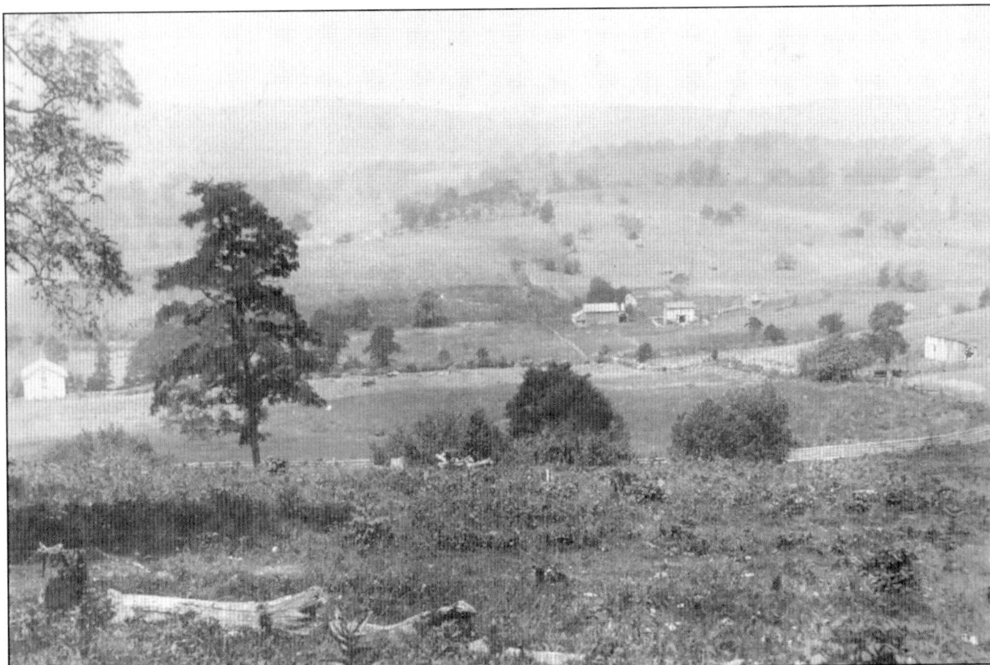

Just north of Blue Grass, Key Run, among other things, is home to New Church Methodist Church. New Church is a former United Methodist church that was used as a youth center in the 1970s and 1980s. (Courtesy of Kent Botkin.)

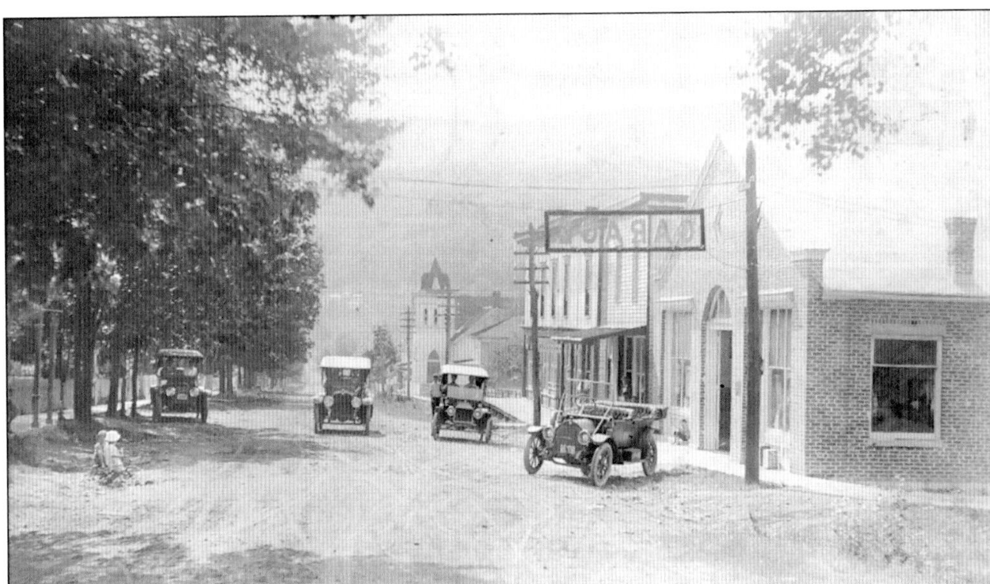

In 1914, Main Street in Monterey was not yet paved, and traffic patterns do not seem to be too strict either. Children play at left, close to the road, in this eastward view down Main. Monterey United Methodist Church stands at the center of the photograph. (Courtesy of Kent Botkin.)

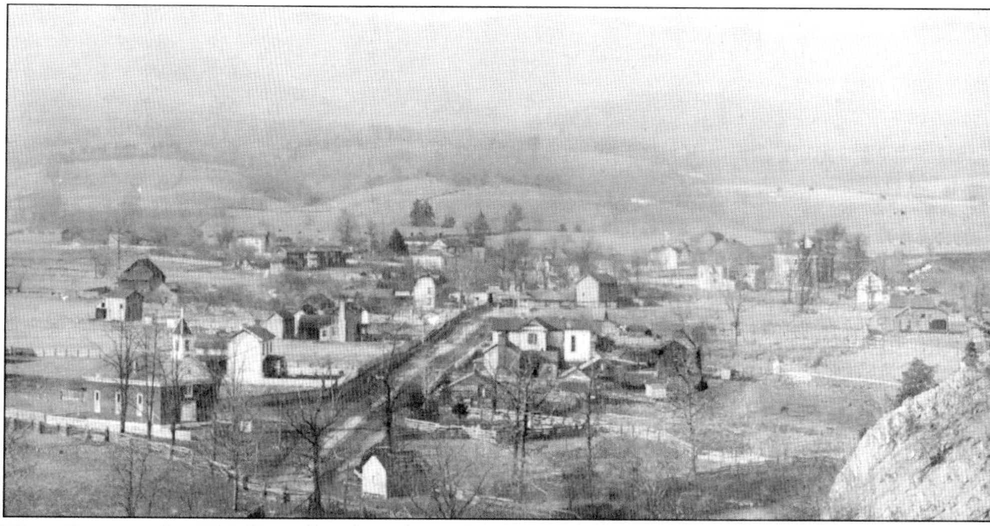

This photograph of McDowell, taken from the top of Sitlington's Hill in 1907, affords a unique view of the town from the McDowell battlefield. The small village unfolds to the west along the Staunton-Parkersburg Turnpike. McDowell Presbyterian Church appears on the left, with the manse just beyond. (Courtesy of Kent Botkin.)

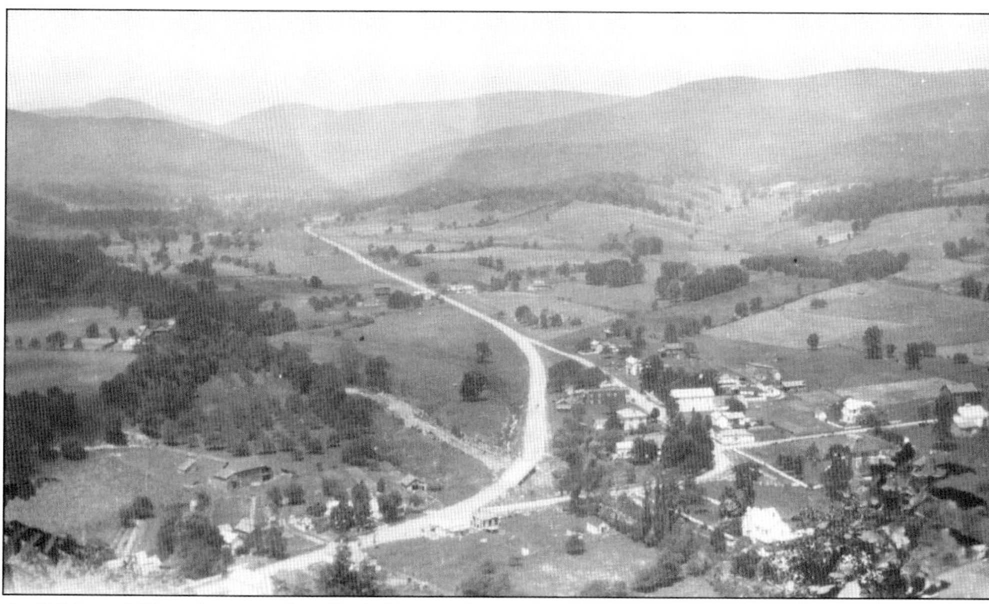

As fields unfold to the west, Swadley's Garage (center) and McNulty's Store (across the road) occupy the commercial section of town. This view gives some perspective on the layout of McDowell and the path of roads through the village. Swadley's was demolished for Obaugh Funeral Home, and McNulty's is known today as Sugar Tree Country Store. (Courtesy of Lyle and Georgianne Maloy Hull.)

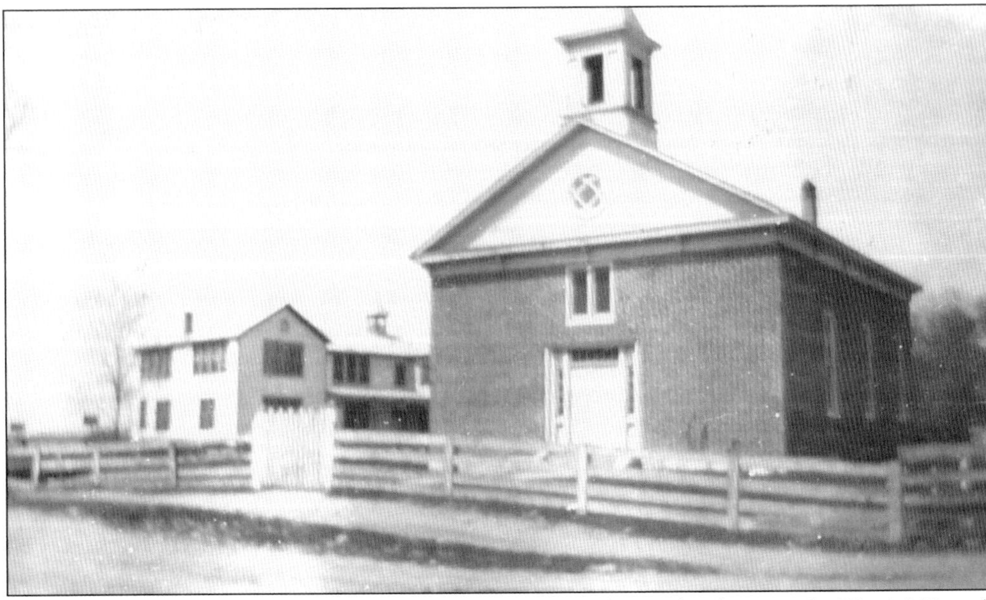

Two iconic images of McDowell stand on the corner in this early photograph. The McDowell High School (left) burned in 1948. McDowell Presbyterian Church (right), with its wood fence, has stood since 1856, when it was built to replace an earlier building just west of the current one. (Courtesy of Lyle and Georgianne Maloy Hull.)

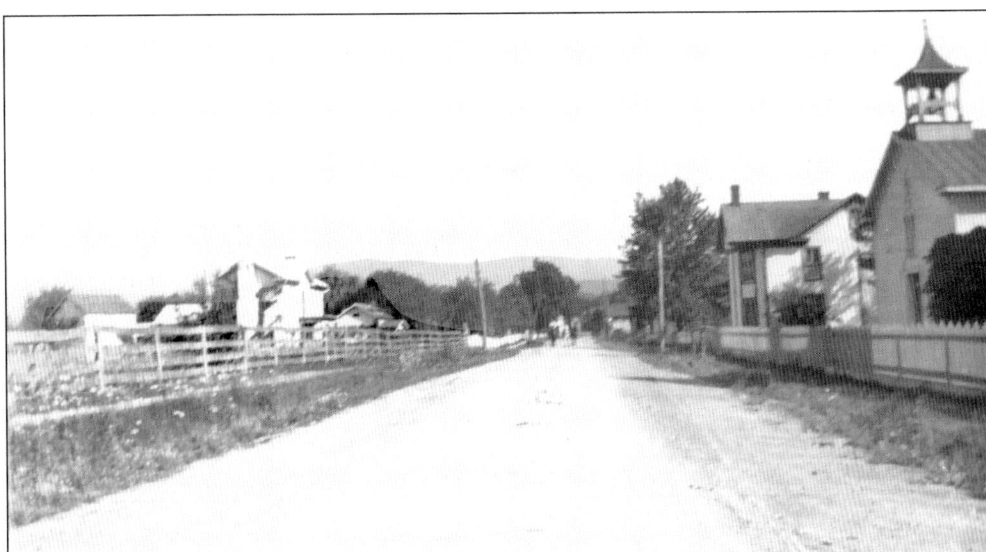

On Main Street in McDowell, McDowell United Methodist Church (right) faces Route 250. The William Helms House stands directly beside the church. The empty field (left) is now occupied by the post office. The church was given a new brick veneer in 1956. Many of the buildings displayed here are still standing. (Courtesy of Lyle and Georgianne Maloy Hull.)

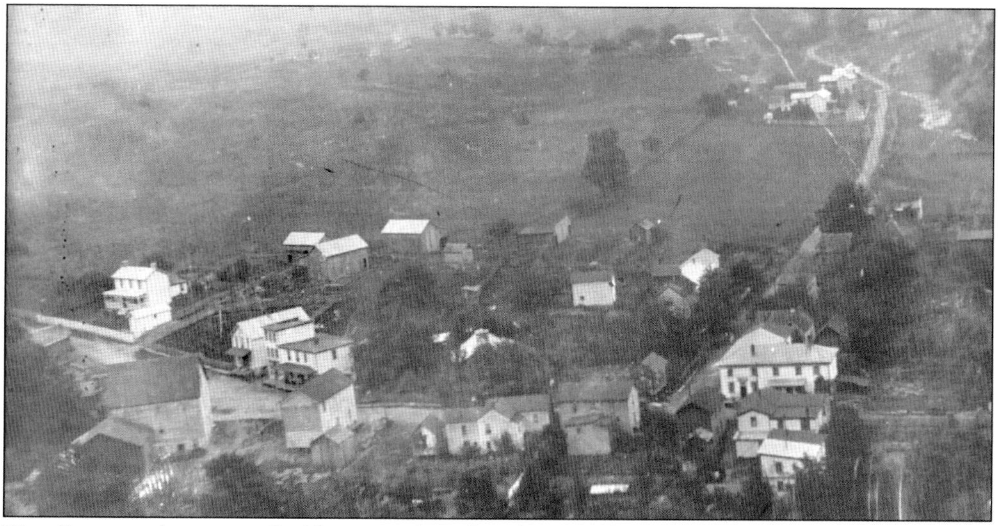

Blue Grass was known as Crabbottom when this photograph of the town's layout was taken. The name was changed in 1945, after servicemen and women returning from overseas convinced the town fathers that outside the county the name was not regarded with a high opinion. (Courtesy of Janet Mullenax.)

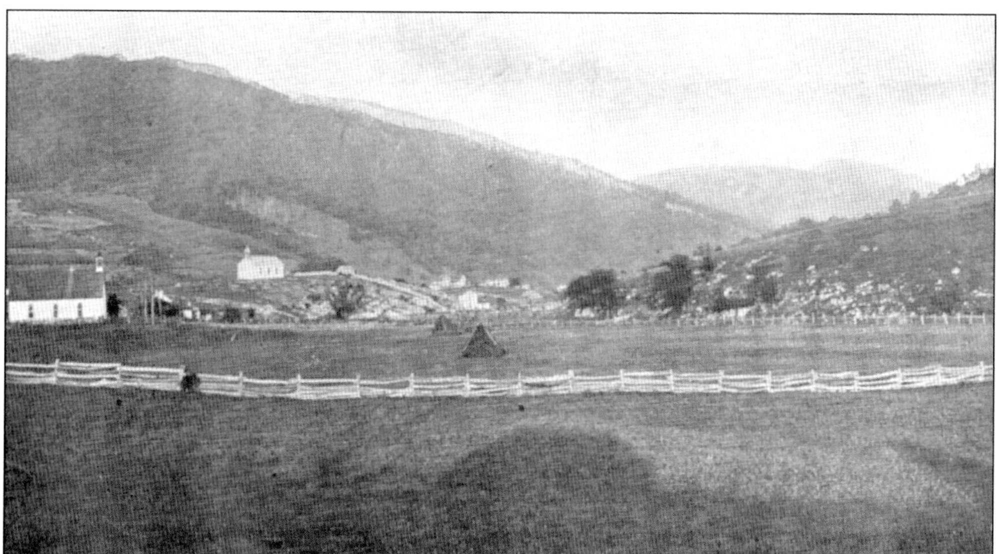

This scene of the Crabbottom Valley, later known as the Blue Grass Valley, reveals the mountainous nature of Highland County. The rock outcropping seen rising toward the left, nicknamed "Devil's Backbone," is a well-known landmark. (Courtesy of the *Recorder*.)

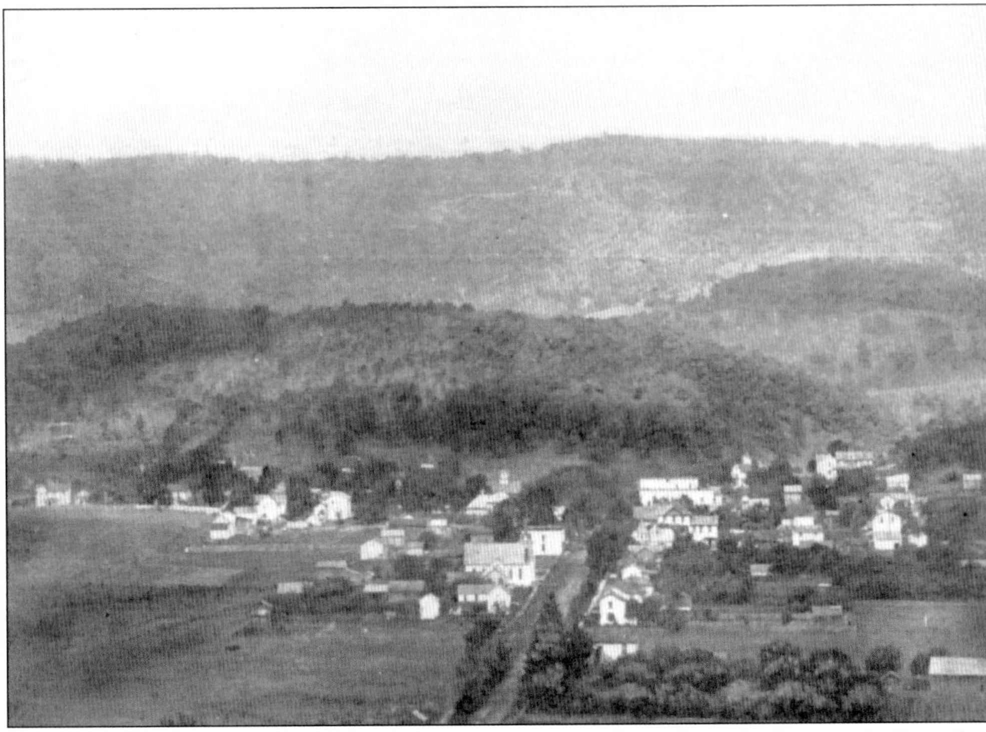

The county seat of Highland County, Monterey is shown in this early-1900s photograph. Recording a population of 246 for the 1900 census, the town had fallen to 158 by the time of the 2000 census. For many years, Monterey has laid claim to being the highest and smallest county seat in Virginia. (Courtesy of Tate Swecker.)

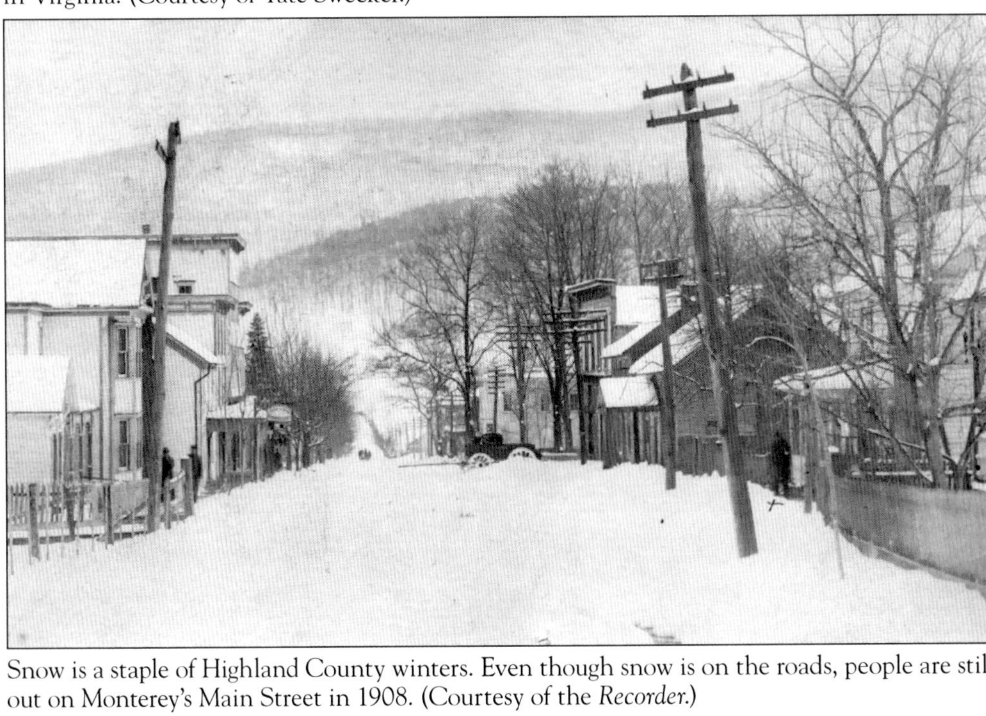

Snow is a staple of Highland County winters. Even though snow is on the roads, people are still out on Monterey's Main Street in 1908. (Courtesy of the *Recorder*.)

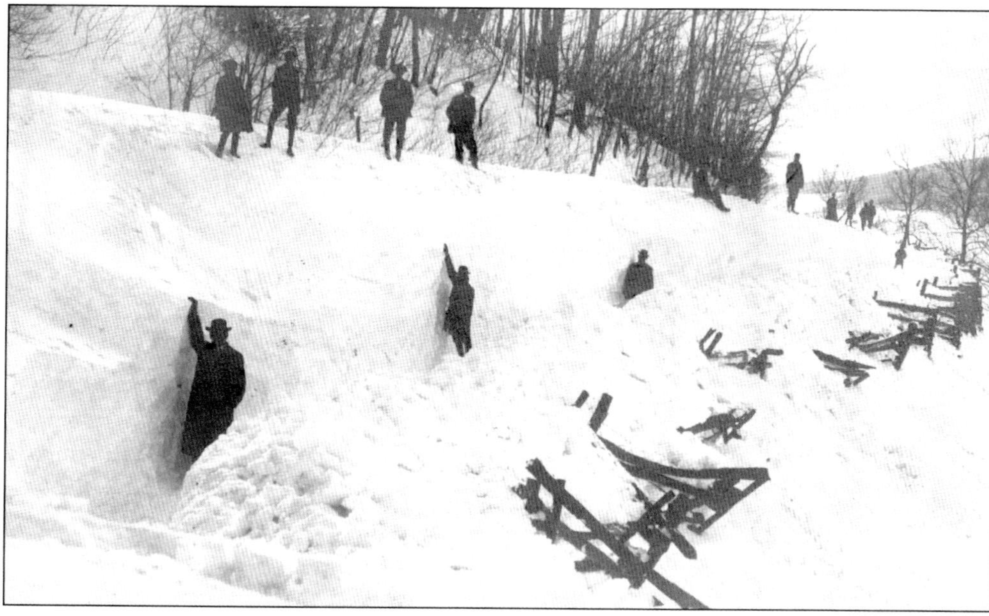

In the mountains, snow can quickly become a major issue. This winter storm in February 1908 produced drifts of snow from 4 to 20 feet in depth for over two miles. These men stand in and on the drifts to demonstrate the amount of snow that hit the west side of Monterey Mountain. Snows such as this one were more common at one time. Many records exist of roads being impassable for weeks at a time every winter before the opening of Virginia Department of Transportation branches around the county. The average annual snowfall in the county at the start of the 21st century was 37 inches. (Courtesy of the Highland County Historical Society.)

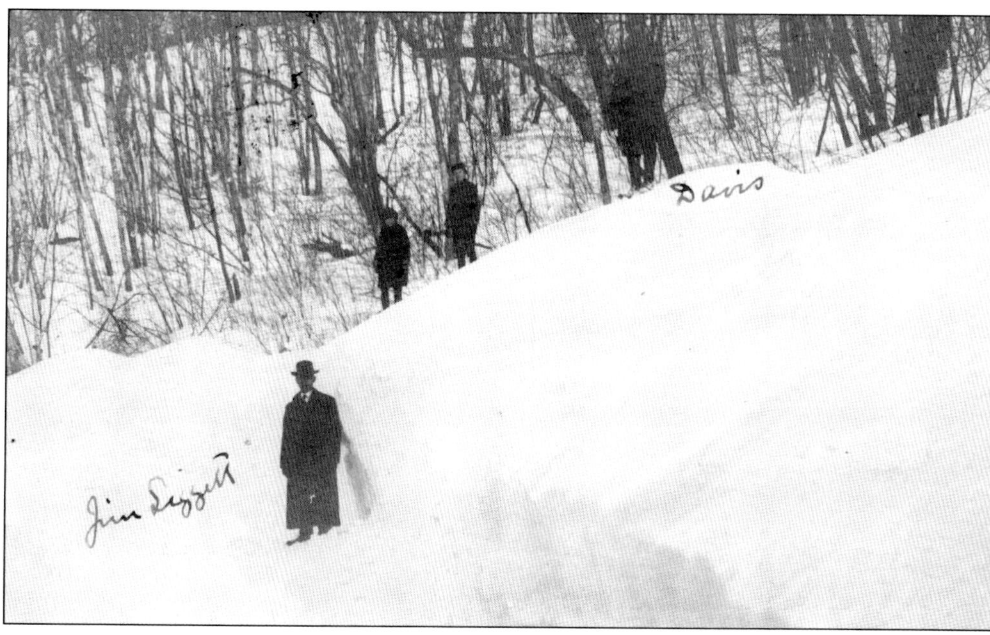

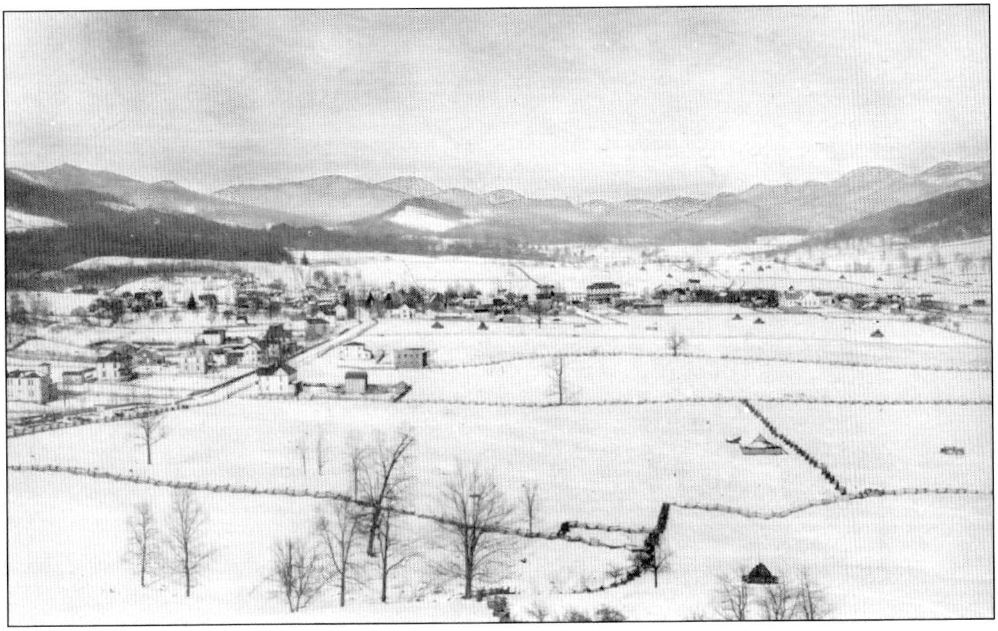

Each season in Highland County brings a different look. These two views of Spruce Street look north toward Monterey. The foliage displayed in the summer (below) contrasts with the empty trees and snow of the winter (above). Monterey looks remarkably the same in these early-1900s photographs as it does 100 years later. Split-rail fences were commonly used to divide fields. (Courtesy of the *Recorder.*)

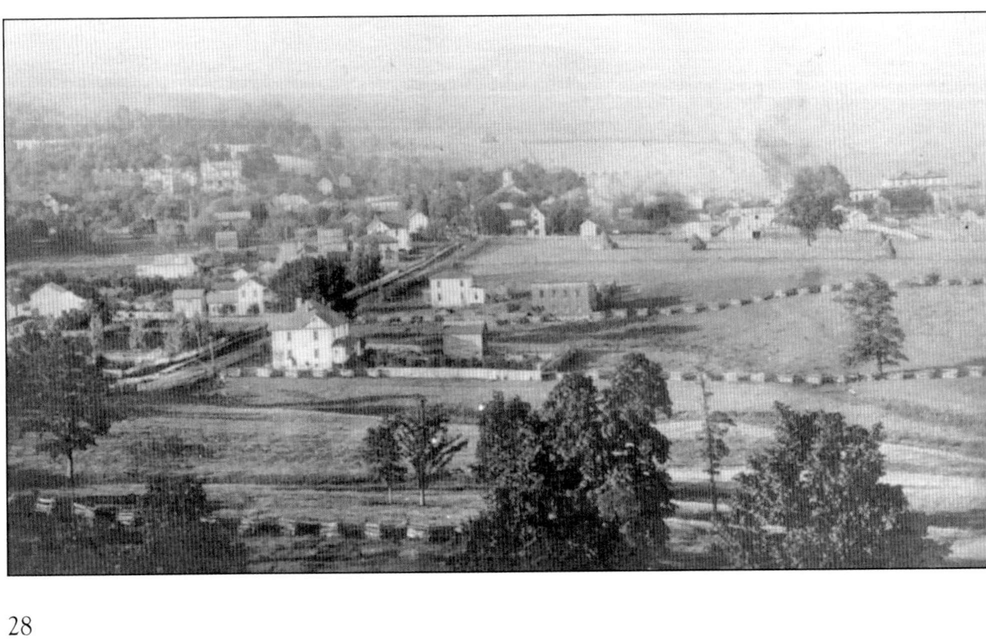

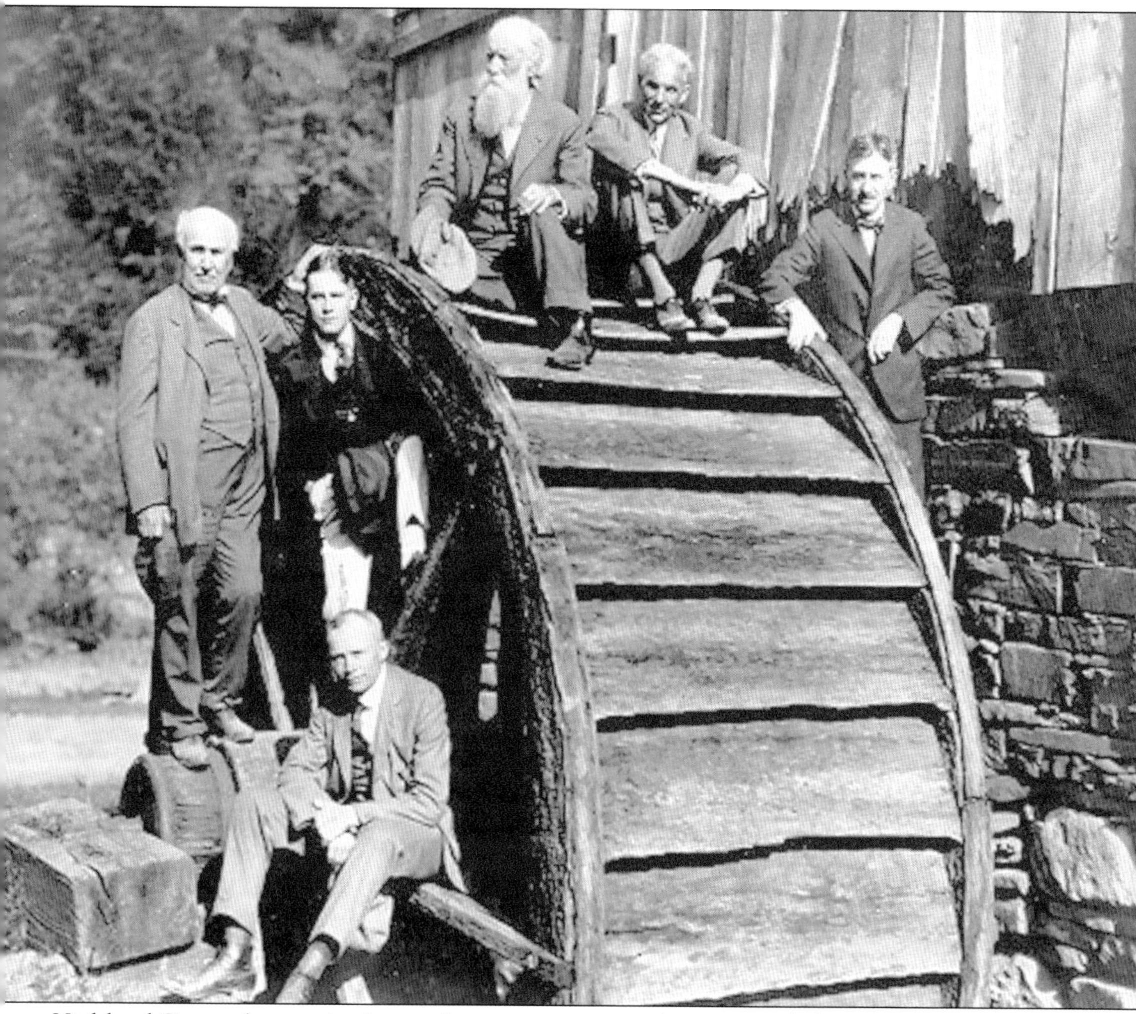

Highland County has received many famous visitors over the years, including, from left to right, Thomas A. Edison, Harvey Firestone Jr., R. J. H. Deloach (seated), John Burroughs, Henry Ford, and Harvey Firestone Sr. This group christened themselves "the Vagabonds." They visited Bolar Springs and stopped to pose on the water wheel at the old Evans Mill on August 23, 1918. During the same trip, the Vagabonds supposedly had dinner at the Hotel Monterey, which later changed its name to the Highland Inn. The group put on a lot of miles on this trip. They drove from Pennsylvania through West Virginia to Tennessee and then over to North Carolina, Virginia, and Maryland. It was one of the group's first such trips. Edison and Ford were instrumental in creating the idea and practice of automobile camping, which eventually became the recreational vehicle industry. Highland County is a part of that history. (Courtesy of the U.S. Department of Interior, National Park Service, Edison National Historic Site.)

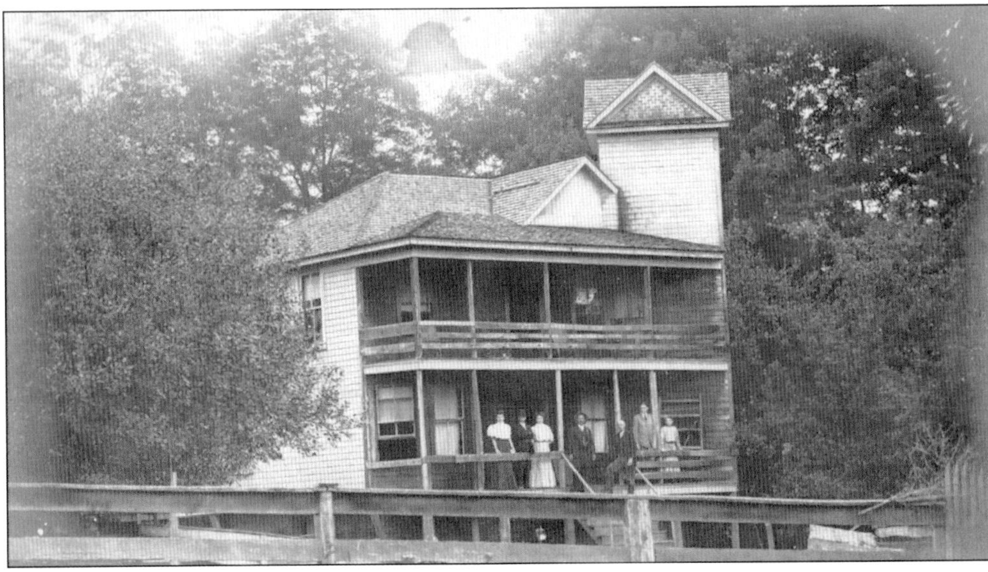

Bolar Springs lies on the dividing line between Bath and Highland Counties, with a bit of the hamlet in each county. Bolar was named after Col. John Bollar, whose wife, Margaret, inherited the land. In the early 1900s, there were several hotels like the ones pictured here in 1908, where tourists flocked to bathe in the mineral springs of the area. Wonderful stories were told of the water's healing powers. The mineral springs' baths run very warm, with temperatures ranging from the mid-70s to more than 105 degrees. The Bolar Hotel charged $1 per night for a room during the first half of the 1900s and burned to the ground in the 1960s. (Courtesy of Kent Botkin.)

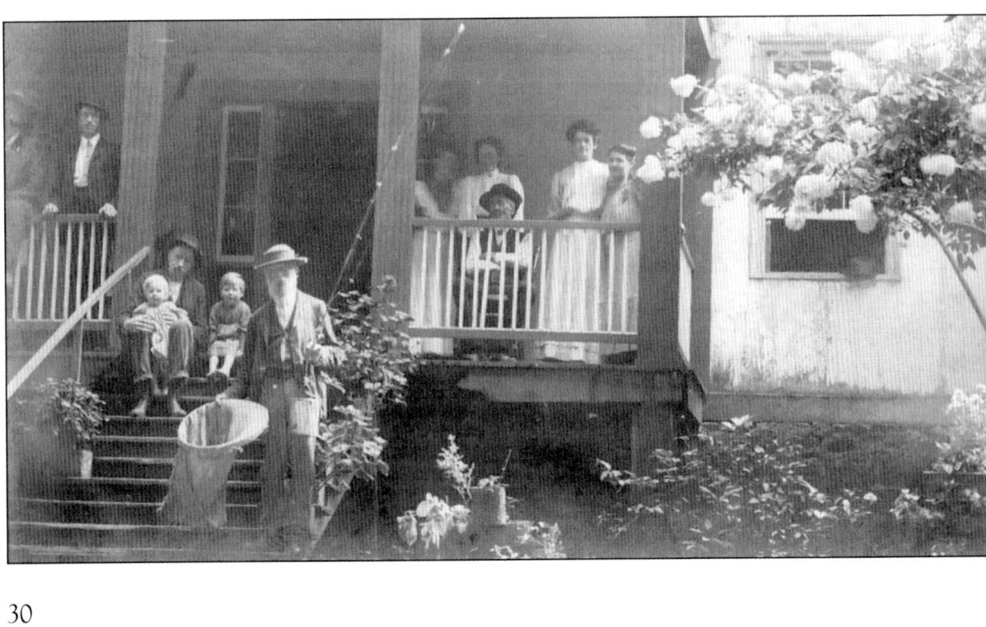

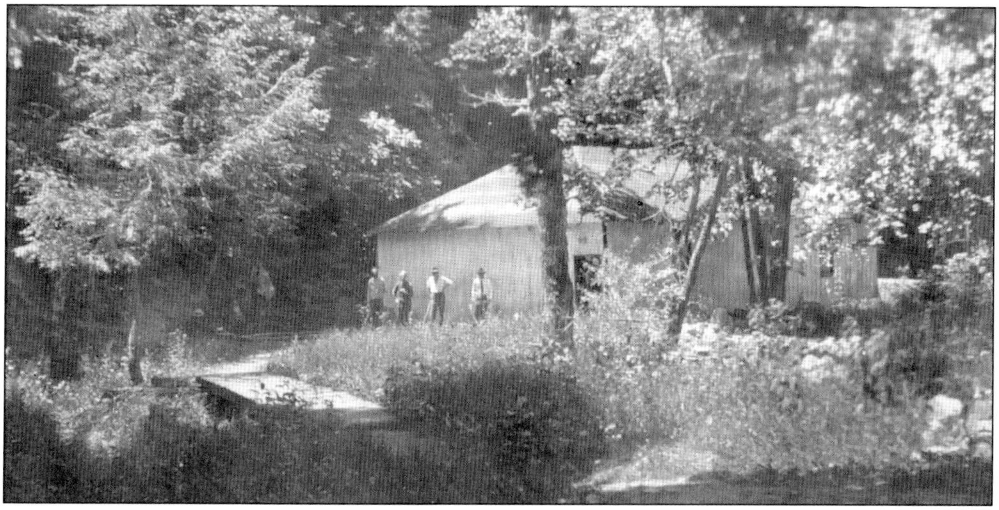

While neighboring Bath County is well known as the location for the natural springs, Highland County has mineral springs as well. Though Bolar does not have a large number of springs, it was at one point a popular resort destination. The bathhouse and grounds, shown here, attracted visitors with promises of the springs' restorative powers. (Courtesy of Kent Botkin.)

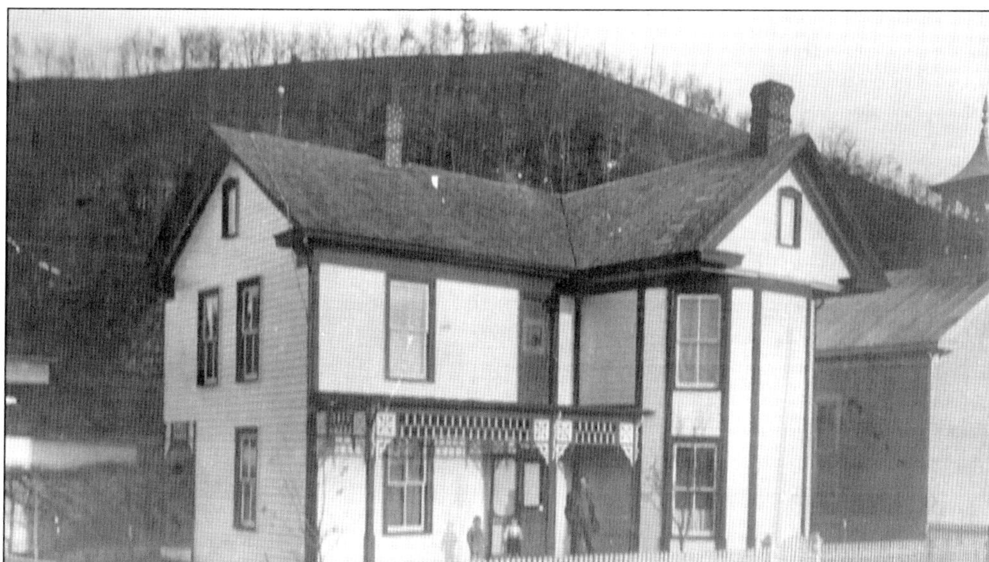

This house, built next to the McDowell United Methodist Church along the Staunton-Parkersburg Turnpike in 1899, displays some wonderful gingerbread work on the front porch that has managed to survive 100 years and several renovations. The people on the front porch are identified only as "Granddaddy Hammer and Henry and Ed." (Author's collection.)

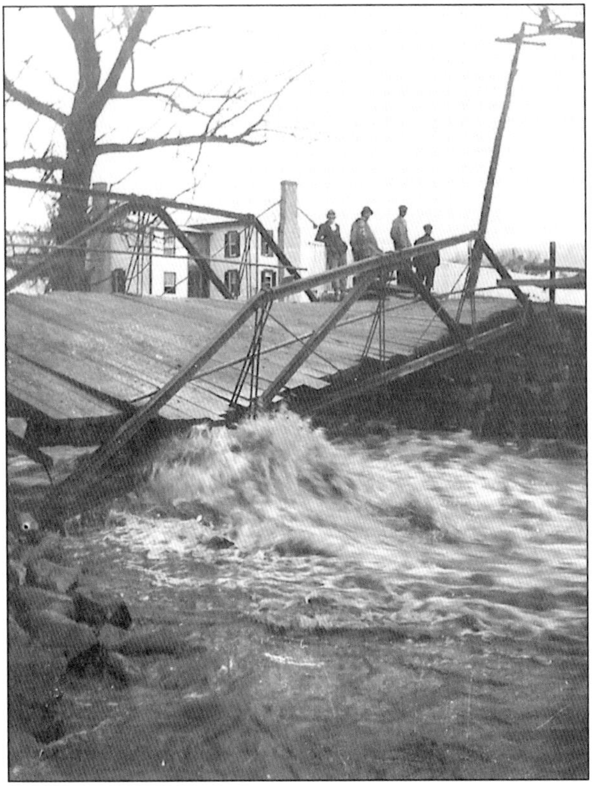

Due to heavy rains, Highland County flooded in 1920. This dramatic photograph captures Crab Run Bridge in McDowell just as it is about to collapse under the weight of the rushing waters of the normally placid stream. In the background stands the Hogshead House. Highland County flooded again in 1985. (Courtesy of Kent Botkin.)

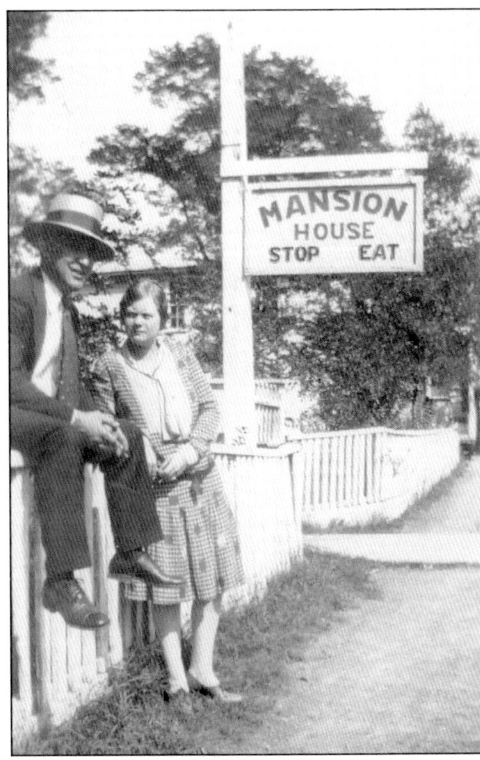

Leola Swadley Maloy and an unidentified man pose next to the sign for the Mansion House in 1930. Both Leola and the Mansion House were McDowell fixtures. Leola was a well-known schoolteacher in town for many years. The Mansion House was a popular restaurant and hotel operating from 1883 to 1931 that served guests with both short- and long-term stays. (Courtesy of Lyle and Georgianne Maloy Hull.)

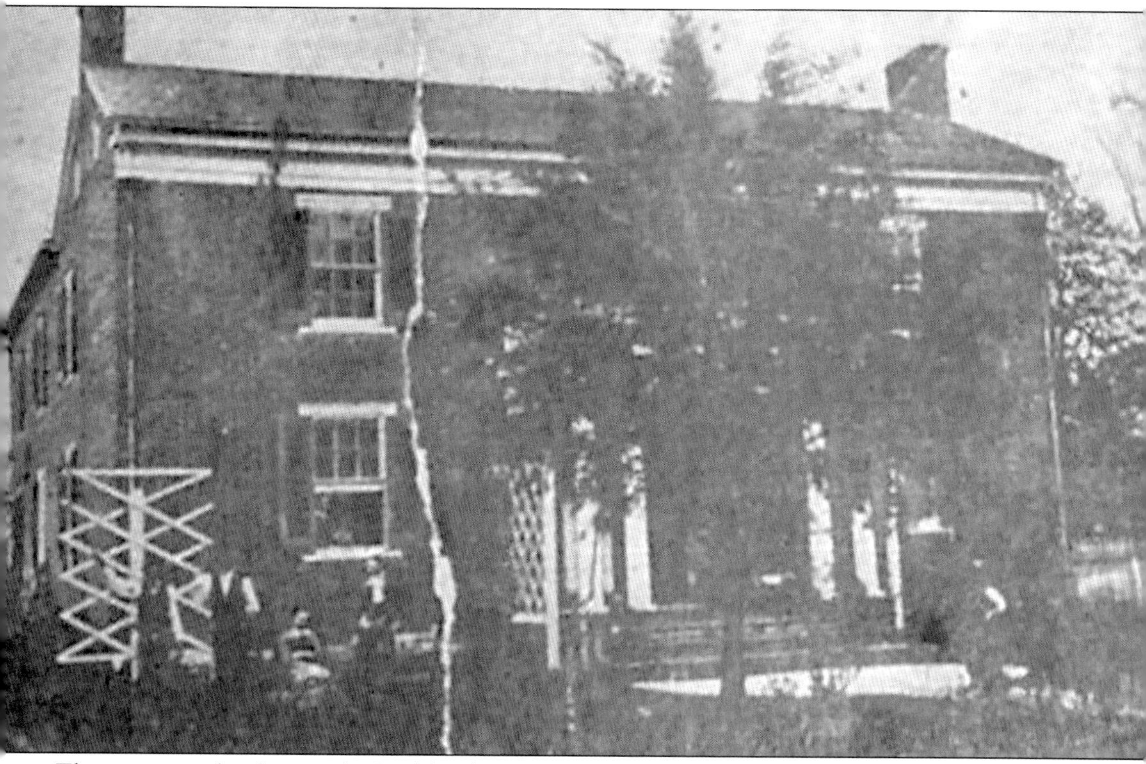

The structure that houses the Highland Museum and Heritage Center has long been a central part of Highland County history. George Washington Hull constructed his home, now known as the Mansion House, facing the Staunton-Parkersburg Turnpike in 1851. Local lore reports that it was called the Mansion because it was the first large brick house in McDowell. The structure was built by slave laborers using bricks fashioned on the Hull plantation. G. W. Hull represented Highland County at the Virginia convention that was called to debate secession from the Union in 1861. The home is shown here as it appeared in 1881. (Courtesy of the Highland County Historical Society.)

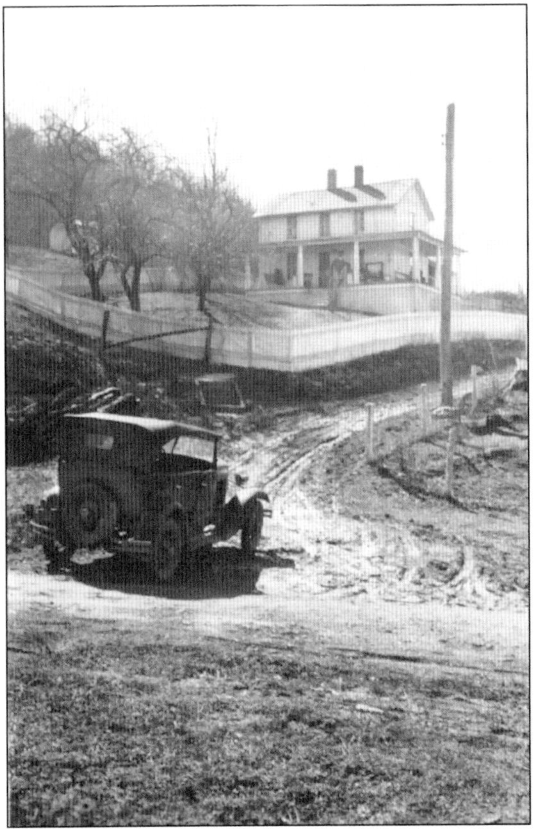

Charles Diggs, along with Huston Wimer, worked as a barber in Monterey for many years. His house is pictured here on what would later become Diggs Lane. He ran his barbershop in different locations over the years, including an office next to what is now High's Restaurant. In an advertisement placed in the *Recorder* in 1919, Diggs gave notice that he was raising the price for a shave to 15¢. (Courtesy of Kent Botkin.)

A horse-drawn wagon carries a load of wool up Main Street toward the Crows Nest (right) about 1909. The Bishop family, owners of Bishops Store in Monterey, built the Crow's Nest in 1908. The note on the back of the photograph calls the horse team "Uncle Bob Bishop's Team." (Courtesy of Kent Botkin.)

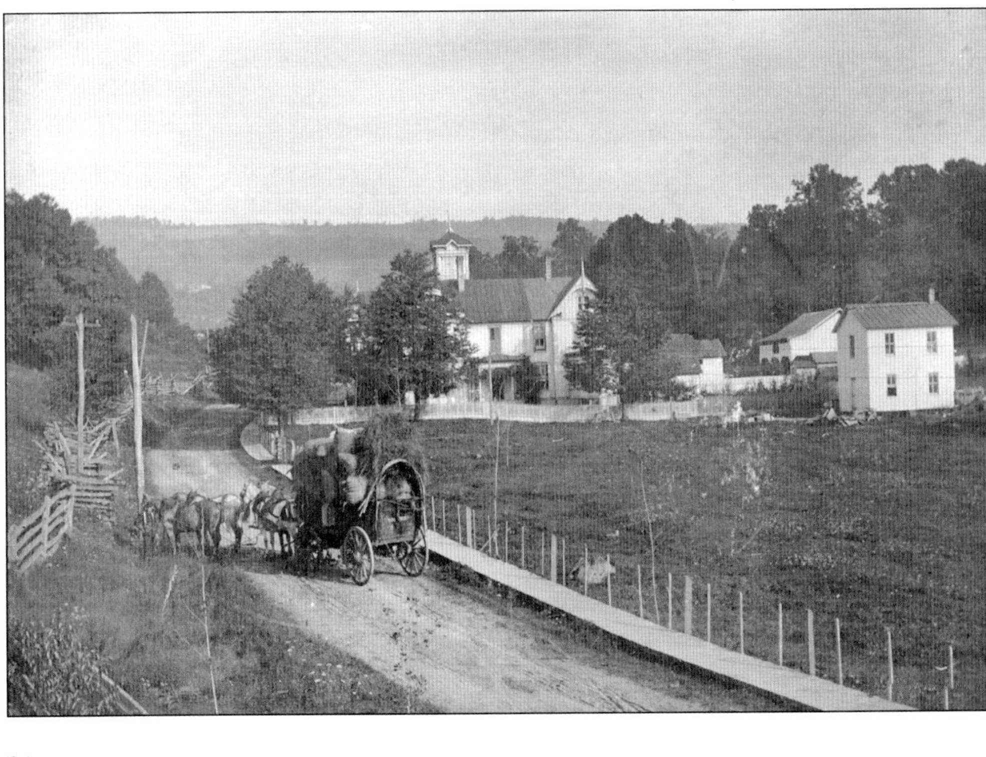

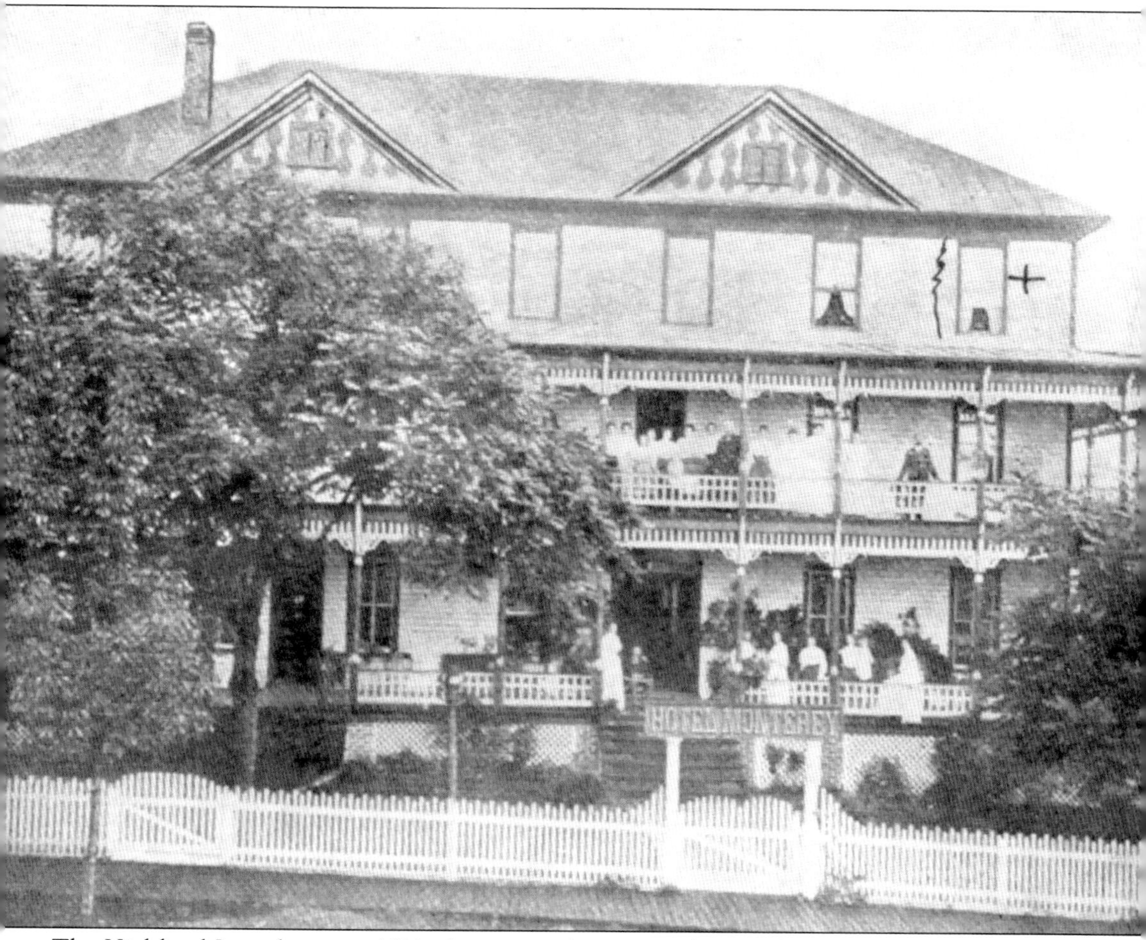

The Highland Inn, shown in 1914 when it was known as the Hotel Monterey, is the largest lodging facility in Highland County. A notice from owner Silas Crummett in the September 28, 1904, *Recorder* read, "I am pleased to announce that my new Hotel building is now completed, furnished and ready for guests. This new hostelry has been flatteringly designated the 'Pride of the Mountains,' and we will spare no effort to back up the appellation. You are cordially invited to stop with us when you visit Monterey. Very Respectfully, S. W. Crummett." The hotel was built in a Queen Anne style at a cost of $6,000. Many stories surround the Highland Inn; one tells of the possible poisoning of the woman who owned the inn with her husband, and the mysterious disappearance thereafter of the husband. (Courtesy of the *Recorder*.)

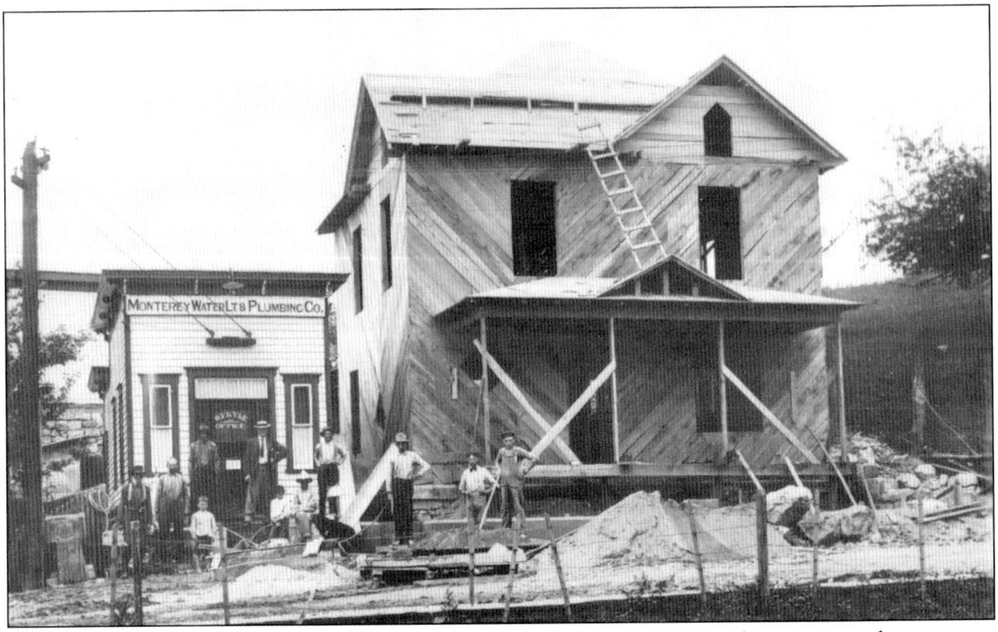

Construction techniques have varied somewhat over the years, but basic principles remain. William F. Kyle (center, with tie) poses above with the crew building his new home in Monterey. Kyle ran the Monterey Water, Light, and Plumbing Company from the adjacent office. To earn a living in Highland County, diversification was a requirement. In addition to the business shown here, he ran Kyle's Garage and owned a Dort dealership in Monterey. The sign (far left) reads "Kyle's Garage: Pure Oils and Gasoline." Kyle, who wed Rosa N. Ward in 1910, sits below with his family on the porch of the finished home. Wooden sidewalks and unused water pipes lie in the foreground. (Courtesy of the *Recorder.*)

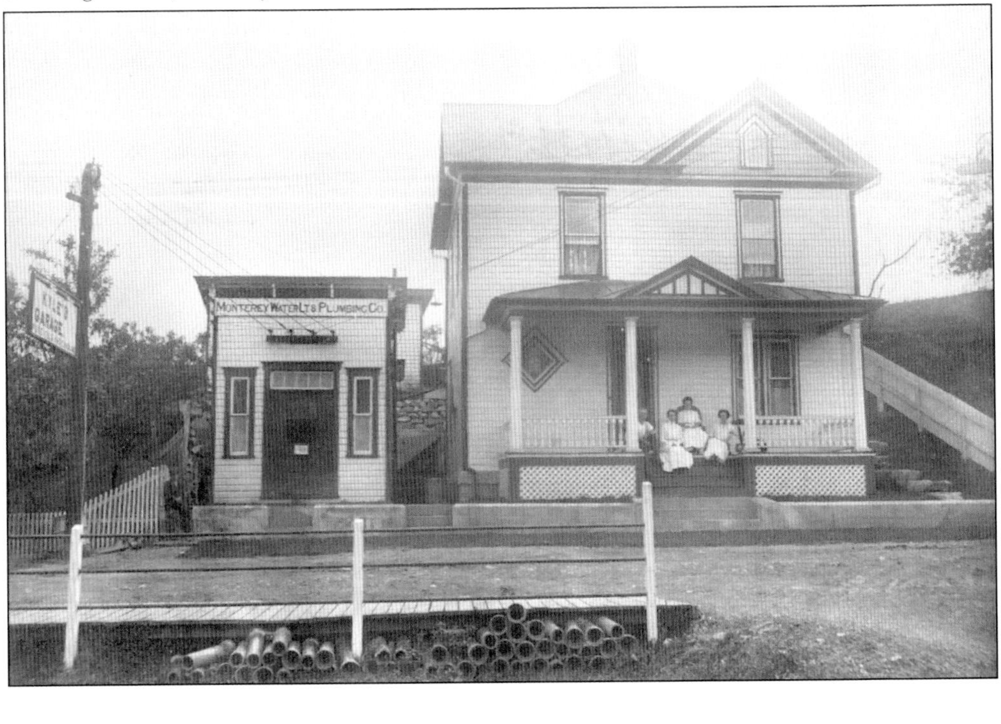

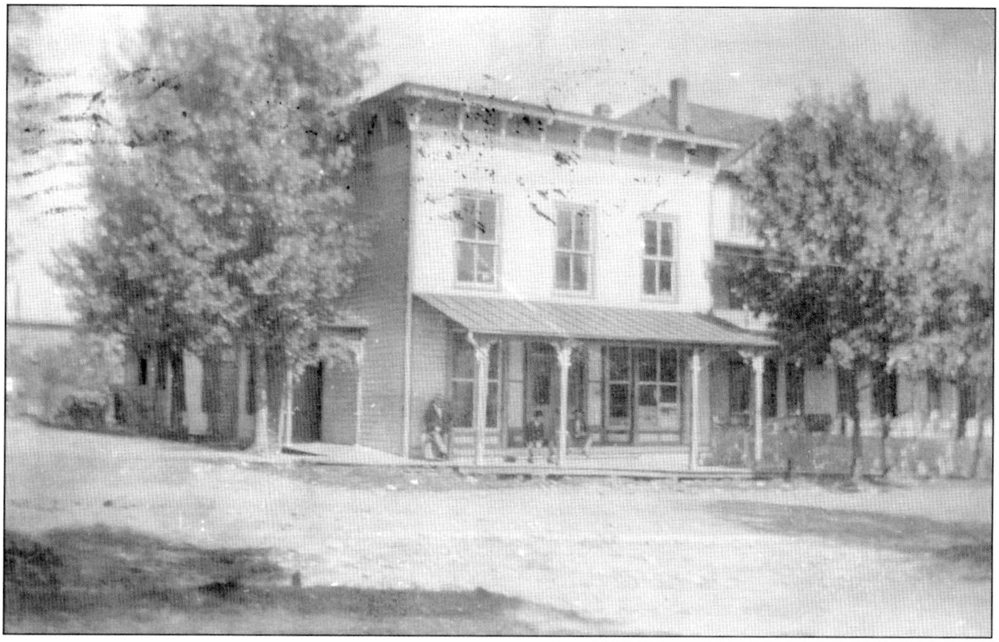

The home of Howard and Daisy Slaven, next to the Monterey Hotel, also housed a jewelry store and post office over the years. Here Howard Slaven (left) sits in his wheelchair next to Charles Lunsford. (Courtesy of the *Recorder*.)

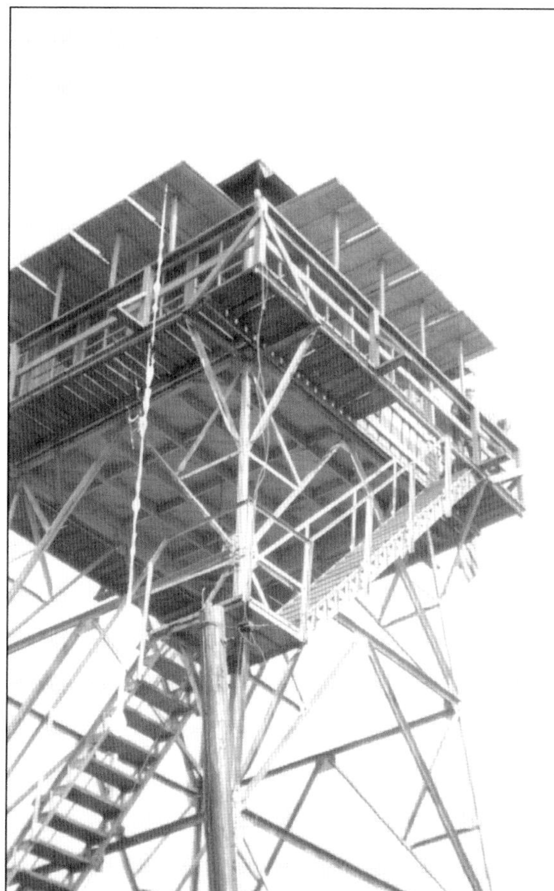

The fire tower was an important early-warning safety feature for a county 75 percent covered by forest. Fire spotters would stay in these elevated towers for months at a time to keep an eye out for forest fires. Patty's Knob Tower stood along the Highland County border with West Virginia on Alleghany Mountain. (Courtesy of Libby Woods Hefner.)

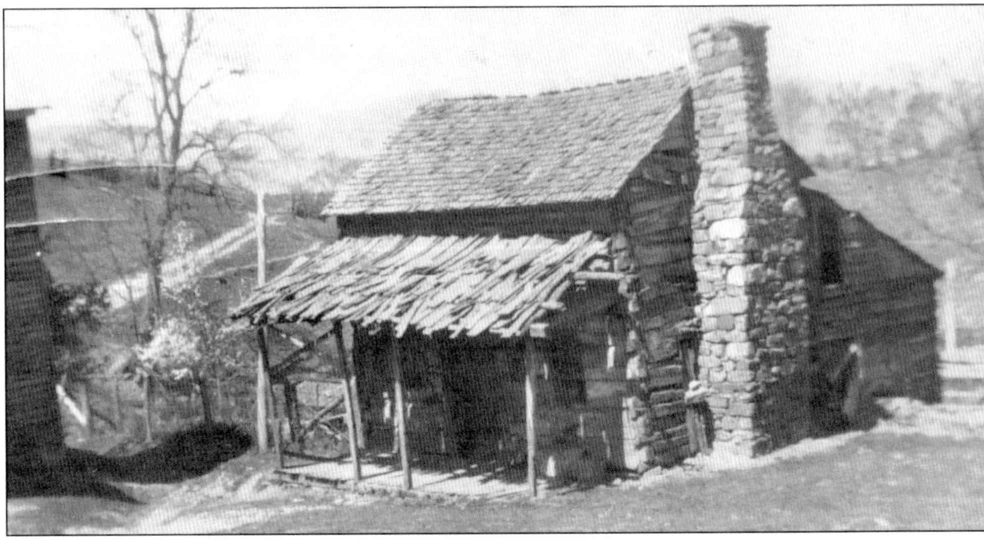

Settlers have carved out an existence in Highland County for many years. This cabin, the Woods family home, was constructed in the Mill Gap area of the county before the Revolutionary War. Inhabited by a continuous line of Woods descendants, it was demolished in the 1930s. (Courtesy of Libby Woods Hefner.)

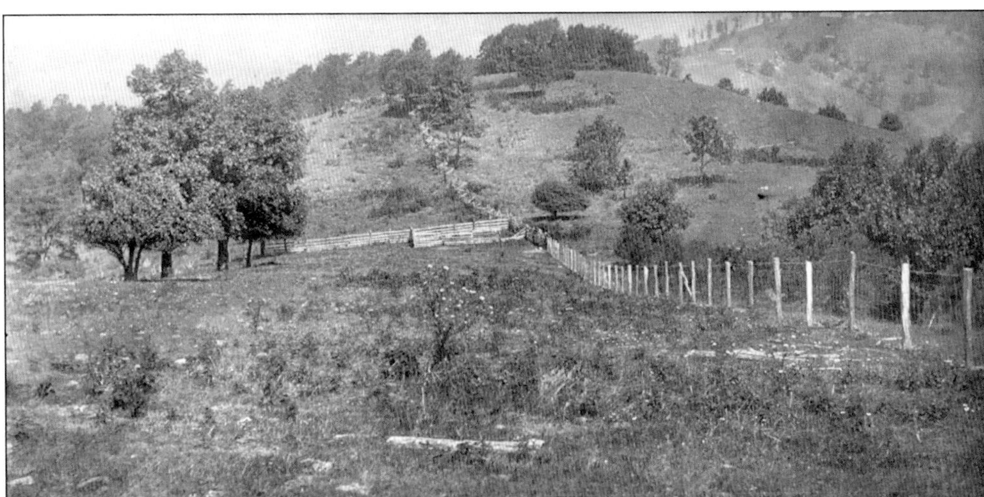

It is rare to find a major Civil War battlefield untouched by the advances of time and encroaching development. Yet the McDowell Battlefield, as seen in 1862, looks remarkably the same today. Most of the fighting took place on this land, just east of McDowell and owned by Robert Sitlington, known as Sitlington's Hill. The one-day battle established Gen. Stonewall Jackson's reputation and caused almost 800 casualties (Courtesy of Kent Botkin.)

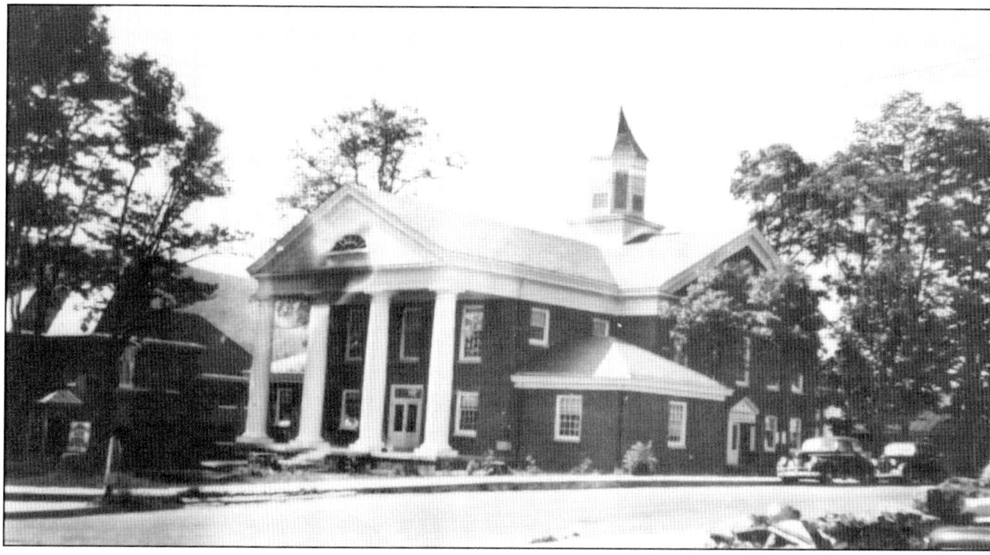

The original courthouse in Monterey burned on February 28, 1947, just a few months shy of the centennial birthday celebration for Highland County planned for May of that year. In 1948, it was replaced with a new building following roughly the same plans and footprint as the previous one. The old courthouse is shown here in different seasons. The winter scene displays the iron fence installed around the lawn in the 1920s. The courthouse lawn was used for visiting, relaxing, and conducting business. The fence was taken down during a scrap metal drive to aid the World War II effort. In 1918, the Highland chapter of the United Daughters of the Confederacy erected the statue of the Civil War soldier facing north. (Courtesy of Lyle and Georgianne Maloy Hull; courtesy of the *Recorder*.)

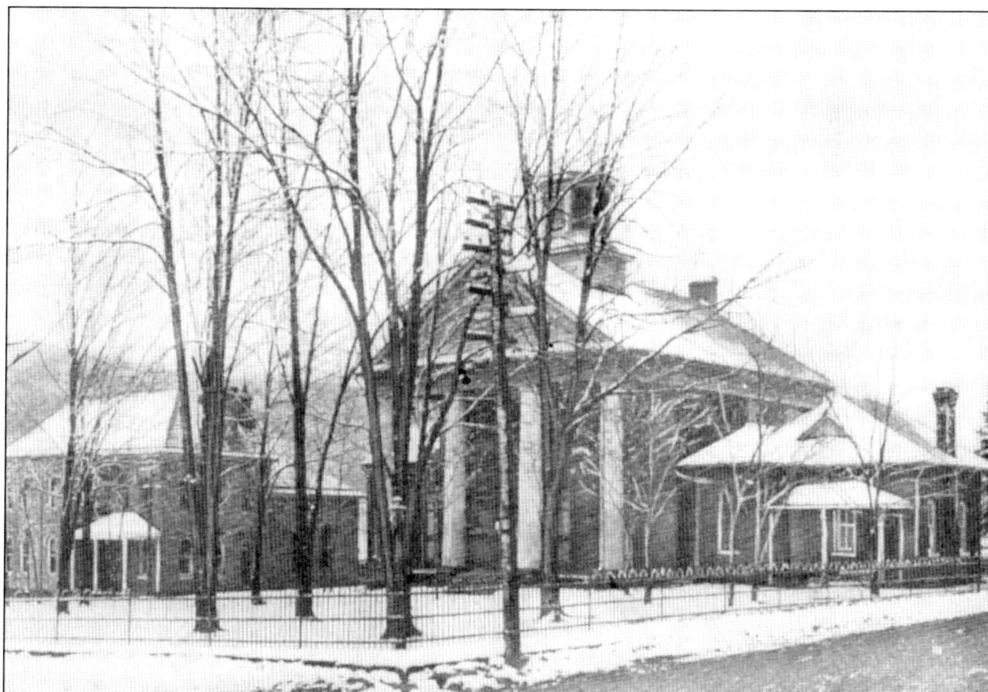

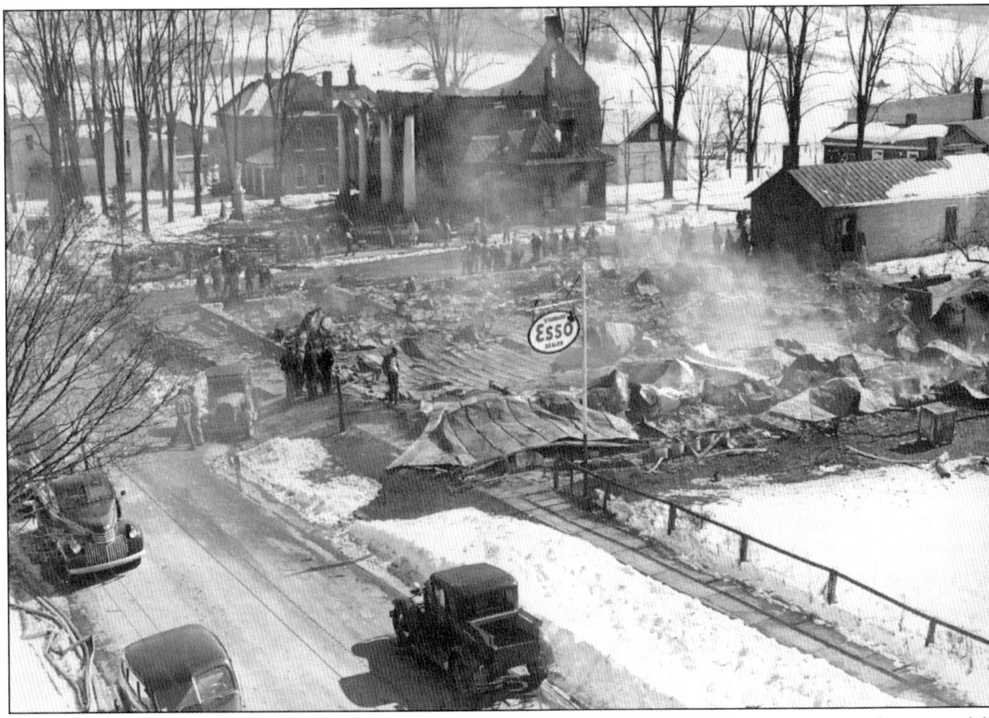

The courthouse fire began in the kitchen of the Star Restaurant in Monterey, spreading quickly to engulf Bishop Brothers Store and the adjacent Beverage Garage. The flames then crossed the road to virtually wipe out the courthouse, causing $40,000 in damage to that structure alone. Though the fire was devastating, no courthouse records were lost because the clerk's office had recently been fireproofed. (Courtesy of Kent Botkin.)

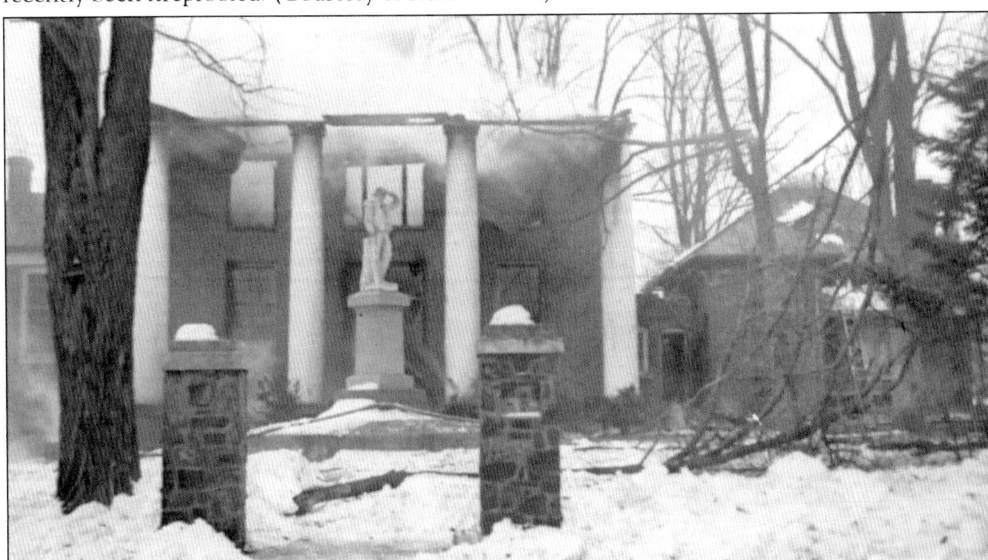

The courthouse was almost a total loss, though some of the shell remained. Several eyewitness accounts saw a visual similarity between that building and the Greek Parthenon with the columns rising into the air. In this photograph taken by the local *Recorder* newspaper, smoke rises from the still-smoldering ashes of the courthouse. (Courtesy of the *Recorder*.)

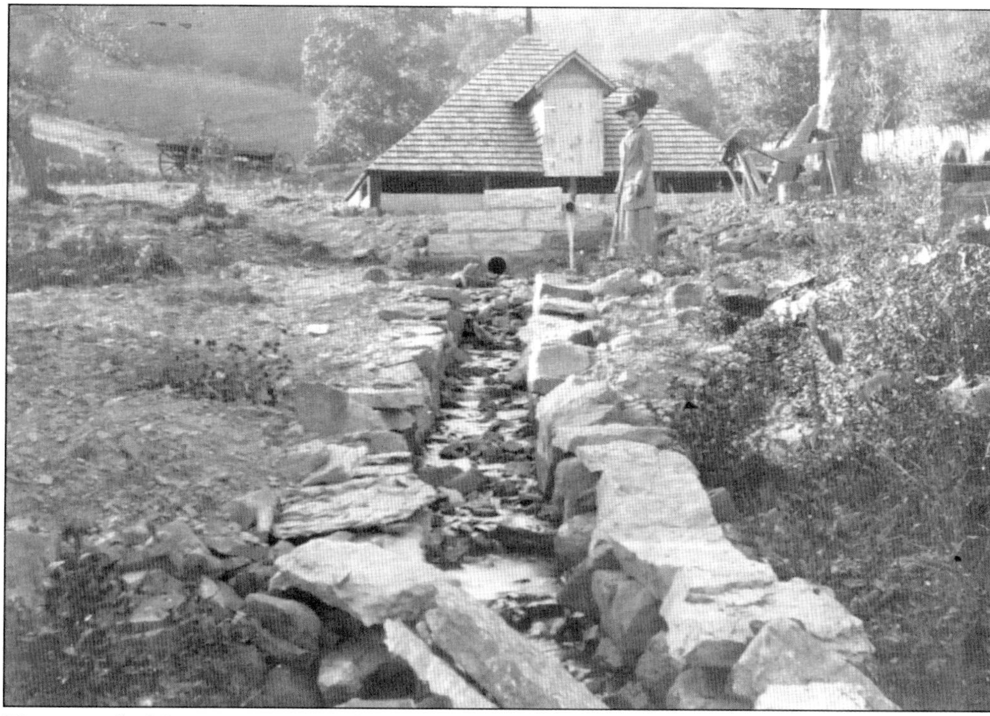

The water for Monterey originated one mile west of town on property owned by William F. Kyle. For many years, Monterey used this fresh spring water. Kyle owned and operated Monterey Water, Light, and Plumbing. (Courtesy of the *Recorder.*)

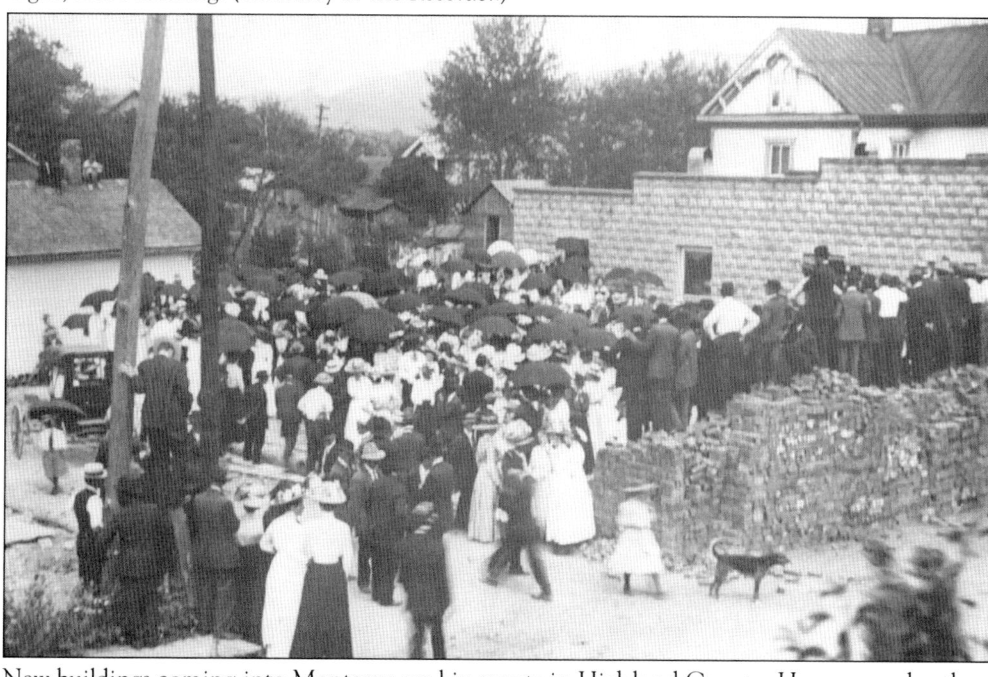

New buildings coming into Monterey are big events in Highland County. Here a crowd gathers on Main Street in Monterey for the ground-breaking ceremony of the Masonic Temple in 1910. (Courtesy of the *Recorder.*)

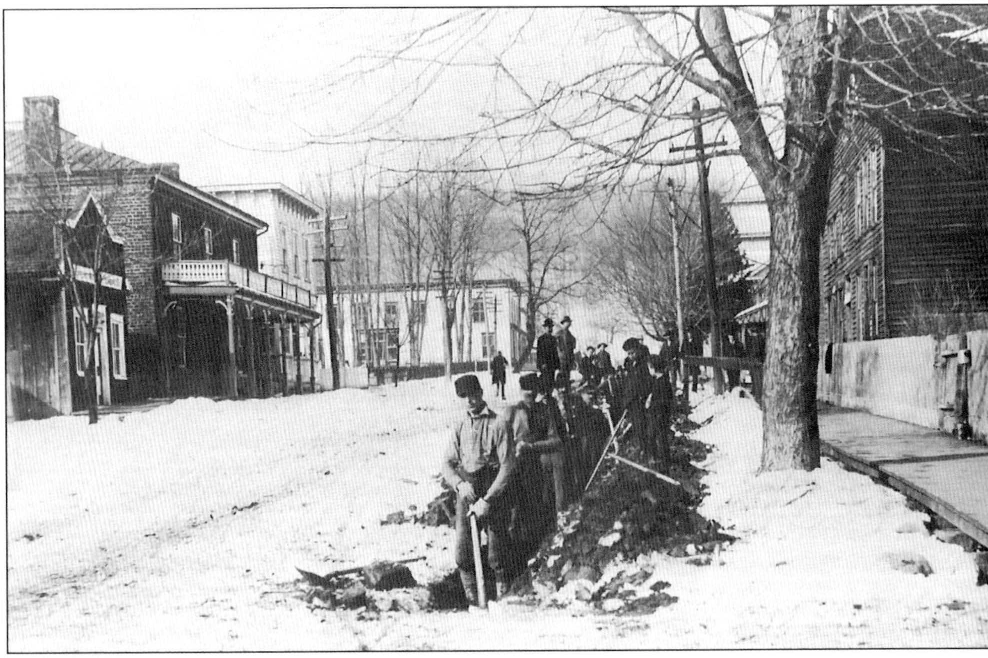

When early residents brought modern conveniences to Monterey, it meant backbreaking labor. Monterey gained running water through workers hand-digging water lines. A long line of men with picks and shovels accomplished the task. The men dug right next to the wooden sidewalks to allow easier access to the houses. The water pipes, brought in by horse and wagon in 1902, were used for many years. (Courtesy of the *Recorder*; courtesy of Tate Swecker.)

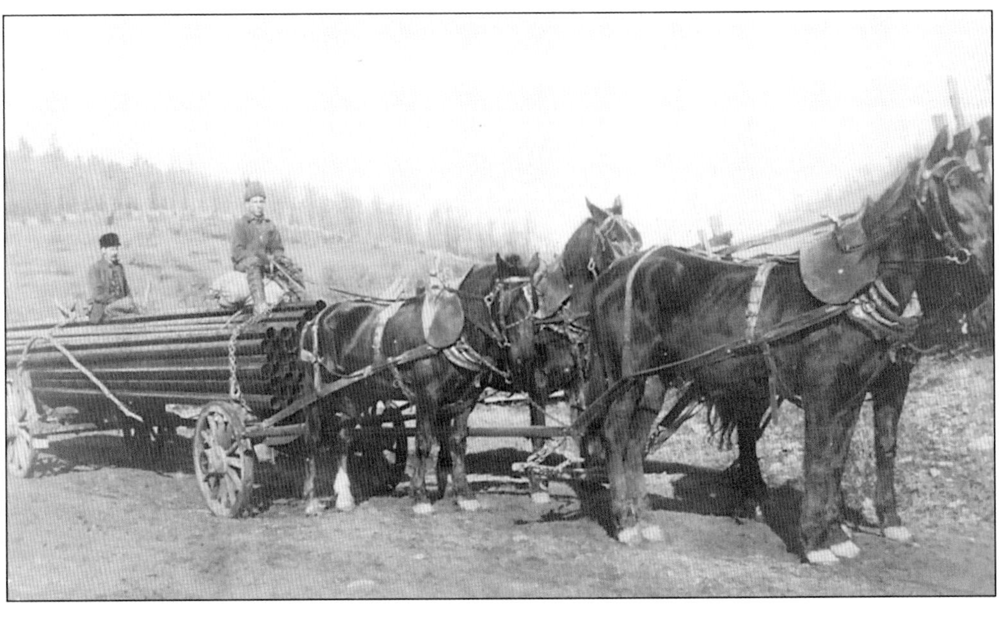

Three

Living off the Land
Farming, Logging, and Maple Sugaring

From the early days of harvesting crops to chopping trees for lumber and tapping maples for syrup, Highlanders have lived off the land.

Farming is a strong presence in Highland County. Traditionally farming was a necessity for all county residents—at least on some scale. Simply put, in order to eat, one needed to grow some crops and raise some cows. Historically cattle and sheep farms have vied neck and neck for dominance in terms of livestock. Poultry operations have grown considerably over the years, with many Thanksgiving turkeys originating in the mountains of Virginia. Recent years have seen the creation of a turkey growers' co-op. In the days before trucks were commonplace, farmers would herd all livestock, including turkeys, to market—about 40 miles away.

Logging has long been a thriving business in the heavily wooded Highland County. In the early days, just about every community in the region had a sawmill, but only a few remain. The earliest known sawmill was located in the Mill Gap area. The New Hampden Mill was recorded in a will in 1842. Like many early sawmills in the area, it relied on water to help fuel its production. The Chestnut Blight from the early part of the 1900s affected the logging industry.

Every year in late winter or early spring, sugar water is collected from the many maple trees and boiled down into syrup. For sugar water to flow, the temperature must dip below freezing at night and reach above freezing during the day. The season only lasts about four to six weeks. Even before the institution of the Maple Festival in 1958, maple syrup played a significant role in the lives of residents. Formed into sugar cakes, maple syrup operated as a medium of exchange in stores and was even carried over the mountains and sold. A staple of the Highland County diet for many years, maple syrup was often used in cooking. Highland residents understand the importance of the maple tree.

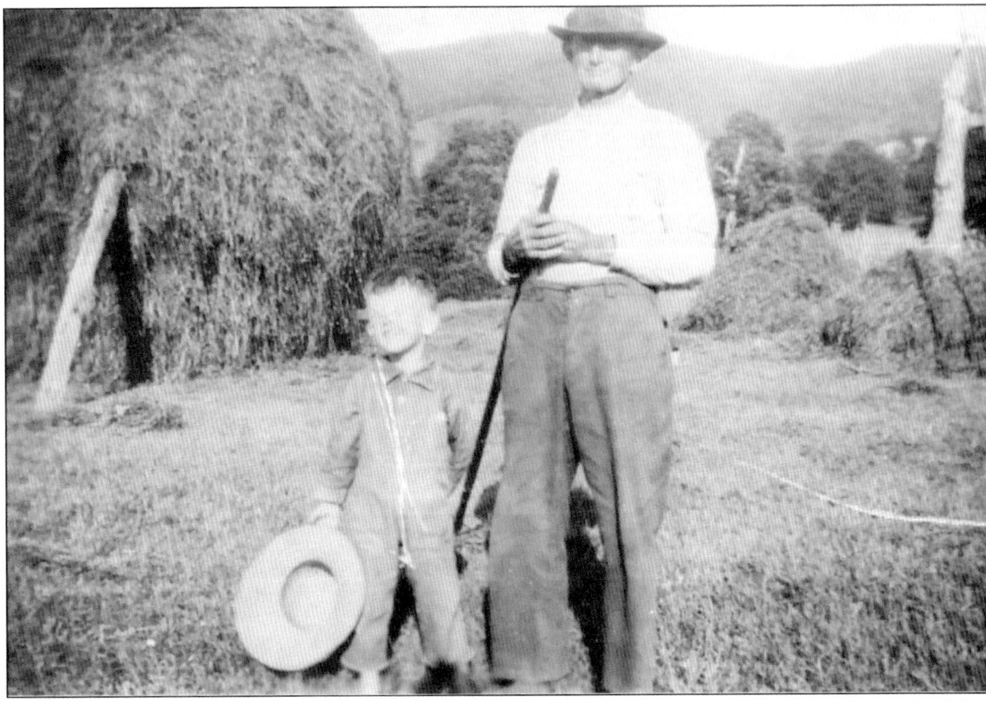

Farming was a family affair in Highland County. Large families meant more mouths to feed, but also more hands to help with the immense workload. Here members of the Swecker family farm together in the Blue Grass Valley in the 1950s. (Courtesy of Tate Swecker.)

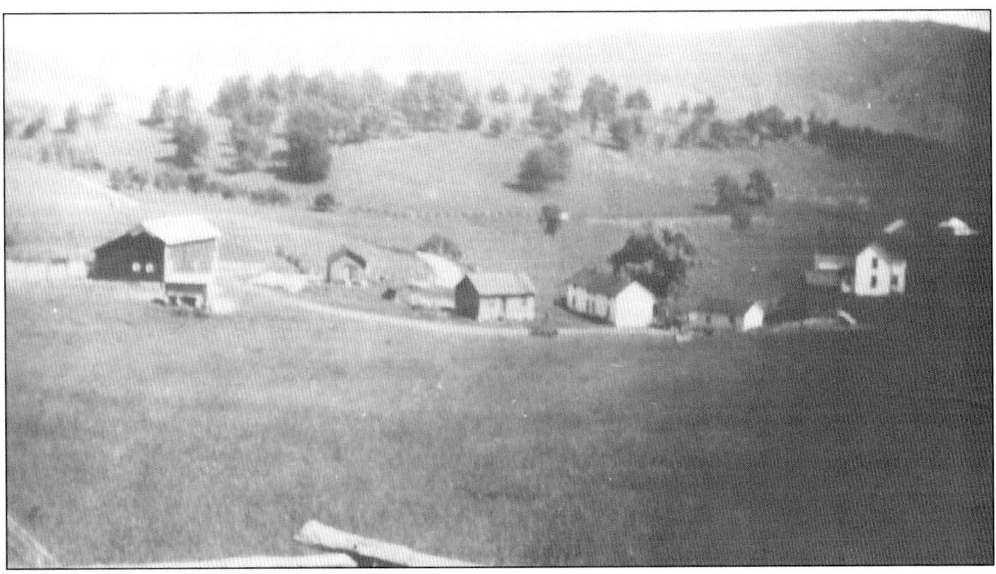

Highland County has a long history, going back to its initial founding in 1847, of taking care of the poor in its midst. At this time, a poor farm was established for the truly destitute. Henry Walter and Mamie Catherine Mullenax ran the farm from 1913 until their son Joseph took over operation in the 1950s. The buildings included, from left to right, the barn, corn crib, grain house, chicken house, inmate quarters, spring house, and caretaker's house. (Courtesy of Janet Mullenax.)

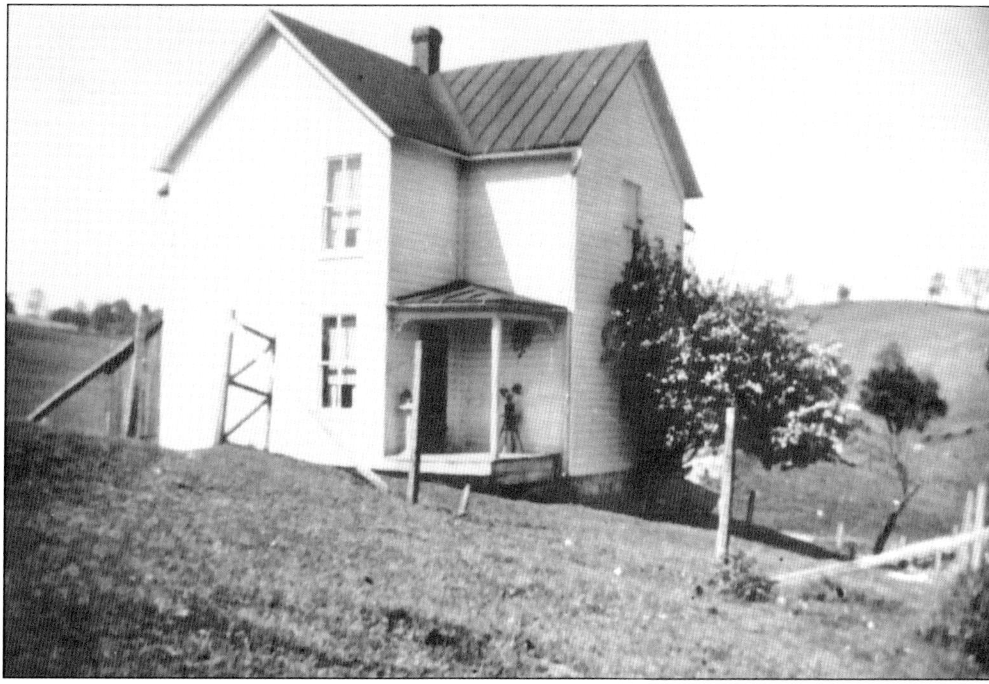

The caretakers of the poor farm in Highland County were given a house on the grounds. Henry and Mamie Mullenax lived in this home and raised their family here for the 40 years that they served as wardens. The poor farm operated like a typical farm. (Courtesy of Janet Mullenax.)

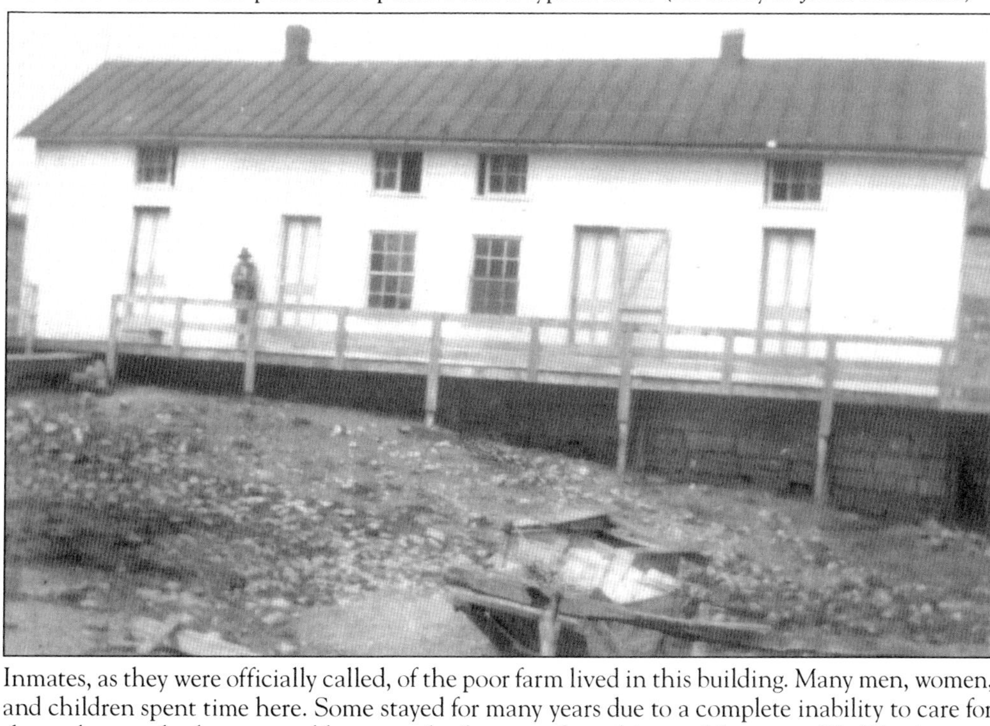

Inmates, as they were officially called, of the poor farm lived in this building. Many men, women, and children spent time here. Some stayed for many years due to a complete inability to care for themselves, and others were able to use the farm as a launching pad for a new life. The inmates performed many of the chores. (Courtesy of Janet Mullenax.)

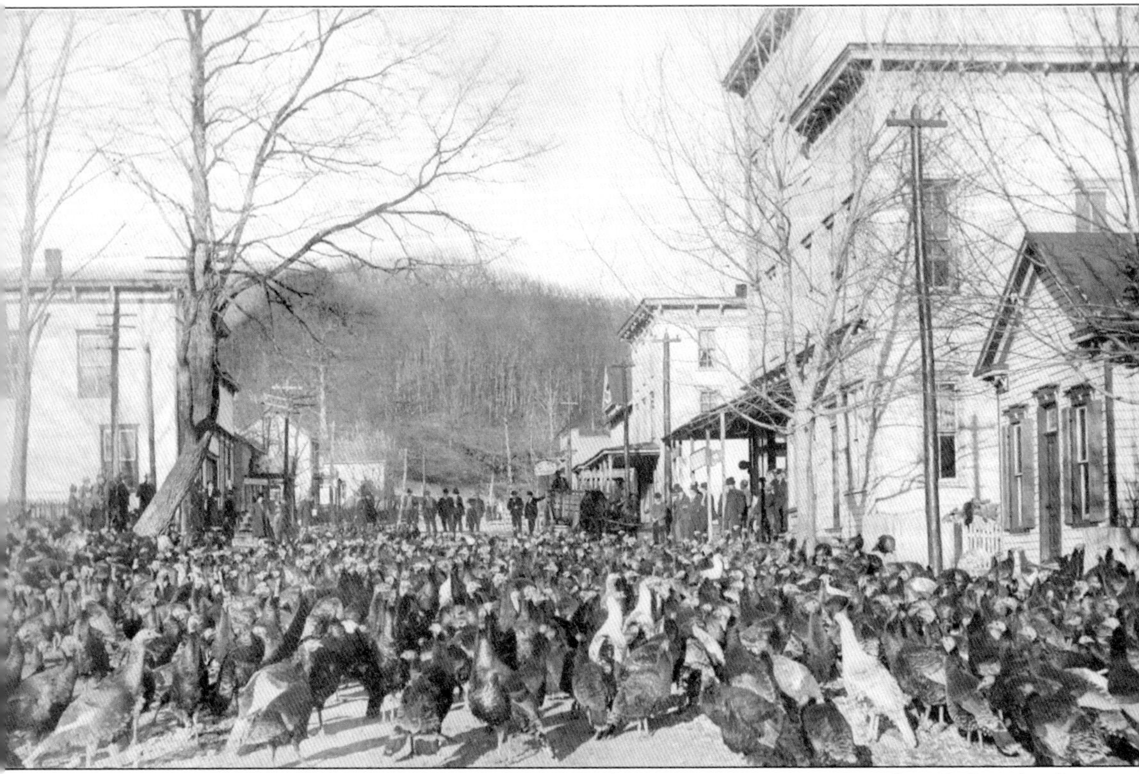

Everything from Highland County had to cross the mountains to get to market. Before the days of big trucks, turkeys were herded on foot over the mountains, and that meant being driven right down Main Street in Monterey, the county seat. The flocks of turkeys would walk all day and roost in the trees along the sides of the road at night. The farmers made what they called "turkey shoes" to protect the turkeys' feet. Walking the turkeys through hot tar and then immediately over sand created tough, protective layers. The note on the back of this postcard sums up the motivation for herding turkeys: "1,361 turkey's sold to Swift and Co of Chicago by Highland Merchants. Dec 10, 1909. A nice little bunch for the rich to eat at Christmas." Turkey houses dot the landscape of the county; to this day, poultry continues to be an important "cash crop" for the farmers of Highland County. (Courtesy of the Highland County Historical Society.)

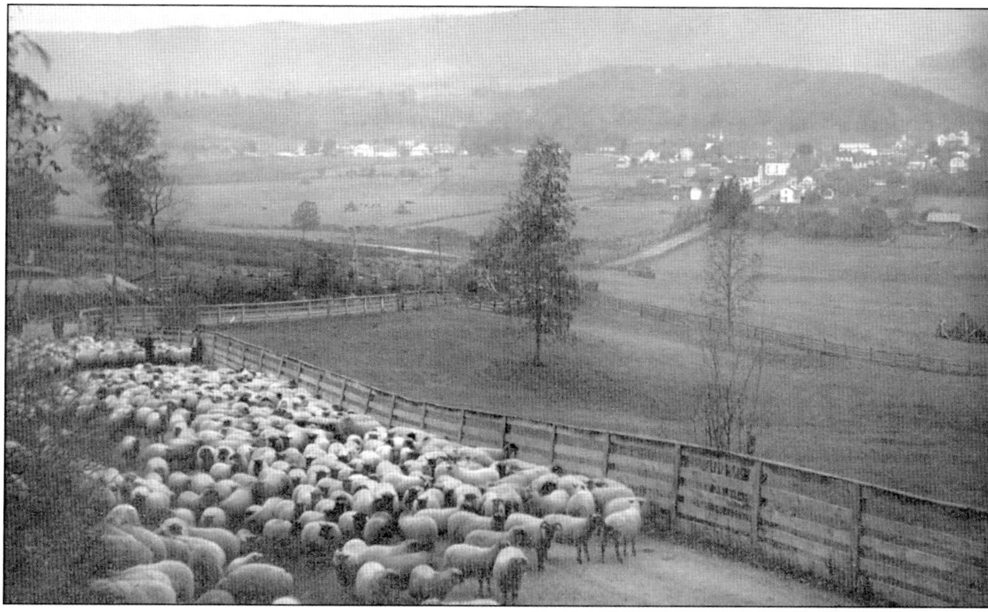

Highland County sheep were driven to market, usually in Staunton, on main county roads such as Spruce Street (below) and (above) Route 250 (Staunton-Parkersburg Turnpike). Wool and sheep have been the backbone of Highland's economy for many years. In 1990, the county ranked third in the state in its number of sheep. Every farm at one point raised at least a few sheep. Sheep brokers would go from farm to farm buying a few animals and then moving on. At the same time, some farmers needed to take their sheep to market to sell on a larger scale. (Courtesy of the Highland County Historical Society; courtesy of Libby Woods Hefner.)

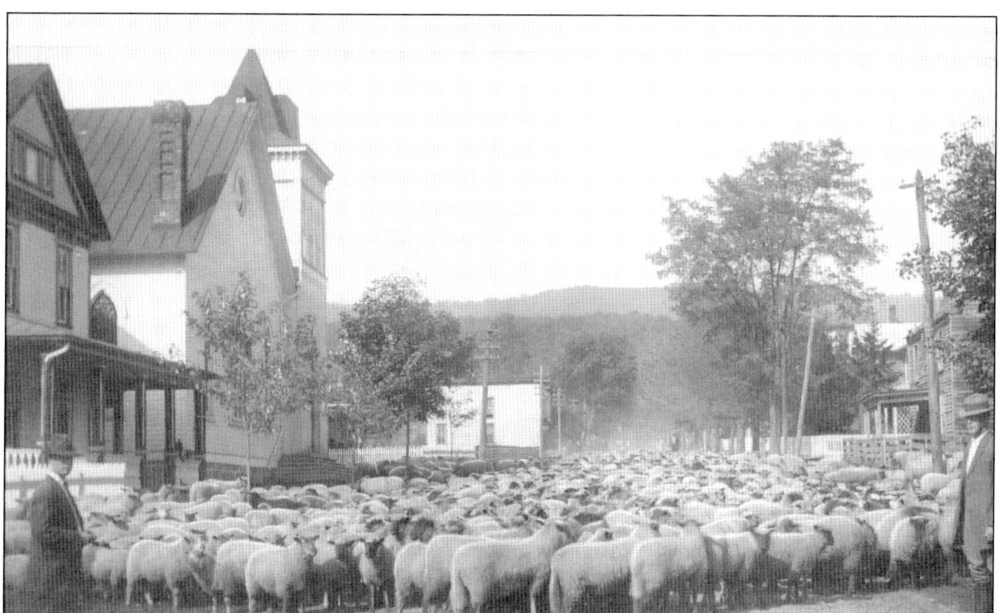

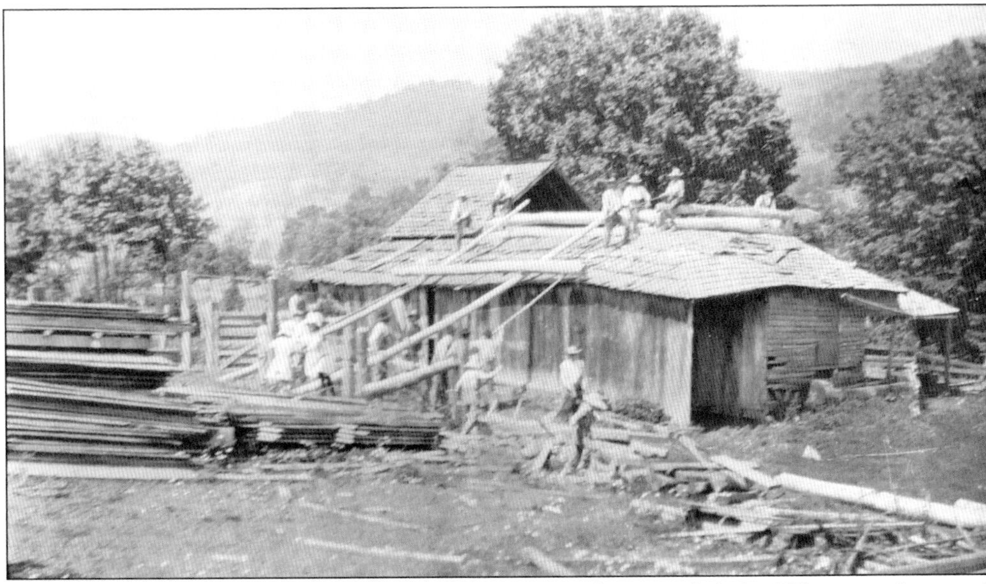

Communities come together when one person among them needs help. Whatever that need, neighbors were expected to help each other in Highland County. Here people from the Mill Gap area gather to raise a barn at the Woods/Wade place. (Courtesy of Libby Woods Hefner.)

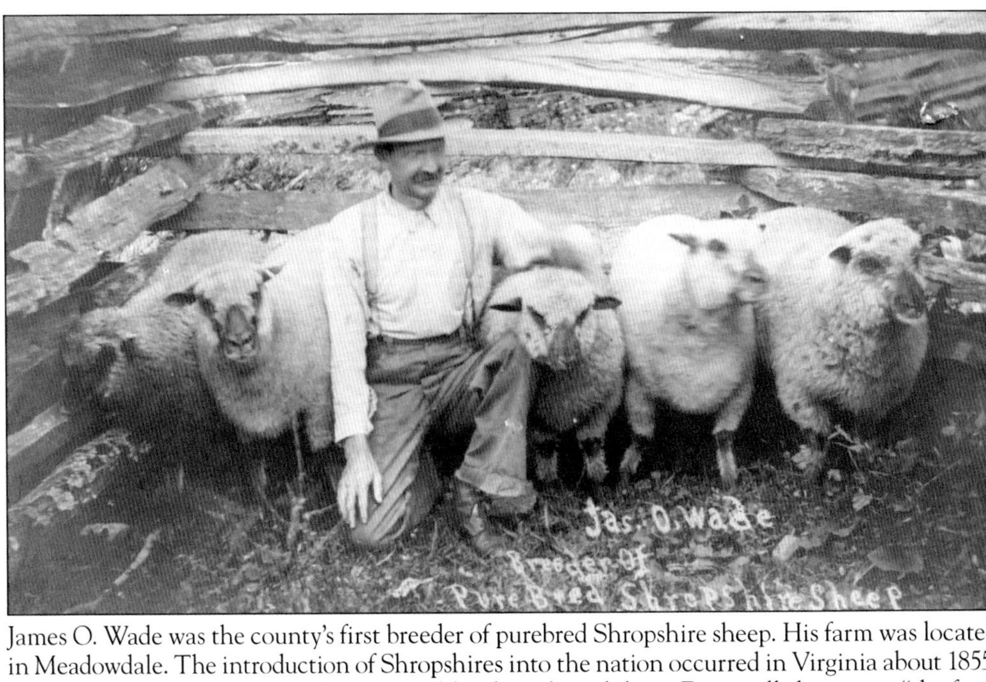

James O. Wade was the county's first breeder of purebred Shropshire sheep. His farm was located in Meadowdale. The introduction of Shropshires into the nation occurred in Virginia about 1855, though the animals did not make it to Highland until much later. Eventually known as "the farm flock favorite," they boasted "wool from the tip of the nose to the tip of the toes." (Courtesy of Libby Woods Hefner.)

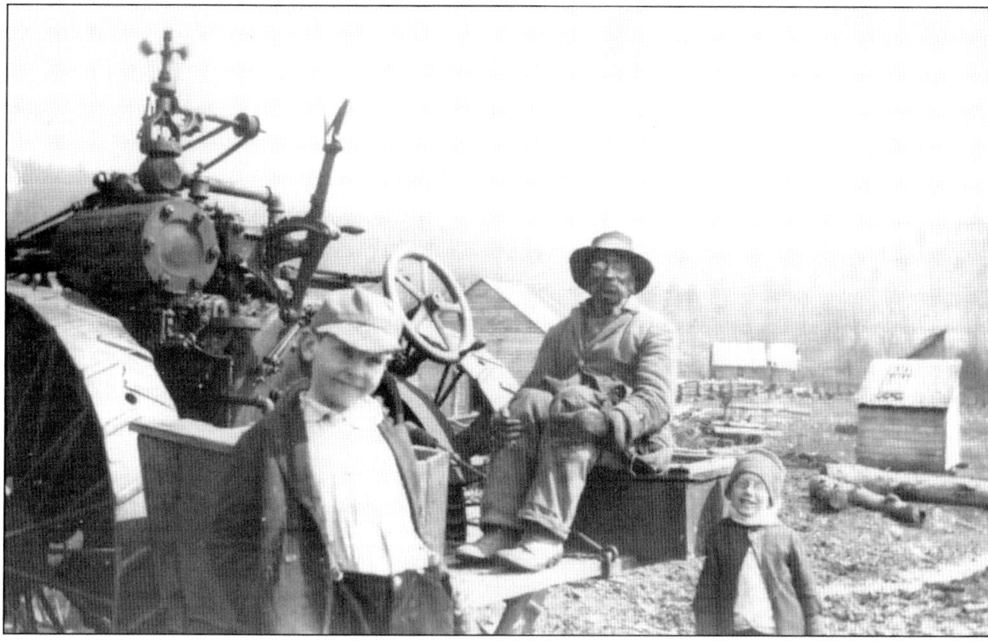

Keeping a farm going in Highland County meant relying on many different people, different ages, and different ethnic backgrounds working together. Lohr Vance (left), Morg Dawson (center), and Josephine Vance (right) pose on the Vance farm. The father of Lena and Mutt Dawson, Morg lived on Davis Run and helped out on farms around the community. (Courtesy of Robin and Nancy Vance.)

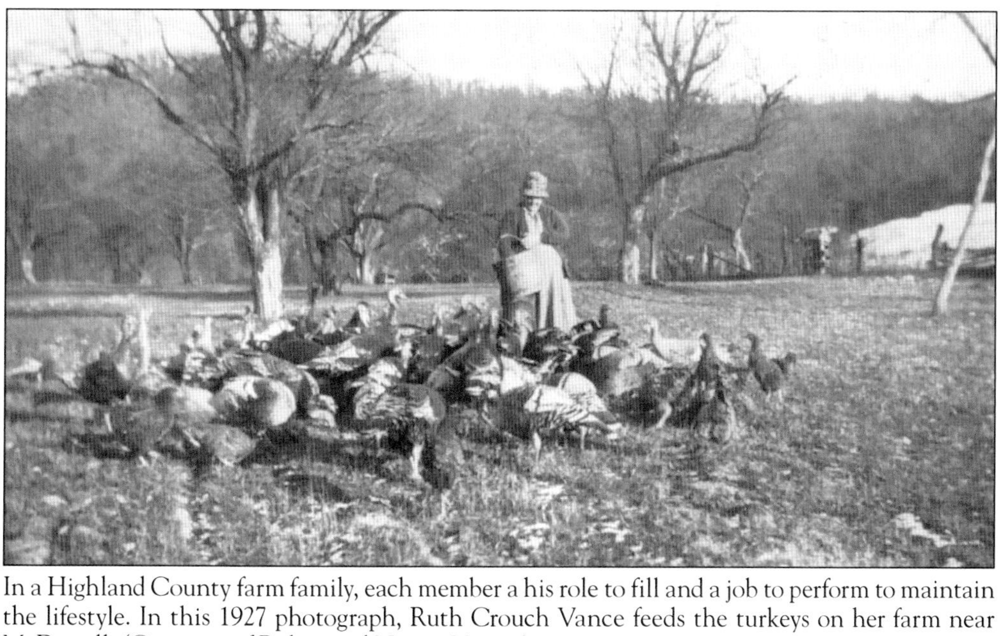

In a Highland County farm family, each member a his role to fill and a job to perform to maintain the lifestyle. In this 1927 photograph, Ruth Crouch Vance feeds the turkeys on her farm near McDowell. (Courtesy of Robin and Nancy Vance.)

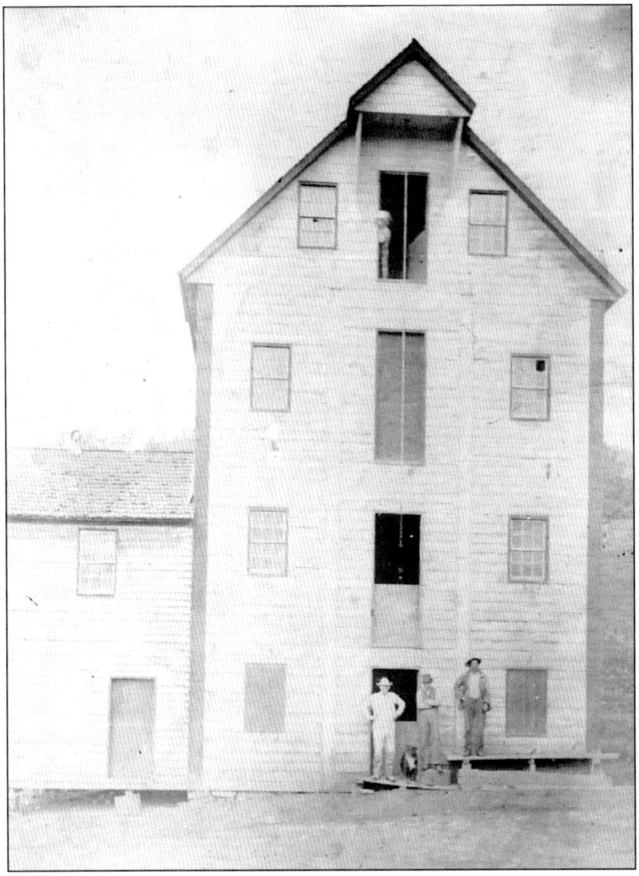

At one point, each village in Highland County had its own mill that served as a meeting place for the rural community. Mill records tell a lot about the economic life of the time. This mill stood in Blue Grass for many years. (Courtesy of Kent Botkin.)

The North Fork of the South Branch ran through a farm owned by Troy Waybright near the foot of Hardscrabble. Waybright would say he was going "up on the Fork to feed" near Roaring Springs. He was born on November 27, 1887, and died on November 22, 1971. (Courtesy of Nancy Mullenax Hedges.)

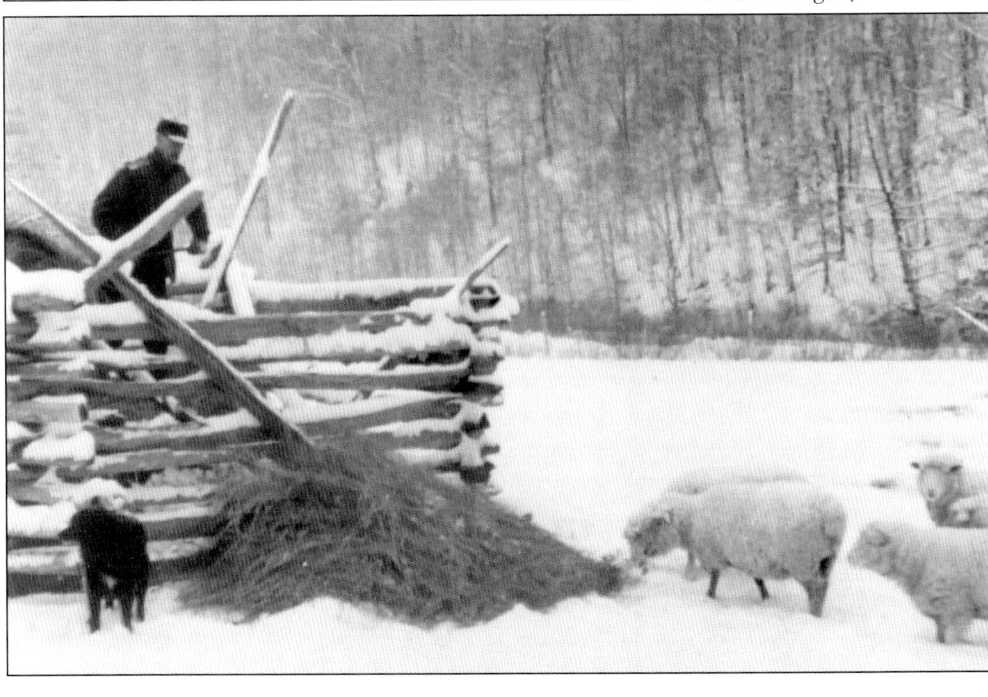

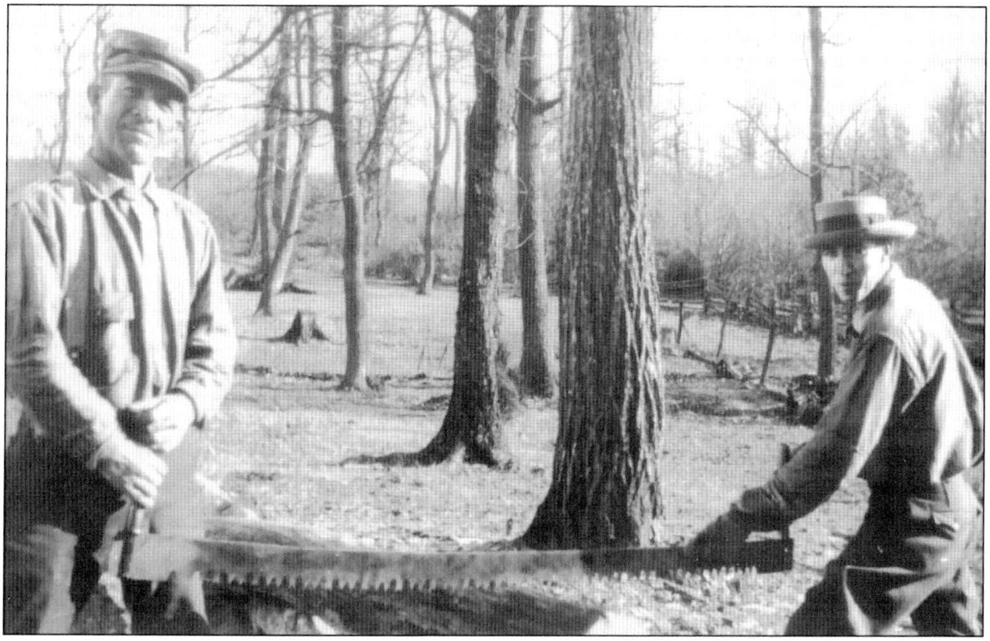

Many people in Highland County have spent considerable time in the woods. Timber is vital to life in the county. From firewood for home use to lumber for commercial purposes, trees have many uses. Here William A. Mullenax (left) and Floyd "Ted" Mullenax (right) cut wood with a two-man saw. (Courtesy of Janet Mullenax.)

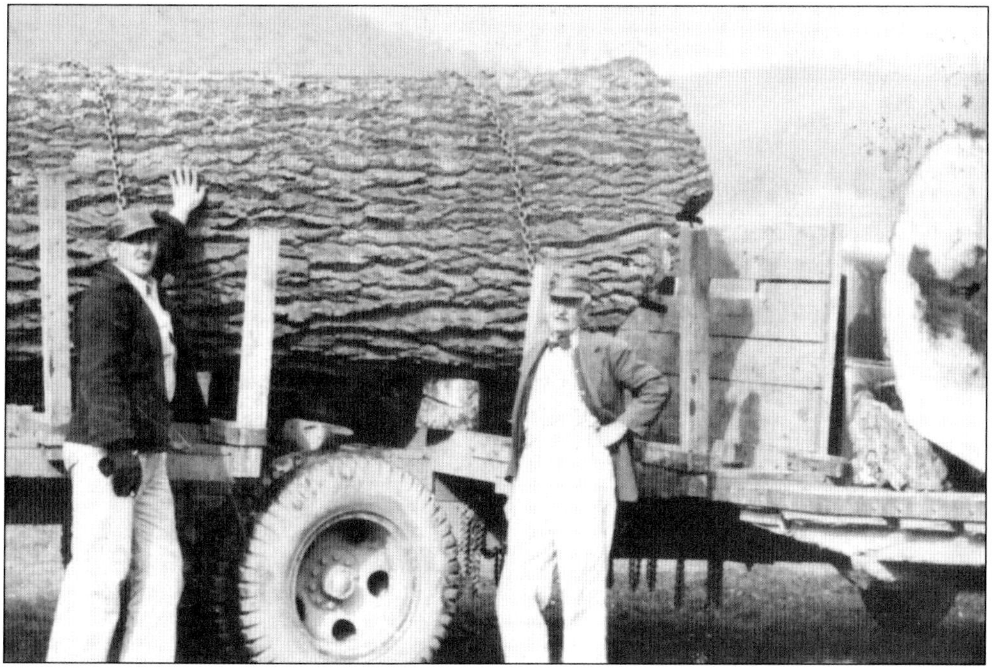

John Mullenax (left) and Henry Walter Mullenax pose in early summer 1953 with what is considered the widest log ever taken out of the woods. The log was displayed in a parade on a 1954 Chevrolet to advertise the trucks being offered for sale that fall. Henry suffered a massive stroke in July 1953. (Courtesy of Janet Mullenax.)

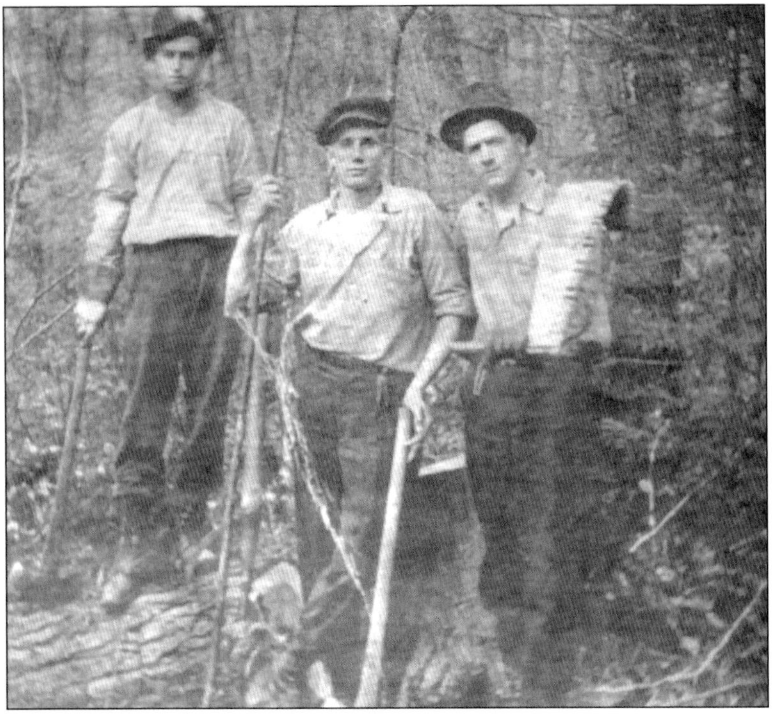

In 1916, Pete White (left), Clarence Lantz (center), and Cecil Rexrode worked on the north side of Cheat Mountain, earning $2 for every thousand feet of lumber cut. The men had to walk several miles to work each day; one week the temperature never rose above -18 degrees. (Courtesy of the *Recorder*.)

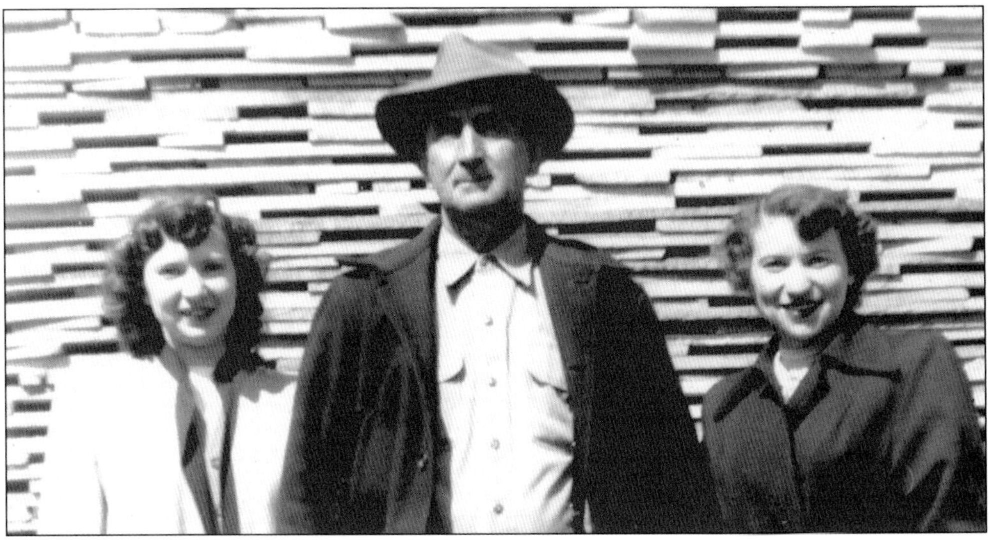

James Edward Mullenax (center) poses with his daughters Avis Mullenax Veli (left) and Grace Mullenax Smith in front of a pile of lumber at his mill in 1950. In the early 1940s, Edward and his cousin Walter Mullenax started the Mullenax Lumber Company near the intersection of Wimer Mountain Road and Hardscrabble, beside what was then the Colaw Store. Edward later sold out to Walter and his son John sometime after John returned from service in World War II. (Courtesy of Nancy Mullenax Hedges.)

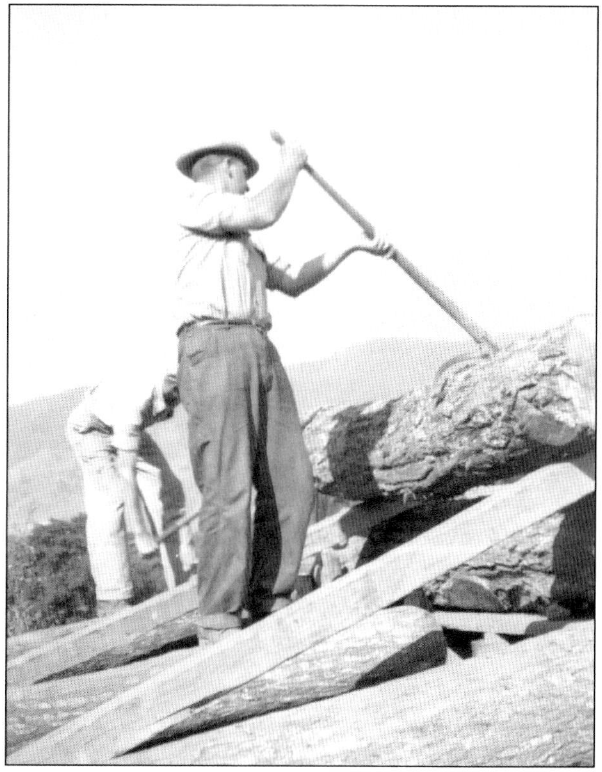

Paul Herold (left) and Dick Woods roll logs from the stock farm in Mill Gap by hand onto trucks. The owner of Woods Store in Mill Gap, Woods was very proud of the fact he never had to use loading machinery. J. W. Sheffer of Vanderpool transported the logs to the sawmills. Sheffer was a part owner with Woods in the store; at that time the name was Woods and Sheffer Store. Many Highland County residents have held several occupations at once out of necessity. (Courtesy of Libby Woods Hefner.)

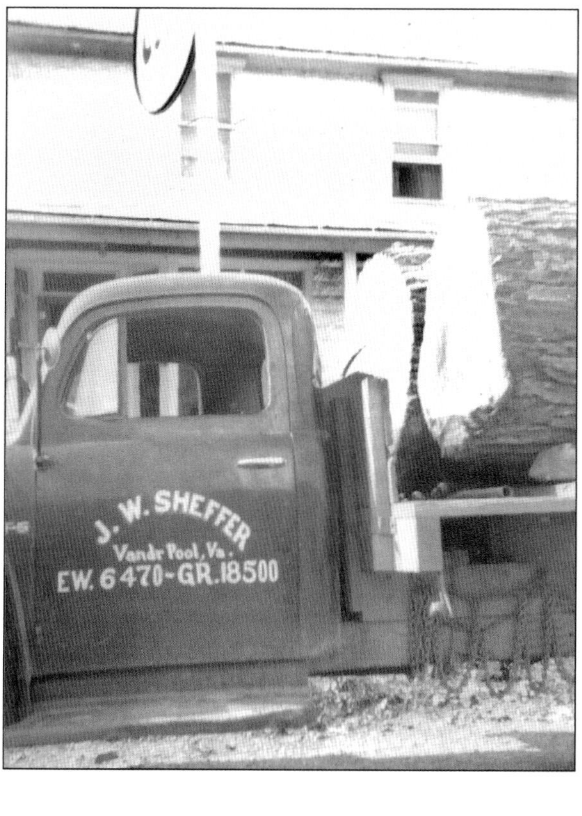

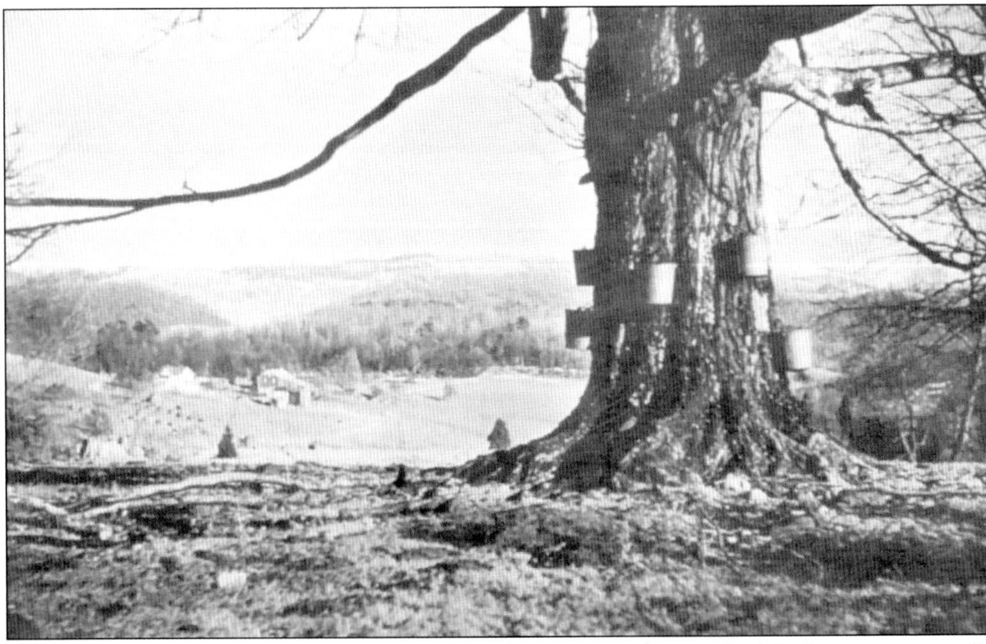

Arguably the most important tree in Highland County is the maple. Maple syrup is usually produced only in February and March. A sugar maple is large enough for tapping when it is 10 inches in diameter at four and a half feet from the ground; no permanent damage is done to the tree during tapping. The process requires 40 to 50 gallons of sugar water to produce just 1 gallon of syrup. (Courtesy of the Highland County Historical Society.)

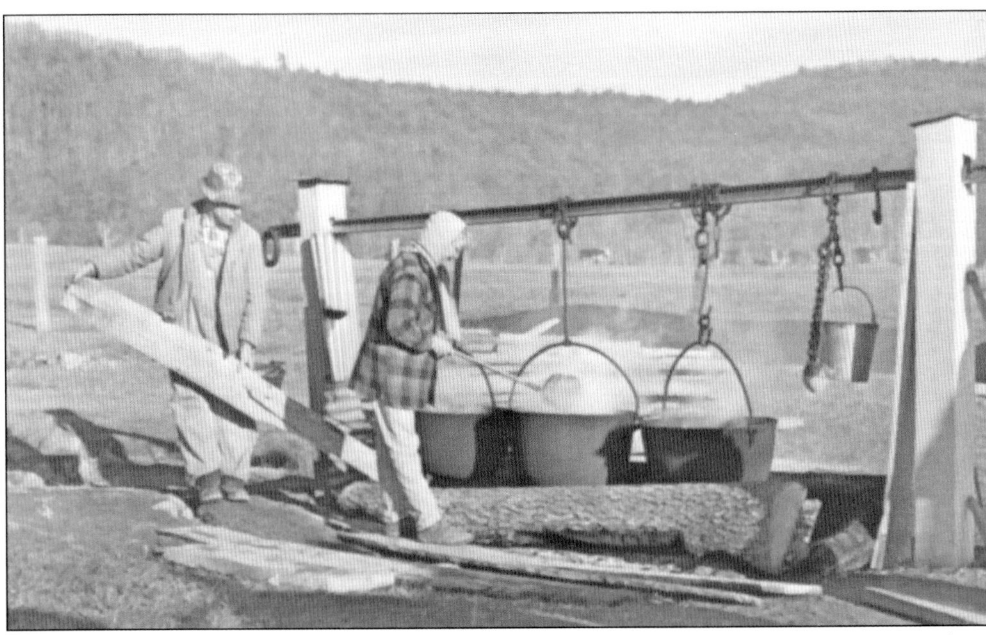

Once collected, the sugar water requires boiling down. Though not done this way on any large scale anymore, the water was traditionally boiled over an open wood fire. Here Lohr and Alice Vance of Vance's Sugar Camp tend to their kettles. (Courtesy of Robin and Nancy Vance.)

The maple syrup–making process has changed from the Native Americans' method of cutting a diagonal slit in the tree bark, allowing the sugar water to run out. For the most part, an elaborate system of taps, hollow tubing, and large tanks are now employed to collect the water. A modern evaporator, pictured here, is used at Puffenbarger's Sugar Camp to process the collected sugar water. (Courtesy of Kent Botkin.)

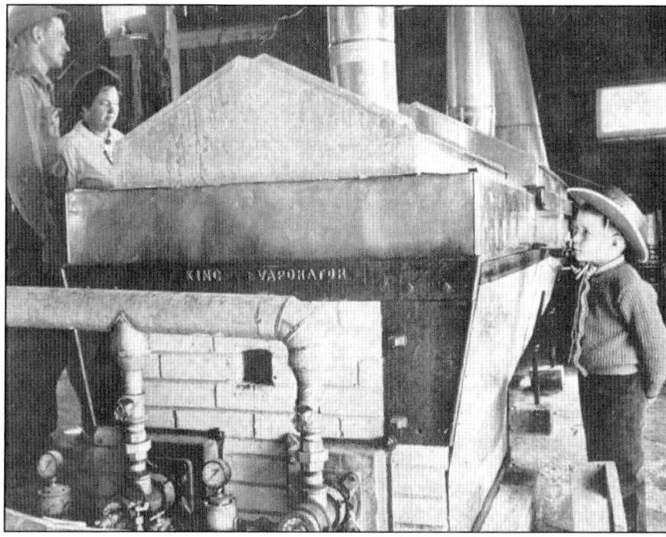

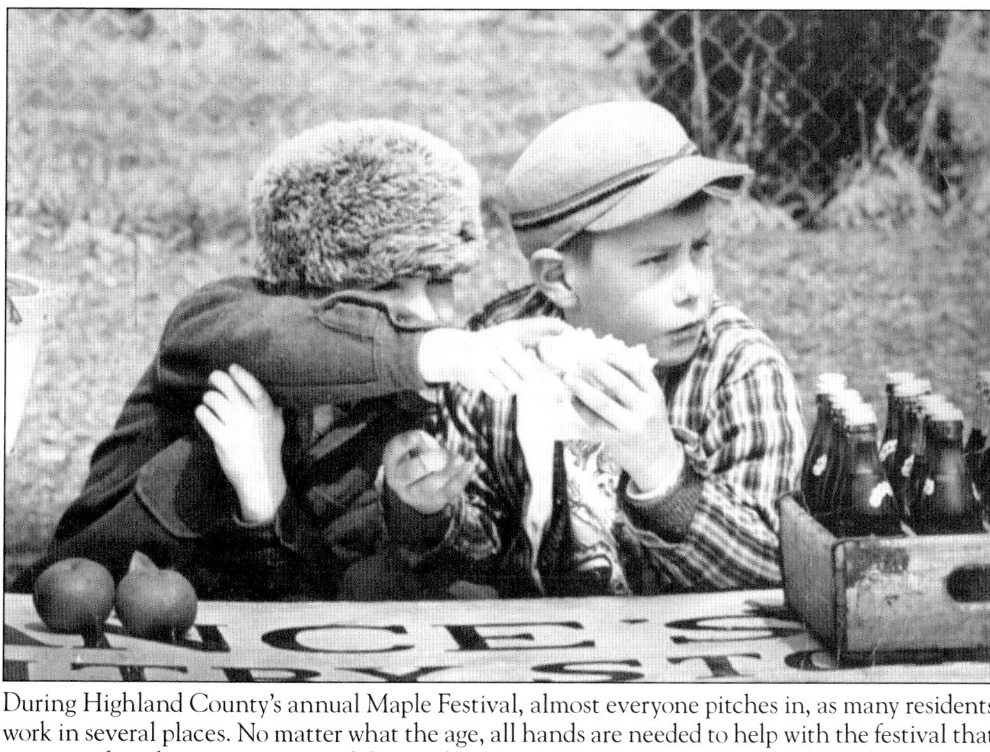

During Highland County's annual Maple Festival, almost everyone pitches in, as many residents work in several places. No matter what the age, all hands are needed to help with the festival that accounts for a large percentage of the residents' annual incomes. Kyle Obaugh (left) and Robin Vance sell apples and drinks at Vance's Country Store. (Courtesy of Kyle and Karla Obaugh.)

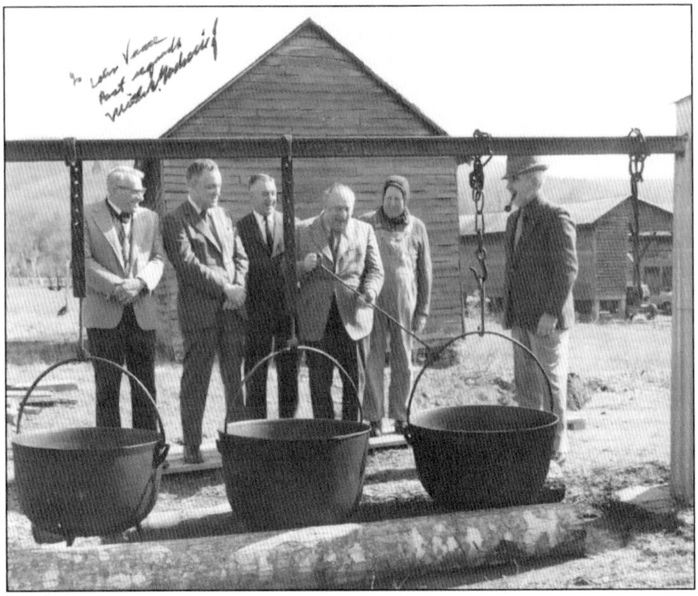

Among the many thousands of visitors who turn out for the annual Maple Festival are numerous politicians and dignitaries. Governors and other state-elected officials come to shake hands. Here former Virginia governor Mills Edwin Godwin Jr. (second from left) visits Lohr Vance at Vance's Sugar Camp on a tour of the county. Godwin served Virginia from 1966 to 1970 and 1974 to 1978. (Courtesy of Robin and Nancy Vance.)

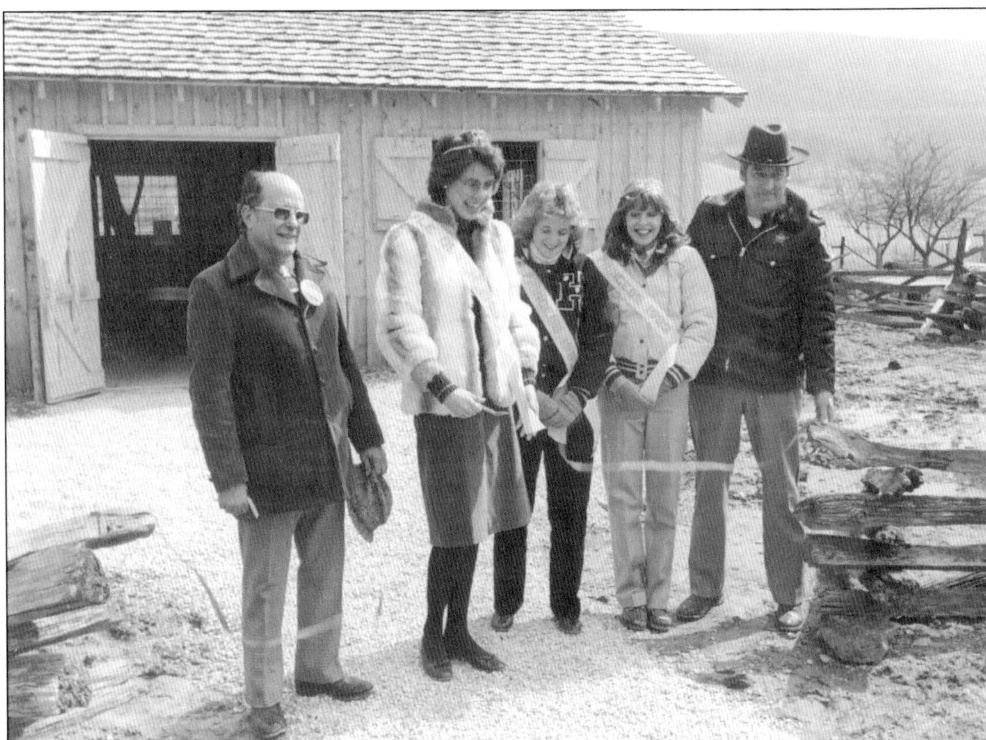

In 1983, Highland County opened a maple museum. The museum displays the history of maple syrup making in a replica of an old-time sugarhouse. Shown at the ribbon-cutting ceremony are, from left to right, Dr. Thaine Billingsley; Sherry Whitelaw, 1983 Maple Queen; Mary Angela Shultz, princess and first runner-up; Crystal Gail Warner, princess and second runner-up; and Deputy Sheriff Edwin "Mick" Williams, president of the chamber of commerce. (Courtesy of the Highland County Historical Society.)

Four

Buying and Selling
Stores and Industry

Country stores have always been an important part of rural life. It was here that purchases of all kinds were made—from clothes to seeds to books. Country stores served as the social centers of their day in many ways, with customers catching up on the latest news or gossip, old men playing checkers, and young people falling in and out of love in the time it took to eat a sundae. Patrons could pick up their mail and food staples, meet the neighbors, get informed (maybe misinformed), and buy a plow all in one visit. These were the days before the Wal-Marting of America. The woodstove became the gathering place in winter, the front porch the place in summer. The porch also provided a spot to post official notices. The porch posts at Sugar Tree Country Store are full of these tack holes.

Highland County, Virginia, is a county made of small towns, and at one point every one of these little towns had one or two stores and possibly some industry. In the area's early days, families were forced to be entirely self-sufficient. When the first country stores came along, the locals deemed them a helpful advance. These shops have thrived in the county from the earliest times. Peter Hull opened a store in Blue Grass (Crabbottom) in 1788. And Doe Hill had a store before 1835.

As the late 19th and early 20th centuries unfolded, industry of all kinds dawned in Highland. Residents of the county were nothing if not entrepreneurial. Inhabitants took in boarders and started millinery shops. Mill Gap boasted several country stores, as did the diminutive town of Headwaters. Though attempted in Virginia's Little Switzerland, a cheese factory in McDowell withered and closed. Skilled craftsmen were suddenly very much in demand. Men such as Lank Simmons became well known to their communities for the precision they brought to their craft.

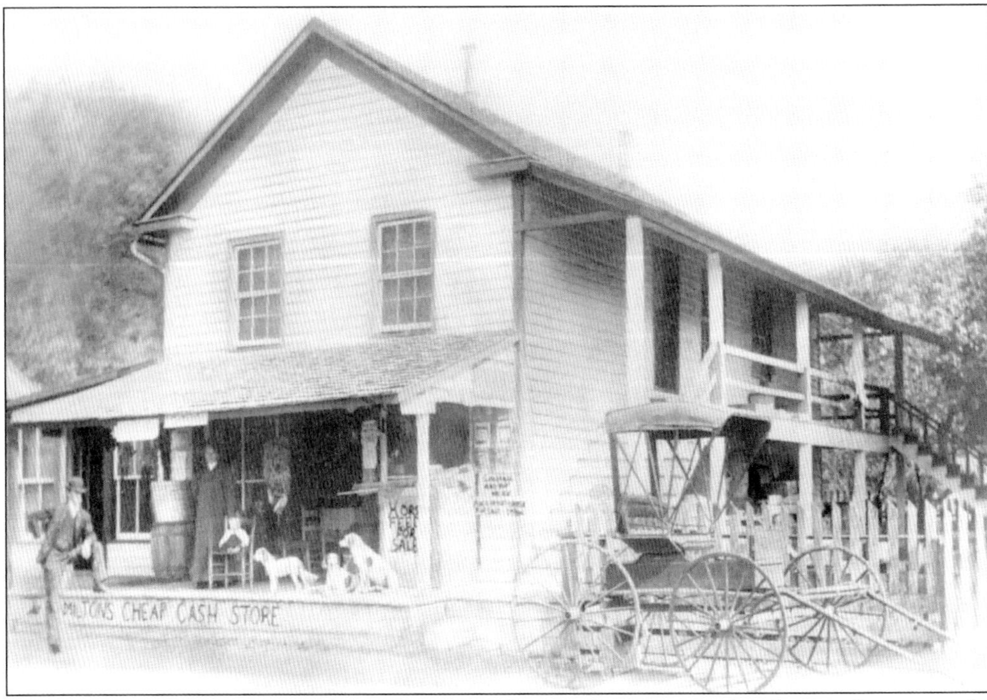

Now known as Millers Store, this shop, post office, and gas station has been a fixture in the Headwaters community for many years. Based on square footage, the store contains the smallest post office in the country. The Hamilton family ran Hamilton's Cheap Cash Store here in the early 1900s. (Courtesy of the Highland County Historical Society.)

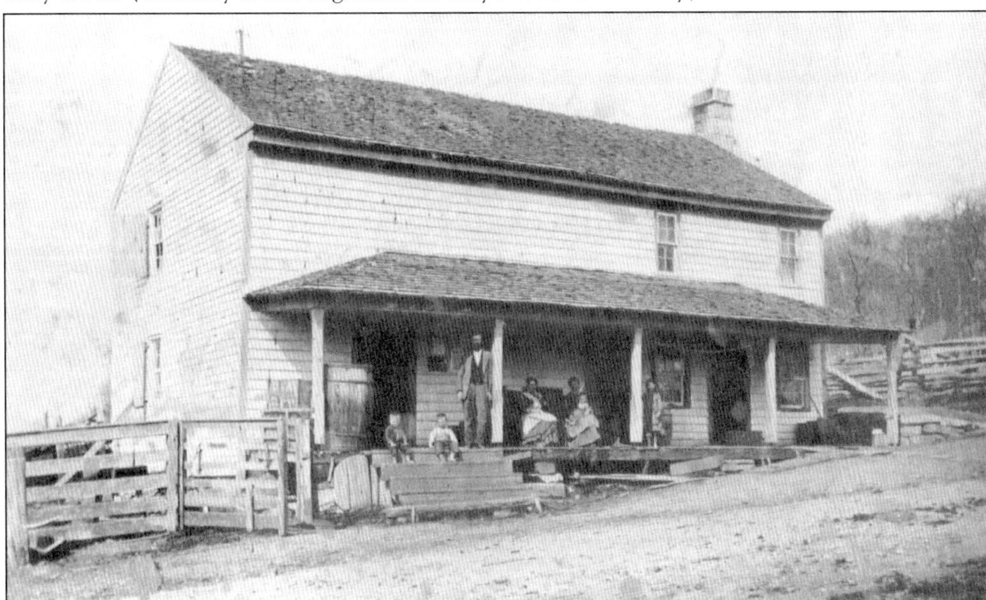

The Hevener family operated a general store in Hightown for five generations. The chain began before 1820, when Jacob Hevener cleared some land on his farm and erected a log store. The shop housed the post office, and successive Heveners served as postmaster until descendant Jacob Hevener retired in 1992. (Courtesy of the Highland County Historical Society.)

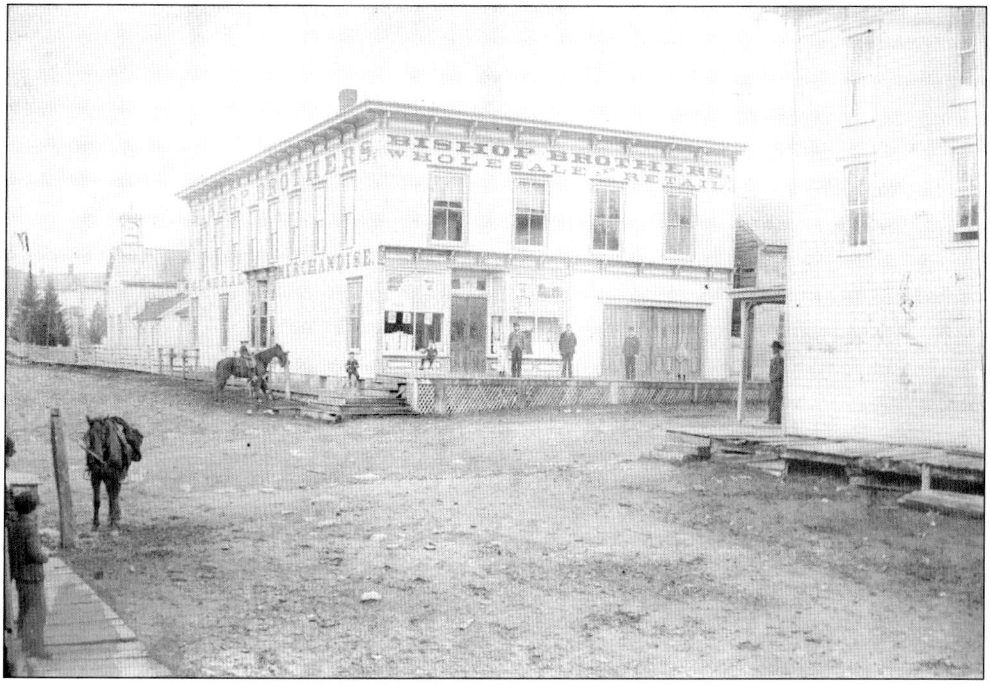

The Monterey fire of 1947 destroyed the Bishop Brothers Wholesale and Retail Store, which served as a general store, among other offerings. First and Citizens Bank is located on this corner spot today. (Courtesy of Kent Botkin.)

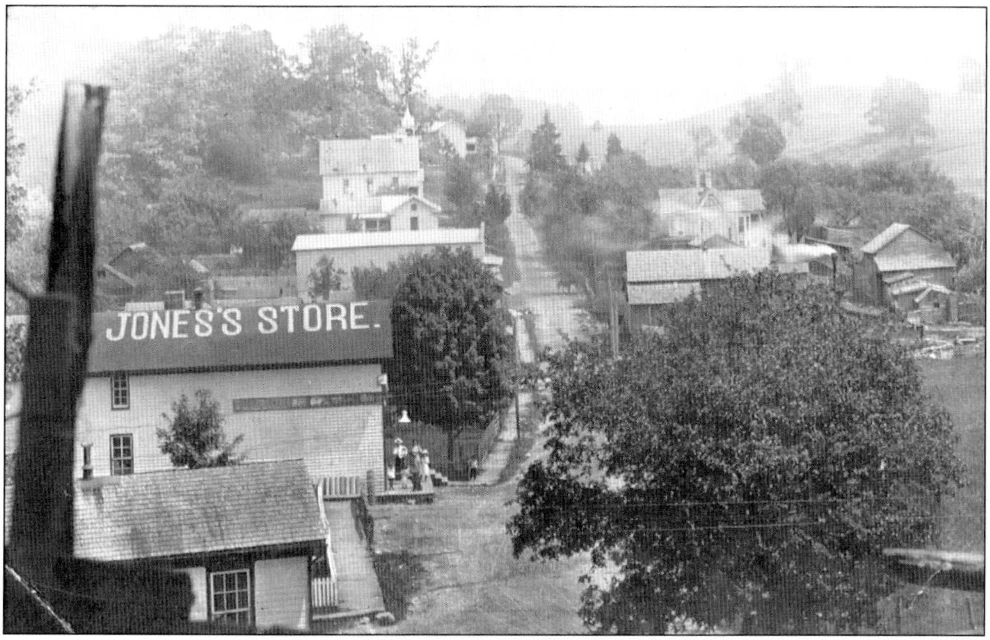

Alpheus Seybert Jones filled many roles in the Doe Hill community. He served as postmaster, worked as a farmer, led as a trustee at Doe Hill United Methodist Church, created the Doe Hill Cemetery Association, and ran Jones's Store. The Jones's Store building housed many different shops over the years, including L. W. Shoulder and Company. (Courtesy of Kent Botkin.)

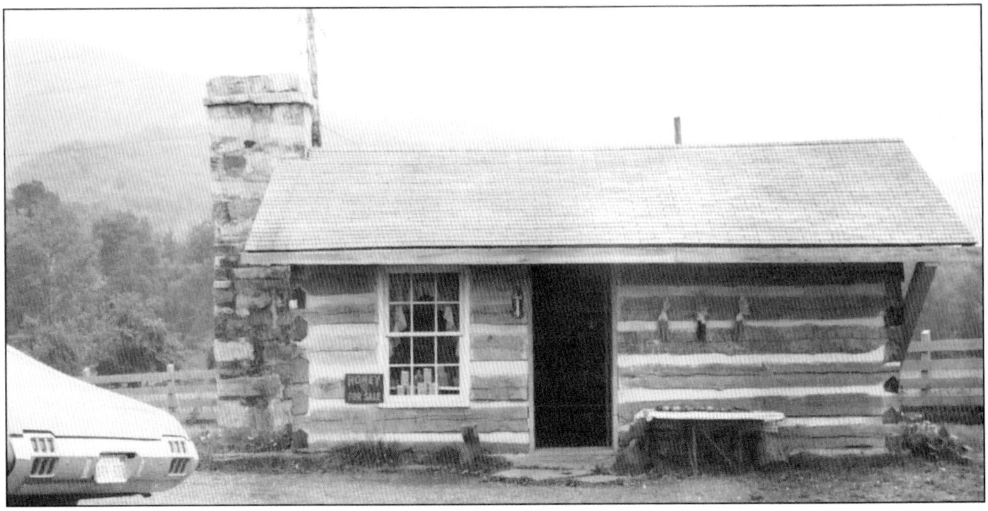

Previously used as a school, the log building that housed Vance's Country Store was moved to this spot in order to educate a generation of Vance children. Lohr and Alice Vance later opened their country store and sugar camp here. In the store, the Vances stocked a wide selection of goods. The register was an intricate system with small metal balls used to total up the customers' purchases. Before coming to Highland, Alice worked as a nurse who, along with her father, had developed a system to calm honeybees. In fact, Lohr and Alice met when she was written up in an Ohio newspaper. Lohr wrote to ask her about her methods, addressing the letter to "Alice the beekeeping nurse." A connection developed from there. (Courtesy of Robin and Nancy Vance.)

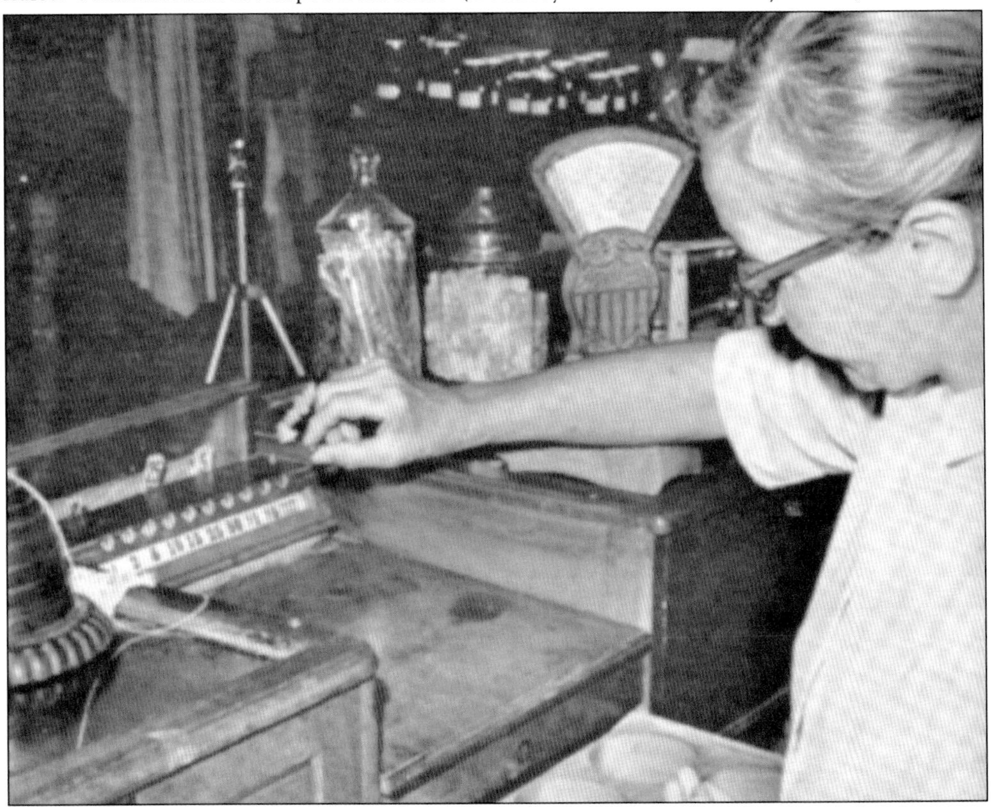

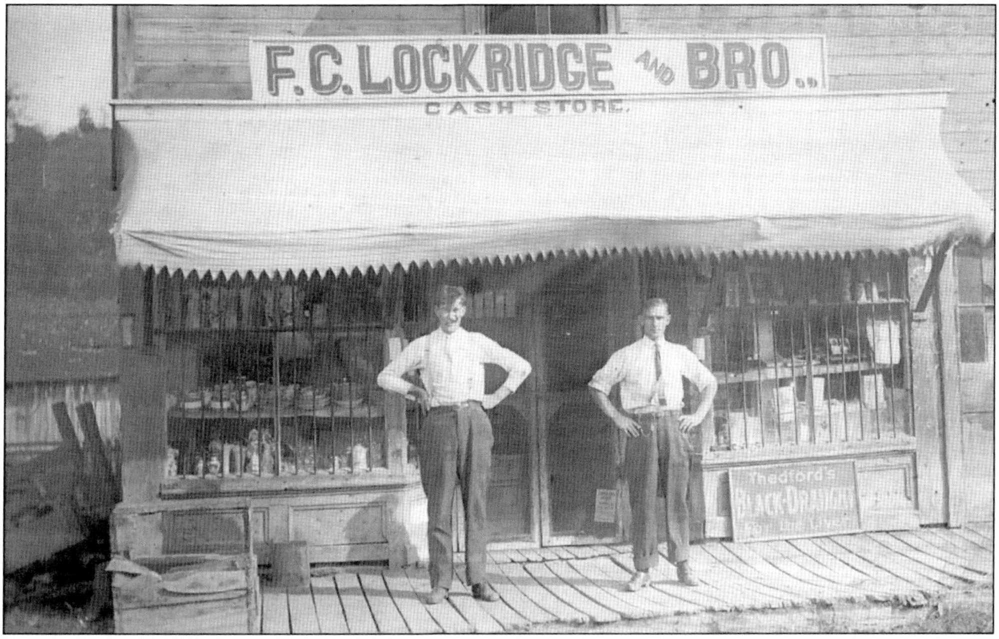

Frank C. Lockridge was the stereotypical entrepreneur retailer. At one time or another, he owned several stores in the McDowell area and a shop on the Doe Hill Road. He built the store and garage that he later sold to William Henry Swadley in the 1920s. He ran F. C. Lockridge and Brother in this location as an all-purpose general store. The building was located on Route 250. (Courtesy of Kent Botkin.)

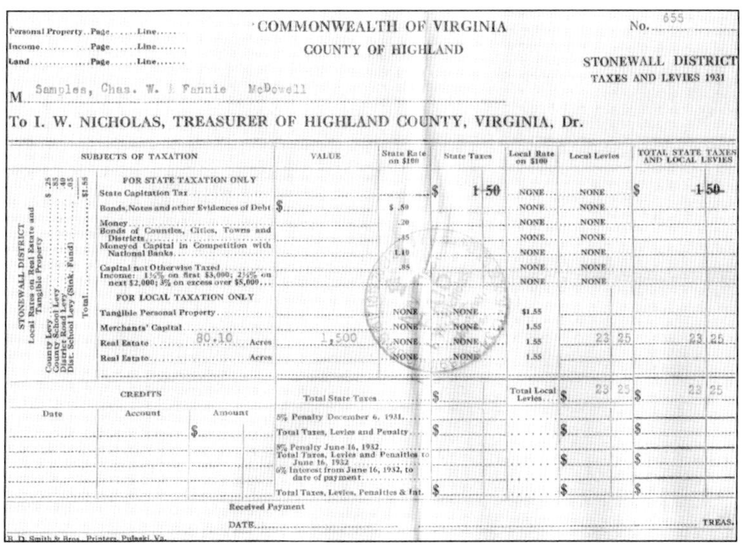

Personal Property..Page......Line.....
Income..........Page......Line.......
Land............Page......Line.......

COMMONWEALTH OF VIRGINIA
COUNTY OF HIGHLAND

No. 655

STONEWALL DISTRICT
TAXES AND LEVIES 1931

M Samples, Chas. W. & Fannie McDowell

To I. W. NICHOLAS, TREASURER OF HIGHLAND COUNTY, VIRGINIA, Dr.

STONEWALL DISTRICT — Local Rates on Real Estate and Tangible Property: County Levy $ .25; County School Levy .85; District Road Levy .40; Dist. School Levy (Sink. Fund) .05; Total $1.55

SUBJECTS OF TAXATION	VALUE	State Rate on $100	State Taxes	Local Rate on $100	Local Levies	TOTAL STATE TAXES AND LOCAL LEVIES
FOR STATE TAXATION ONLY						
State Capitation Tax			$ 1 50	NONE	NONE	$ 1 50
Bonds, Notes and other Evidences of Debt	$	$ .50		NONE	NONE	
Money		.20		NONE	NONE	
Bonds of Counties, Cities, Towns and Districts		.35		NONE	NONE	
Moneyed Capital in Competition with National Banks		1.10		NONE	NONE	
Capital not Otherwise Taxed		.85		NONE	NONE	
Income: 1½% on first $3,000; 2½% on next $2,000; 3% on excess over $5,000				NONE	NONE	
FOR LOCAL TAXATION ONLY						
Tangible Personal Property		NONE	NONE	$1.55		
Merchants' Capital		NONE	NONE	1.55		
Real Estate 80.10 Acres	1,500	NONE	NONE	1.55	23 25	23 25
Real Estate ... Acres		NONE	NONE	1.55		

CREDITS: Date	Account	Amount		State		Local	Total
		$	Total State Taxes	$	Total Local Levies	$ 23 25	$ 23 25
			5% Penalty December 6, 1931				
			Total Taxes, Levies and Penalty	$		$	$
			5% Penalty June 16, 1932				
			Total Taxes, Levies and Penalties to June 16, 1932			$	$
			6% Interest from June 16, 1932, to date of payment				
			Total Taxes, Levies, Penalties & Int.	$		$	$

Received Payment

DATE.......... .... TREAS.

B. D. Smith & Bros., Printers, Pulaski, Va.

The reality of life anywhere in any age is the existence of taxes. All business owners, farmers, and owners of property have to pay the government. In this tax bill from 1931, the tax rate on 80 acres valued at $1,500 was $23.25. This served as an annual bill for Charles and Fannie Samples of McDowell. (Courtesy of Sarah Samples.)

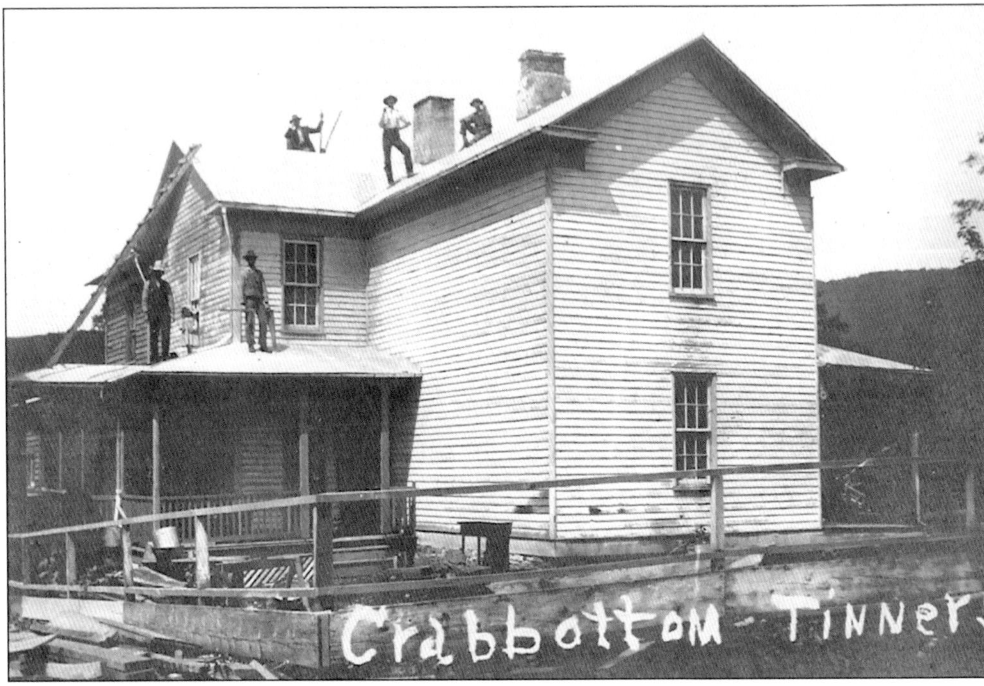

Physically demanding, construction might also be considered an art form when it comes to metal roofing. Here a group of roofers, or tinners, plies their trade in Crabbottom, which would later become Blue Grass. (Courtesy of Kent Botkin.)

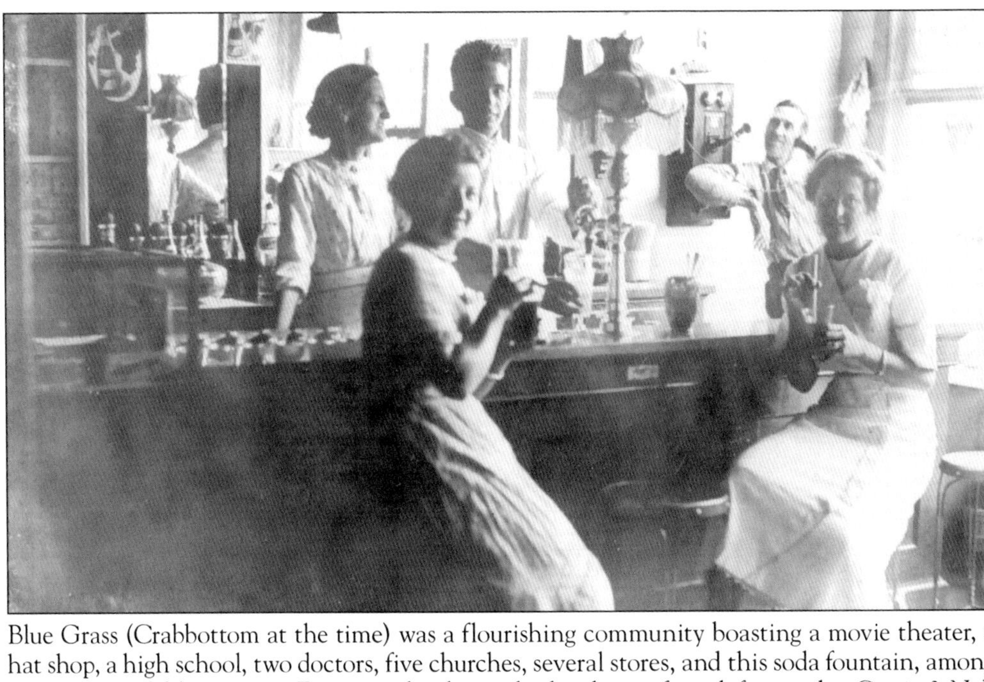

Blue Grass (Crabbottom at the time) was a flourishing community boasting a movie theater, a hat shop, a high school, two doctors, five churches, several stores, and this soda fountain, among other successful businesses. Enjoying the day and a laugh are, from left to right, Carrie ?, Nell Nichols, Charlie Ralston, Sam Ralston, and Maggie Mauzy. (Courtesy of Janet Mullenax.)

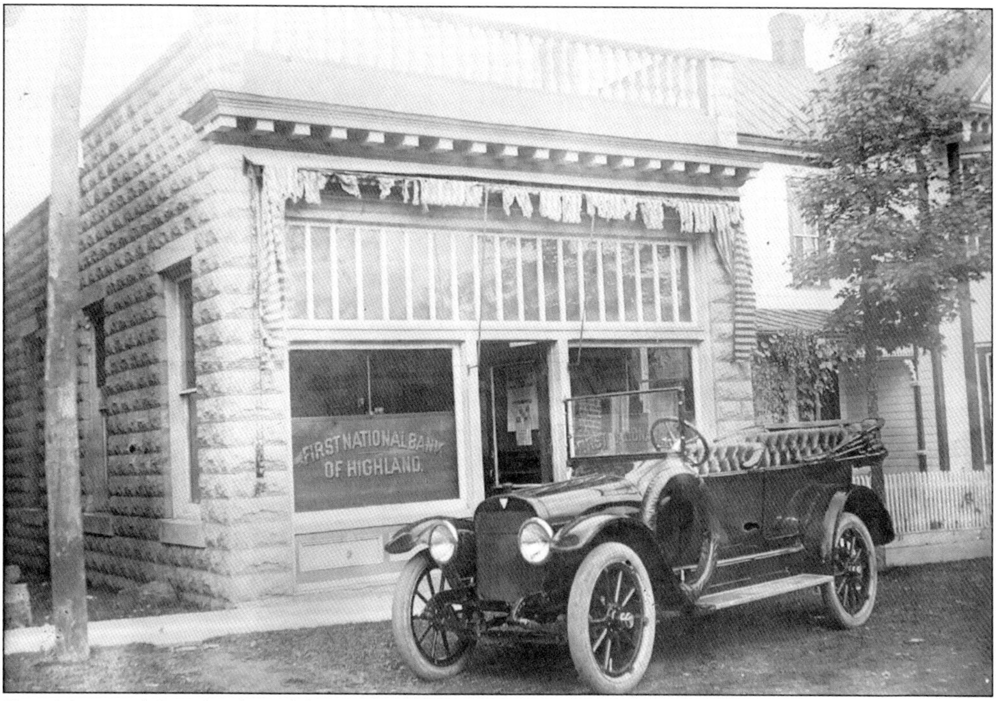

First National Bank of Highland and Citizens Bank of Highland, competing county financial institutions, merged to become First and Citizens Bank shortly after the stock market crash of 1929. The First National Bank building in Monterey was constructed in 1908 and now houses Evelyn's Pantry. Currently there are two different banks in the county. (Courtesy of the *Recorder*.)

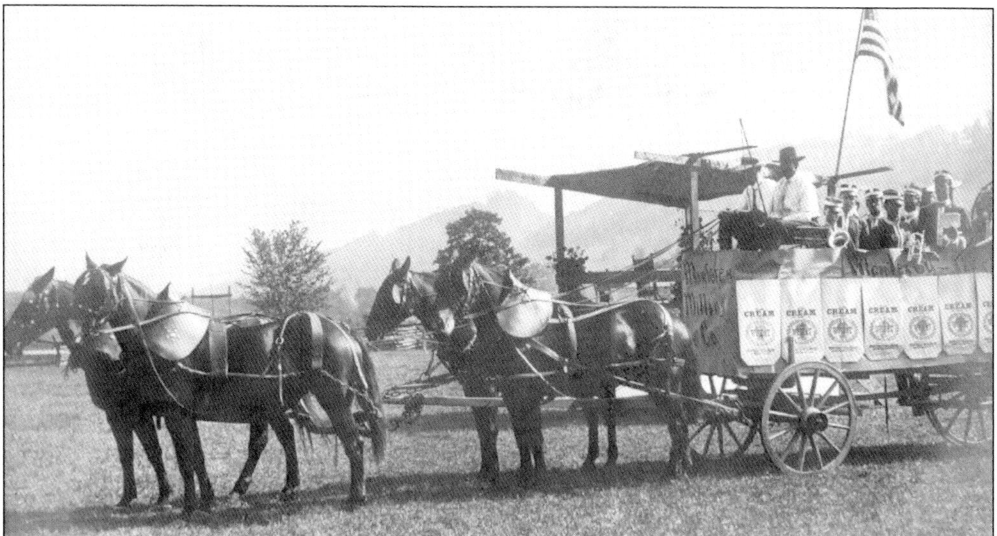

The Circleville Band of West Virginia plays music in a wagon advertising the Monterey Milling Company at the Monterey Stock Show in 1910. (Courtesy of Kent Botkin.)

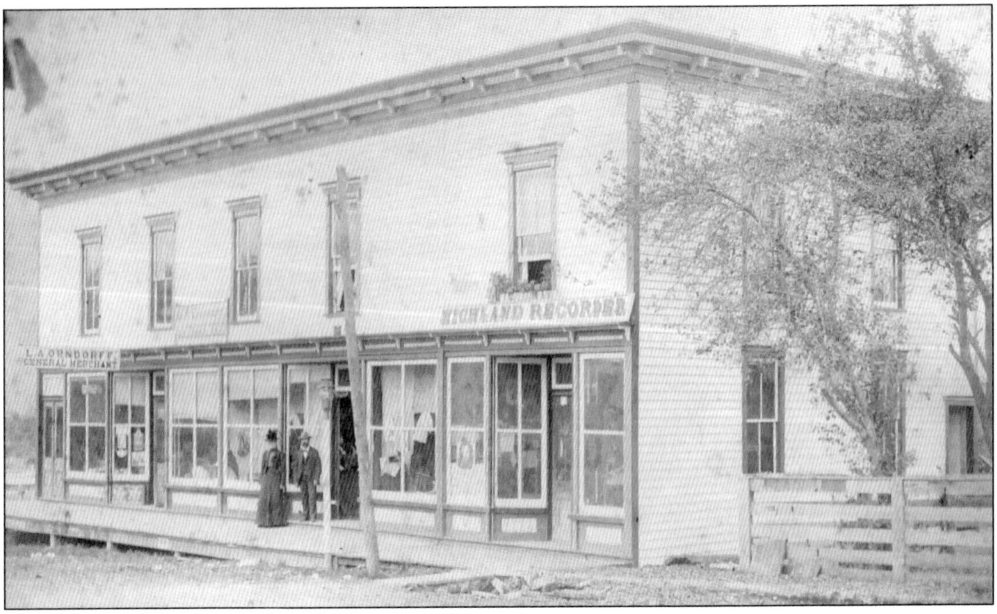

The *Recorder*, shown in the early 1900s in one of its many locations, stands next to the L. A. Orndorff General Merchant Store and the S. W. Crummett Harness Shop. Silas Crummett owned this harness shop before building and opening the Hotel Monterey in 1904. (Courtesy of the Highland County Historical Society.)

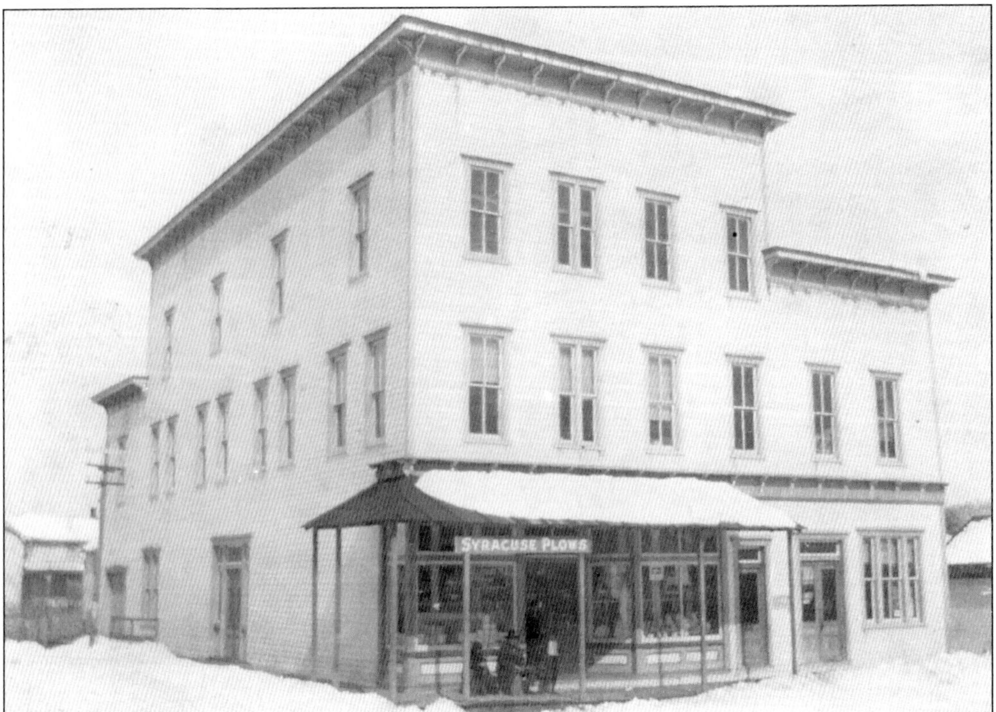

Then known as the D. H. Peterson Store and currently the H&H Cash Store, this building is located on Main Street in Monterey. A sign on the porch advertises Syracuse Plows, a popular brand of plow that is still manufactured today. The upstairs serves as apartments. (Courtesy of the *Recorder*.)

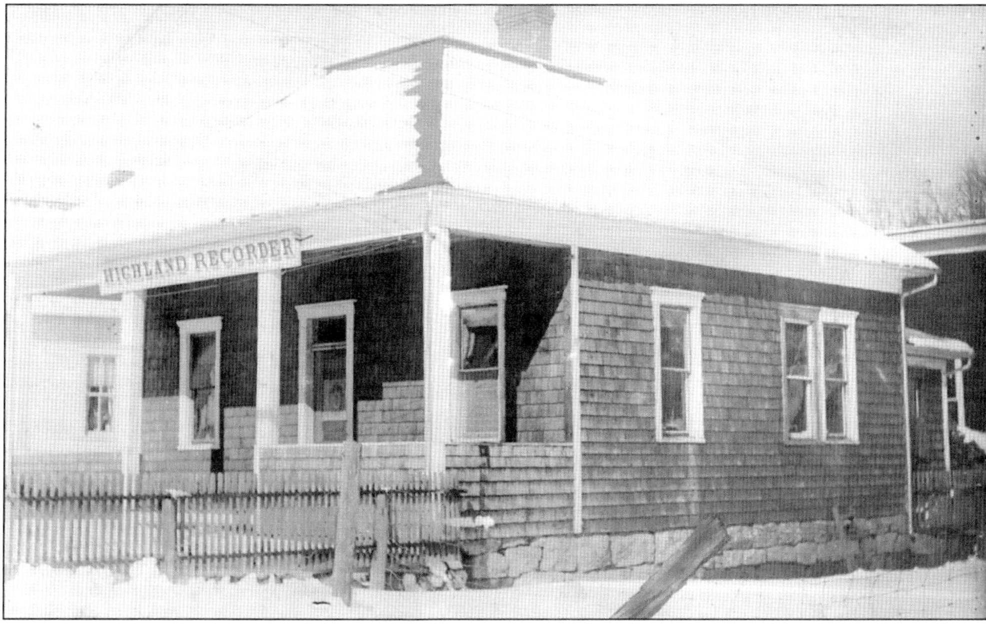

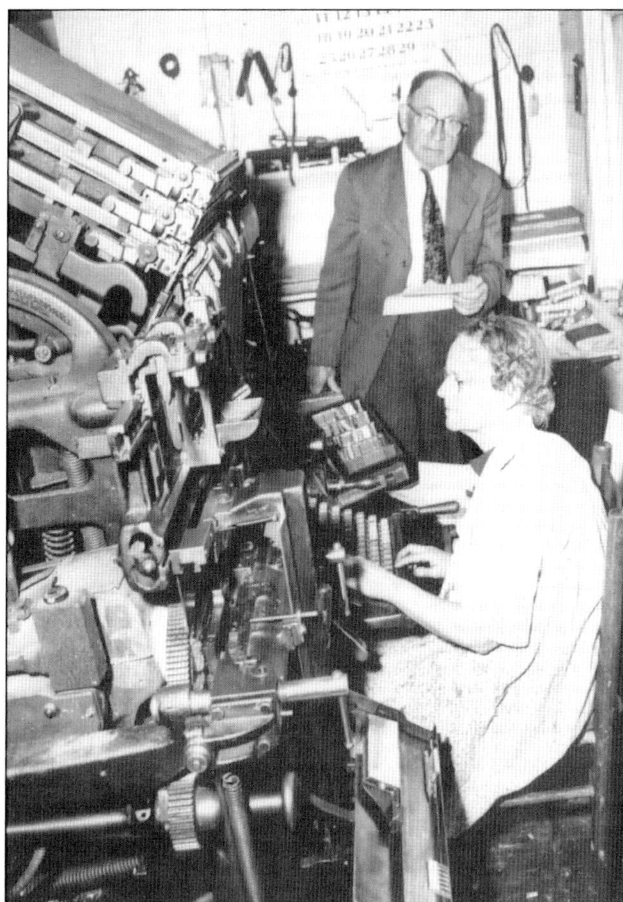

Founded on October 20, 1877, the *Highland Recorder*, as it was originally known, is the weekly newspaper for the county. P. E. Witts and George M. Jordan began the paper after their previous newspaper failed in Pendleton County, West Virginia. The name changed to simply the *Recorder* in April 1972 to reflect that the paper was now serving Bath County as well. The *Recorder* has changed hands several times over the years, with H. B. Wood serving the longest tenure as publisher, from August 12, 1904, to July 24, 1953, and again from August 21, 1953, to October 5, 1953. Wood returned after the unexpectedly short possession of the new owner, Herbert H. Horton. Wood, shown at the time of his retirement, often made the statement that he had come to visit Highland County for a summer and stayed 50 years. This building (above) was the paper's home about 1920. (Courtesy of Kent Botkin.)

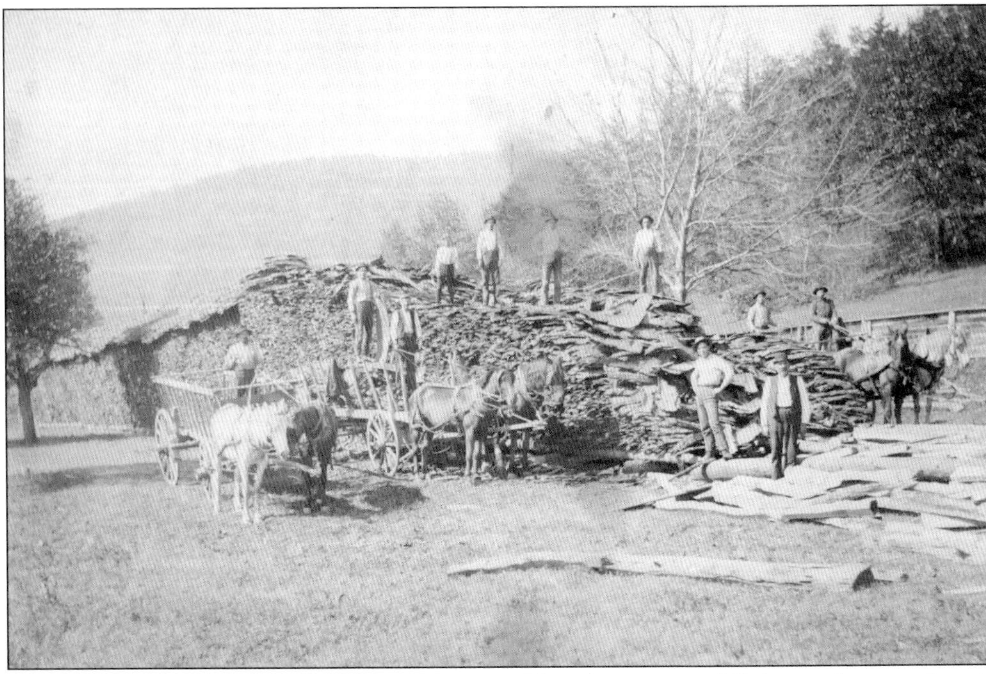

Tree bark was important to the tanning process. After the tree was felled, a worker cut rings in the bark with an ax every three feet and peeled off sections or strips. The inner bark, dripping with sap, was then used for tanning. Unidentified men pose at the tanbark yard in Highland County. (Courtesy of Kent Botkin.)

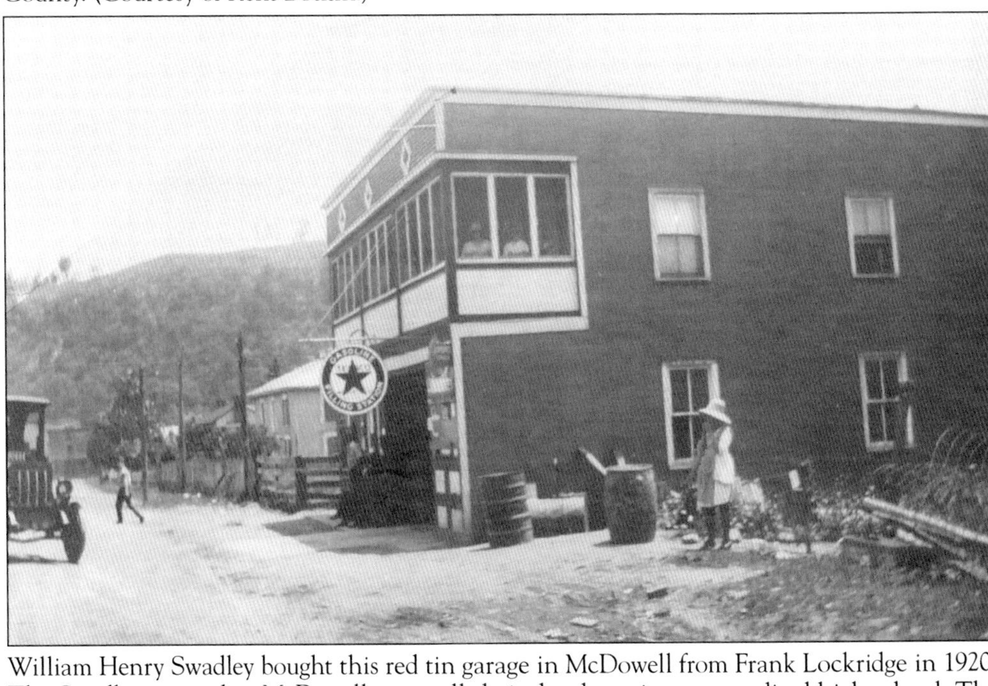

William Henry Swadley bought this red tin garage in McDowell from Frank Lockridge in 1920. The Swadleys moved to McDowell to enroll their daughters in an accredited high school. The family lived in the upstairs of the garage; from this porch, they spotted the fire in the log kitchen adjacent to the Mansion House. (Courtesy of Lyle and Georgianne Maloy Hull.)

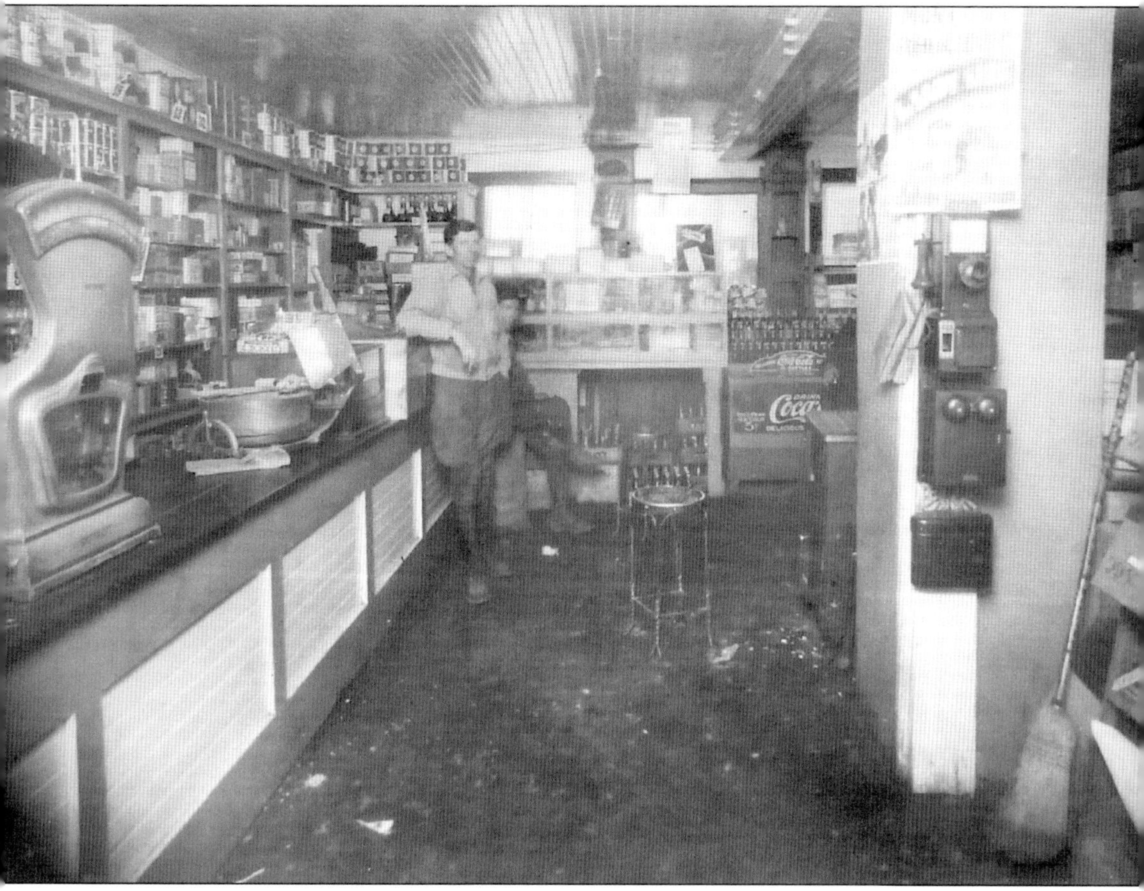

William Swadley leans on the counter of Swadley's Store, located next to his garage in McDowell. His daughters Leola and Virginia worked in the store serving lemonade and ice cream. In this image, the shelves are crammed with offerings. An early public pay phone hangs in the foreground on a support beam. After Swadley closed the shop, E. C. Devericks used the space to house his GE appliances and Rawley products. Devericks boarded with William and Thressa Swadley, as he was a traveling salesman who kept his car loaded with samples. Both the garage and the store building were sold in 1957 to make way for the Obaugh Funeral Home. (Courtesy of Lyle and Georgianne Maloy Hull.)

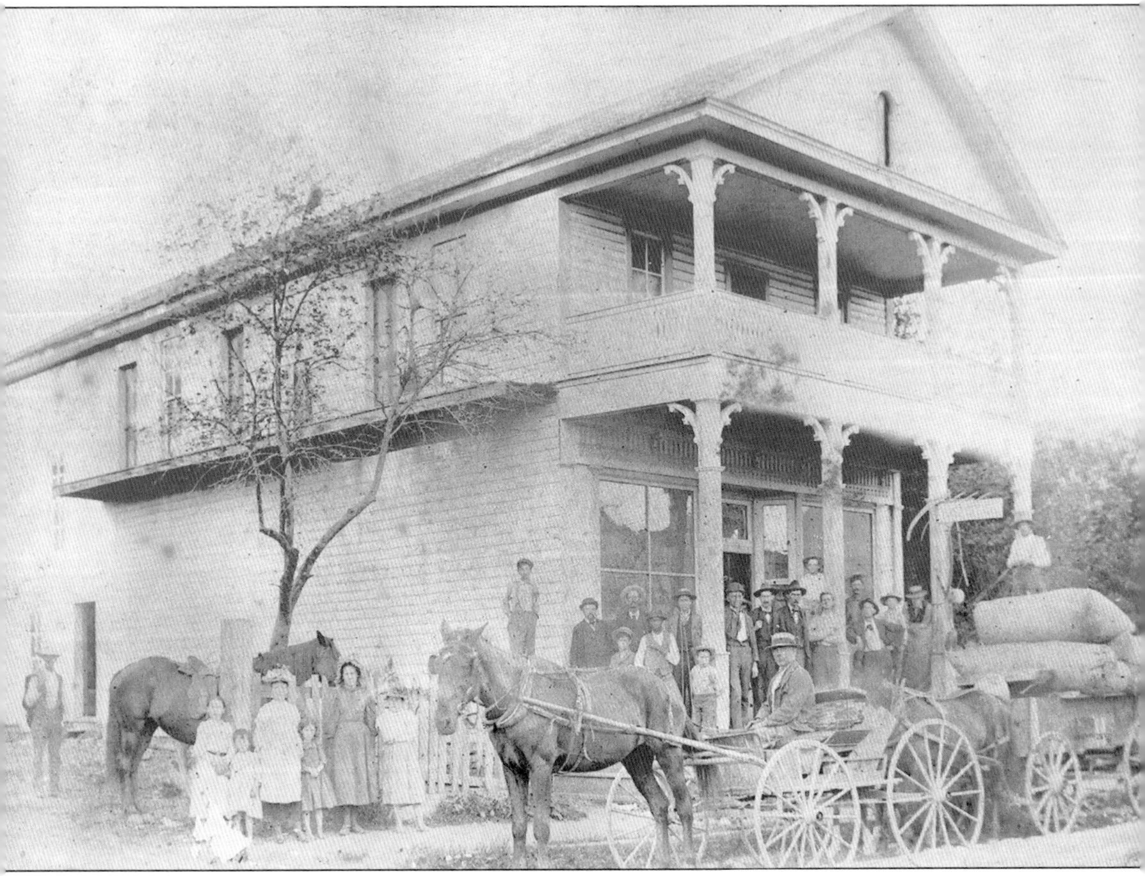

McDowell residents gather at McNulty Brothers Store on March 15, 1905. The group includes schoolteacher Elsie Bryant, shopkeeper E. A. McNulty, and John McNulty, among others. George Washington Hull is believed to have constructed the building sometime prior to 1854, when his father, Peter Hull, specified in his will that the house and storehouse be included in the acreage left to George. The house mentioned is the Mansion House, immediately to the west of this structure. Hull's Store appears on the 1847 map of Highland County. Under a number of owners and tenant merchants, this shop operated as a general store and post office for many years. After the death of E. A. McNulty in the 1950s, his clerk George Hogshead built a new store and post office, and the original space closed its doors. In 1986, Jim and Lorraine White reopened the building as Sugar Tree Country Store in honor of the town's original name. In January 2005, the business passed to new owners, Glenn and Fern Heatwole. (Courtesy of Sugar Tree Country Store.)

Completed in 1911, the McDowell Mill required several years to construct. Edward Ashby Hammer built the mill and died shortly after finishing. His obituary in the *Recorder* included these lines: "He gave employment to more people than any other man in this county. His last effort was building a flour mill at McDowell, which he had completed about the time he took sick." Over the years, the building has been used as a theater, store, and more. (Courtesy of Kent Botkin.)

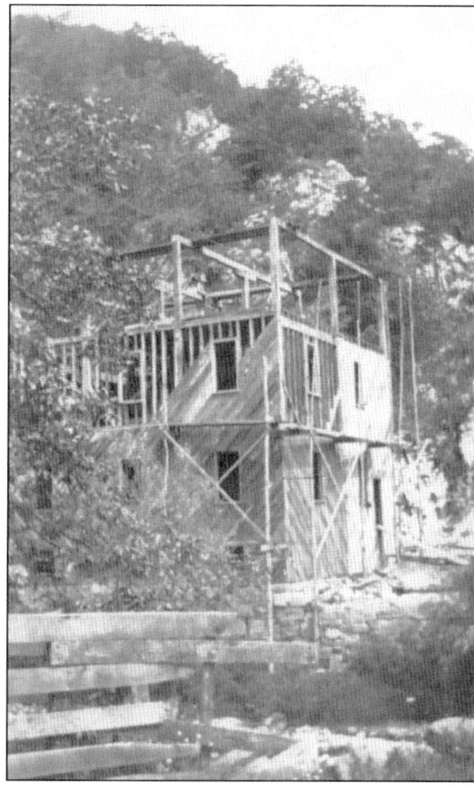

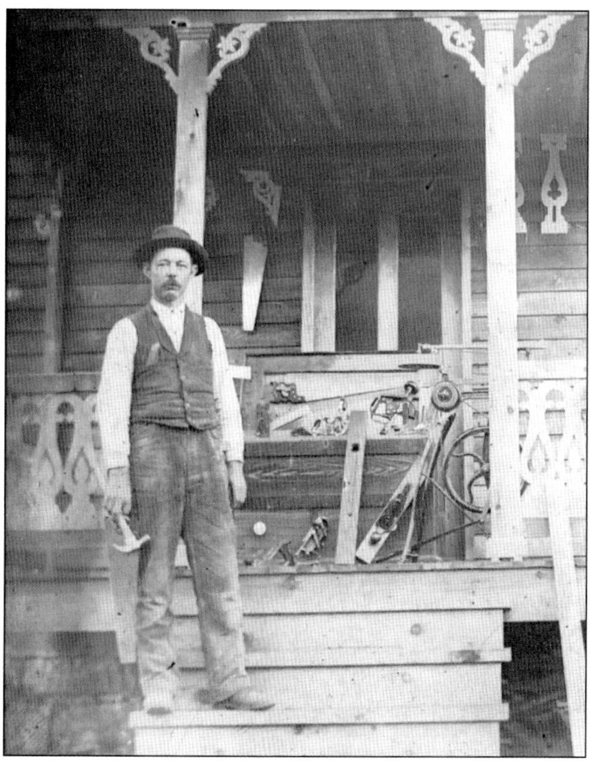

Lank Simmons, standing with his tools on a building project near Palo Alto in 1900, was a carpenter and surveyor in Headwaters. Well known for his insistence on perfection, he once fired a man on the spot for hammering a screw. Simmons constructed Headwaters Presbyterian Chapel in 1900. He was a stalwart pillar of the church, to which he left his estate upon his 1956 death. (Courtesy of Kent Botkin.)

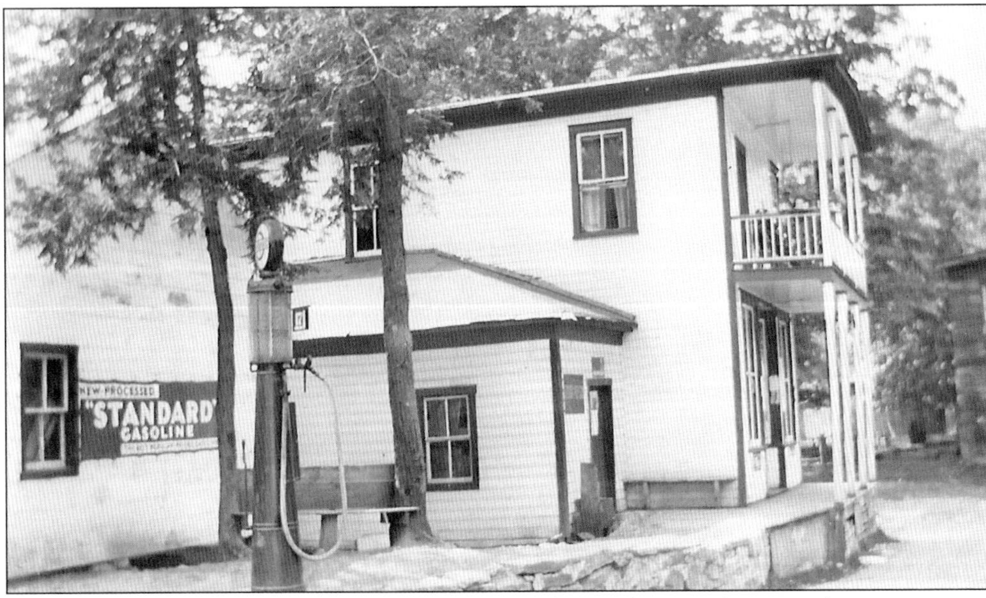

Stephenson's Grocery in Bolar, owned by Charles Omby Stephenson, functioned as a community hub for the town. The store offered groceries and fuel and is now a private residence. (Courtesy of Kent Botkin.)

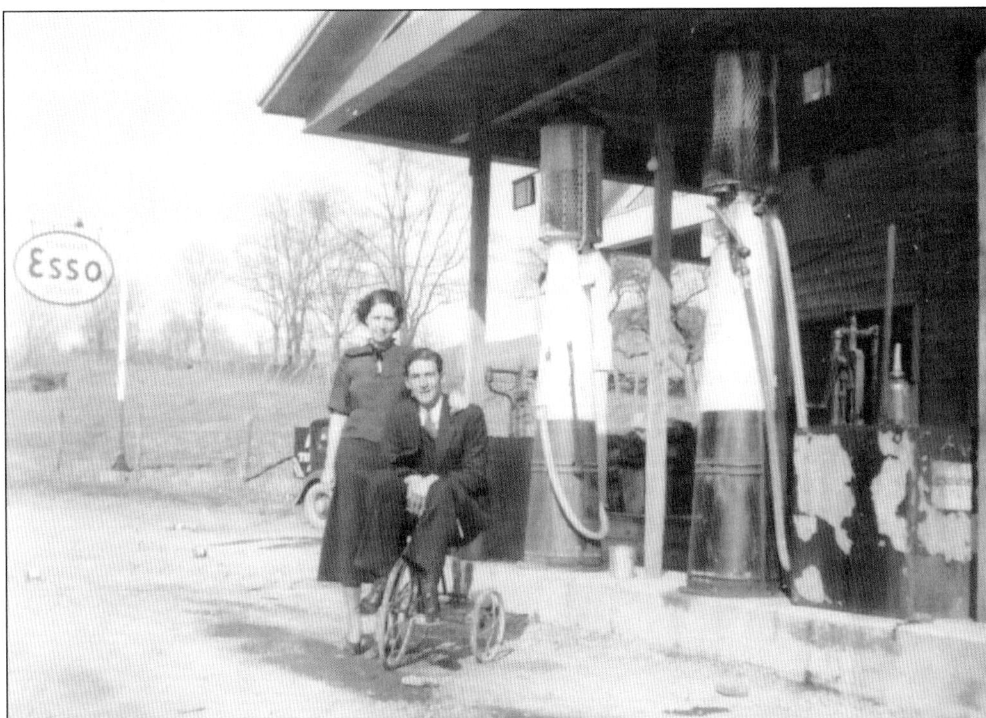

Mill Gap once had several country stores serving its area residents. Here Kenton Schooler has a little fun in front of the Mill Gap Store on a tricycle with an unidentified woman. This store was owned by Minor Gutschall and is currently known as Mill Gap Supply. (Courtesy of Libby Woods Hefner.)

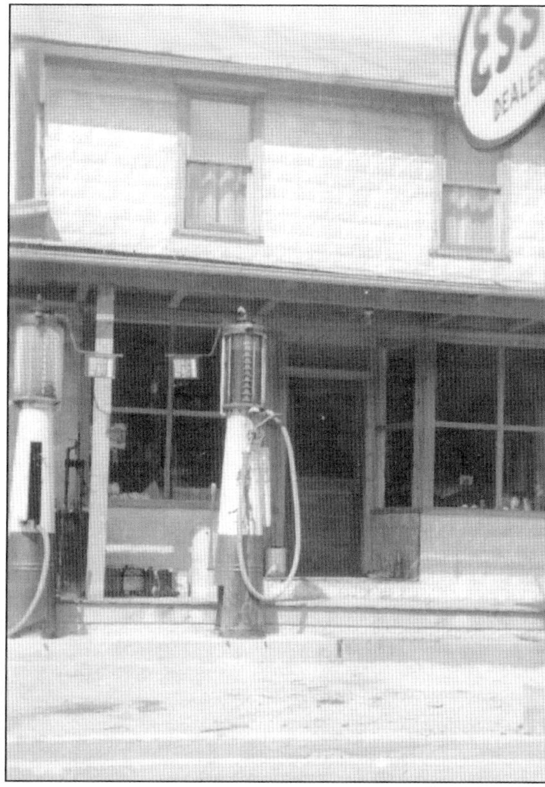

From 1945 to 1960, Howard "Dick" and Ruby Woods offered most everything a family needed from their store on Route 84 in Mill Gap. They also sold the popular Esso gasoline. The store's shelves, behind James Woods, were crammed with the staples of life, from seeds and meat to fabric and paper. Esso became Exxon in the 1970s. (Courtesy of Libby Woods Hefner.)

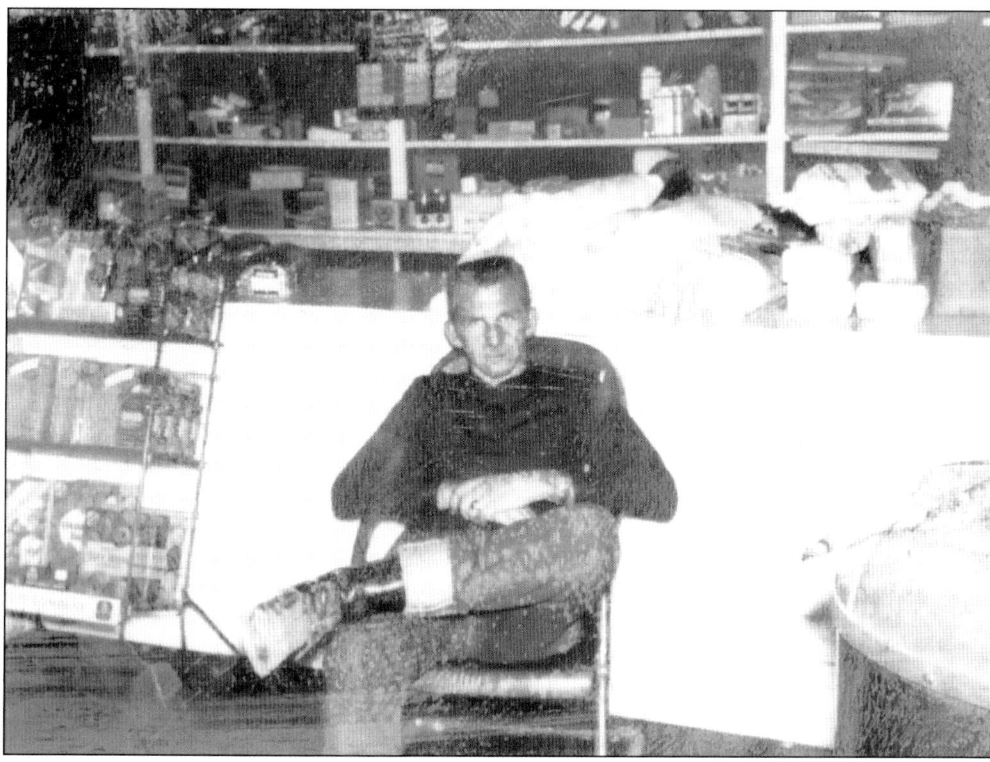

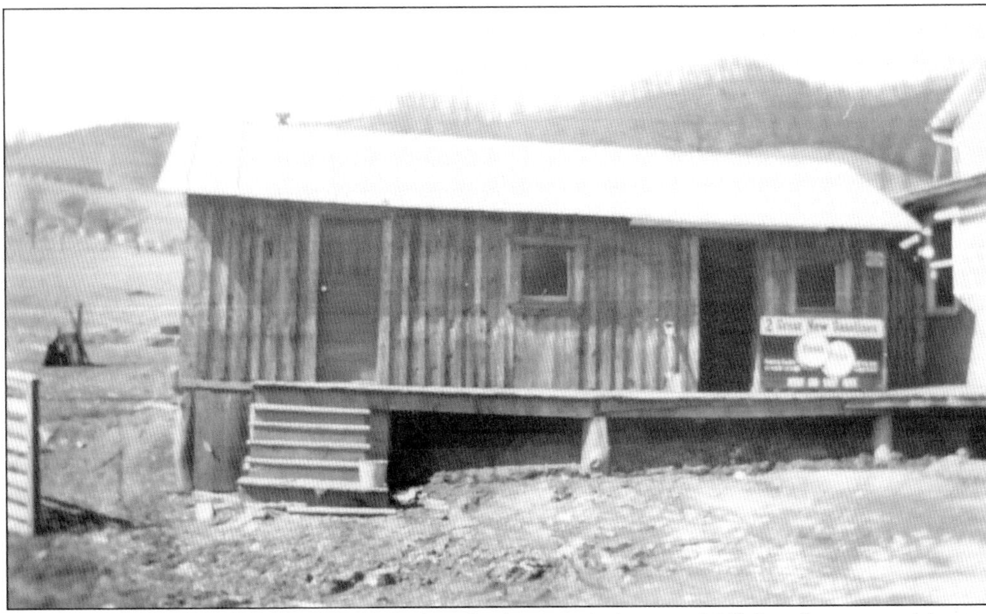

This shack was moved into this location beside the Woods Store in Mill Gap from a neighboring farm. Originally intended for use as a storage shed, it was first rented out for living space. A note on the back of the photograph reads, "This will be our home." Later it was indeed used as storage for the store, with a space in back for butchering chickens. (Courtesy of Libby Woods Hefner.)

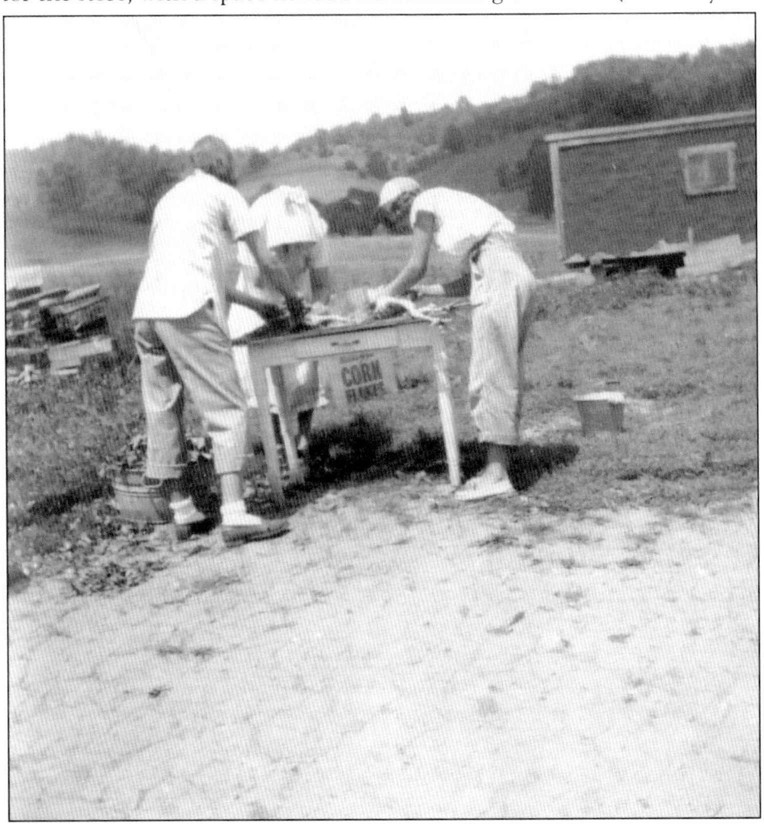

In the early 1950s, Mary Catherine Smith (left), Nina Sheffer (center), and Lucy Carroll cut up chickens to be canned and sold at the Woods Store. The ladies were paid for their efforts with cash and chicken pieces. Sheffer was locally famous for constantly wearing her bonnet. (Courtesy of Libby Woods Hefner.)

Five

Making a Life
Churches and Recreation

While earning a living is important, residents have a full tradition of pursuing a rich quality of life as well. Churches and social activities have always been key components of life in Highland County. Both church and recreation fill different but valid roles.

From church picnics and weddings to Sunday school conventions and hymns, church has long defined life in the county for residents. As in most Southern towns, churches played a significant role for residents, from the obvious spiritual component to a more immediate social one. Sunday may have been one's big chance to catch up on gossip, news, or simple conversation. Churches were usually located five miles apart, a reasonable distance to travel by horse and wagon.

At the time of the settling of the region, the Episcopal church was the officially sanctioned church in Virginia, though after the Revolutionary War, religious life began to open up. Part of the attraction of the Highland County area was that non-Episcopal dissenters were left alone west of the Blue Ridge. The early Scotch-Irish settlers brought their Presbyterian faith with them. Methodists are well represented as well. Many differing denominations have appeared in Highland County at one point or another. There have been several attempts at a Catholic church, with a group meeting in a home in the Crab Run area of the Monterey district and a building in Mustoe. Pisgah Presbyterian and McDowell Presbyterian are the oldest continuously functioning churches in the county. Mennonites began moving into Highland County in the early part of the new millennium.

Outside of church, recreation has proved important. Whether in the form of music, sports, or popular jousting tournaments, diversions are a part of a well-lived life. Highland residents are committed to work, to faith, and to a fully rounded existence. The Highland County Fair is the longest continually running fair in Virginia, held every year without fail since 1951. Some activities that may be viewed as hobbies or recreation, such as hunting, were actually absolute necessities in years past.

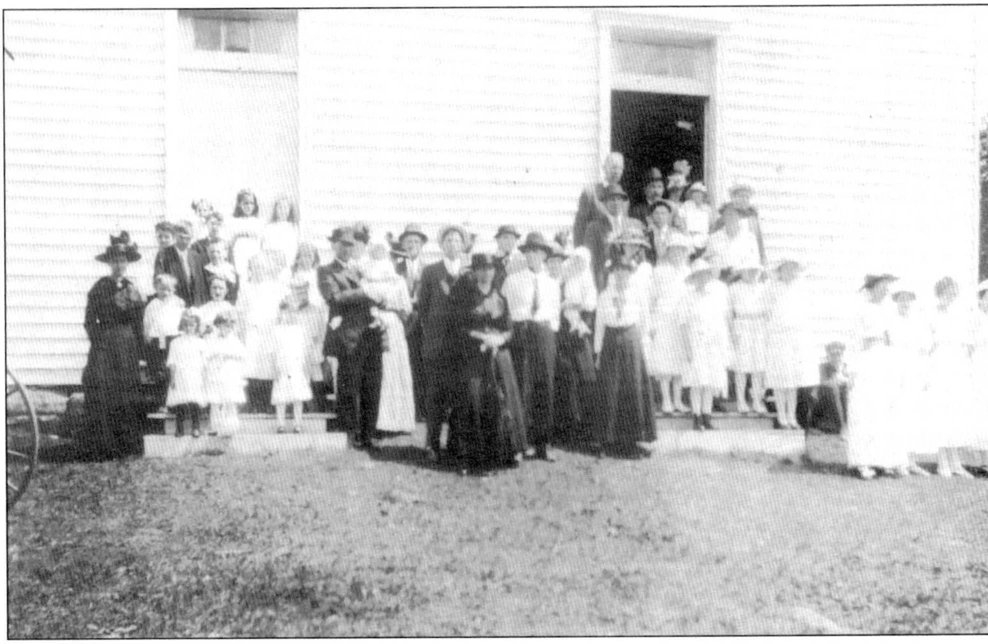

Green Hill Church is now a United Methodist Church located in Mill Gap. The left door was the women's entrance and the right was the men's. The church has since been expanded. The land was deeded to the church in 1843, with this building completed in 1849. (Courtesy of Libby Woods Hefner.)

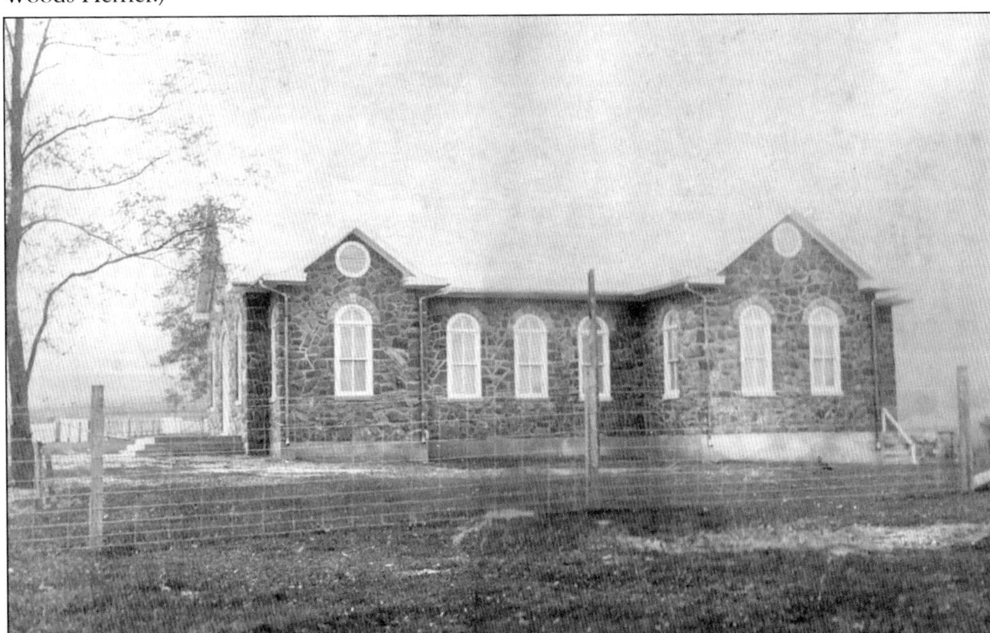

This church prospered through several locations, mergers, and name changes. Known now as Blue Grass United Methodist Church, it was formed when New Church and Central Methodist merged in 1977. Each church had several locations prior to the construction of this, the largest and most recent of the buildings, in 1924. The United Methodist name was added in 1968 when the Methodist church combined with the Evangelical United Brethren. (Courtesy of Kent Botkin.)

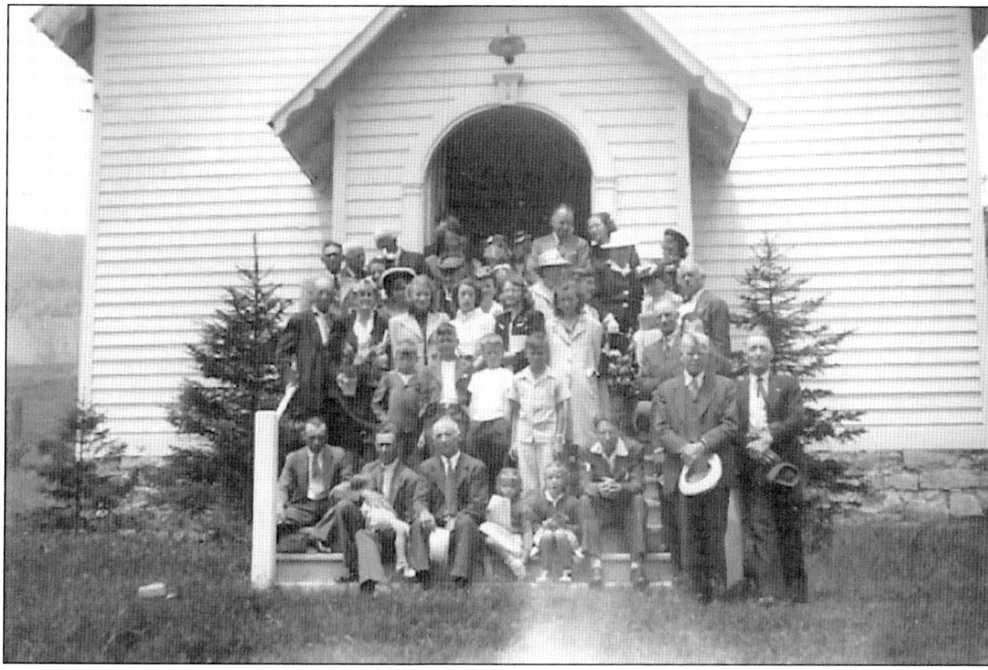

Pisgah Presbyterian Church, organized in November 1831, is considered to be the mother Presbyterian church for the county. It was from this church that Monterey Presbyterian was formed. Several buildings have been used, including a union church built in 1839. This building was constructed in 1878. The congregation poses for a group portrait in 1947. (Courtesy of the Highland County Historical Society.)

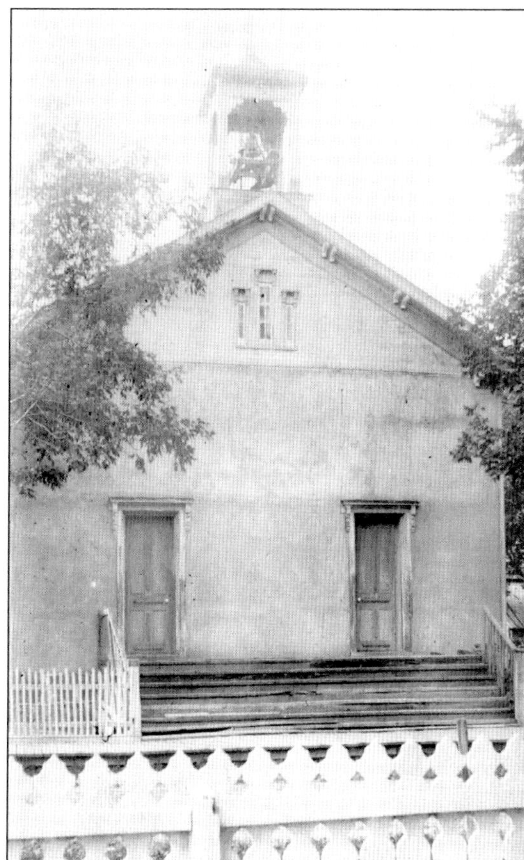

Monterey Presbyterian Church has occupied two different buildings on the same lot on Spruce Street in Monterey. This photograph depicts the first building, erected when the lot was purchased in 1882. It was later razed to make way for a new church building, constructed in 1909 and dedicated on September 10, 1911. Organized in 1878 as an offshoot of Pisgah, the church began with five members from Monterey. (Courtesy of the *Recorder*.)

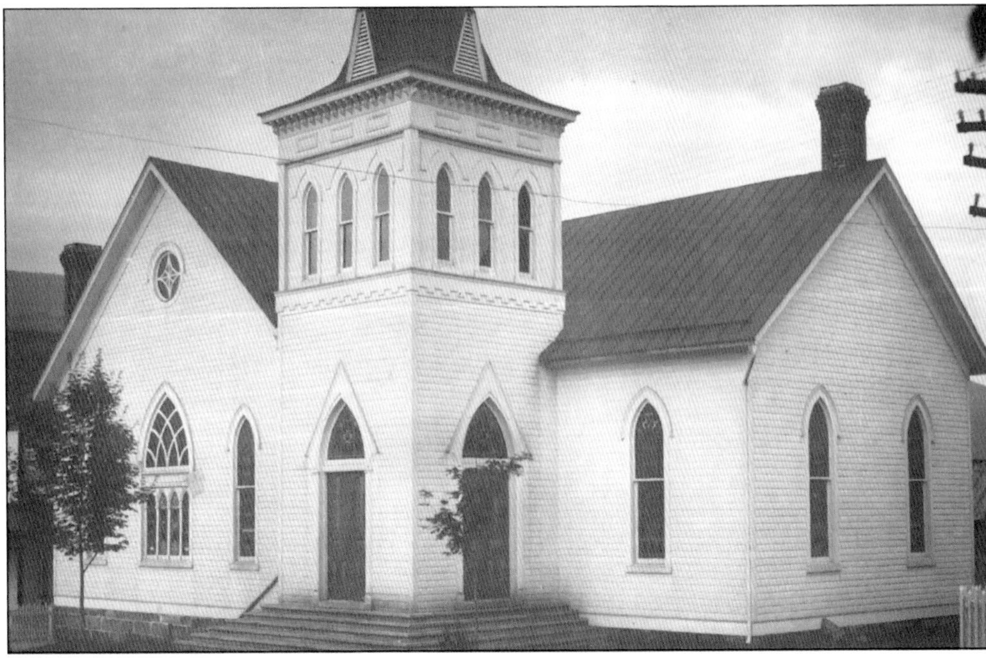

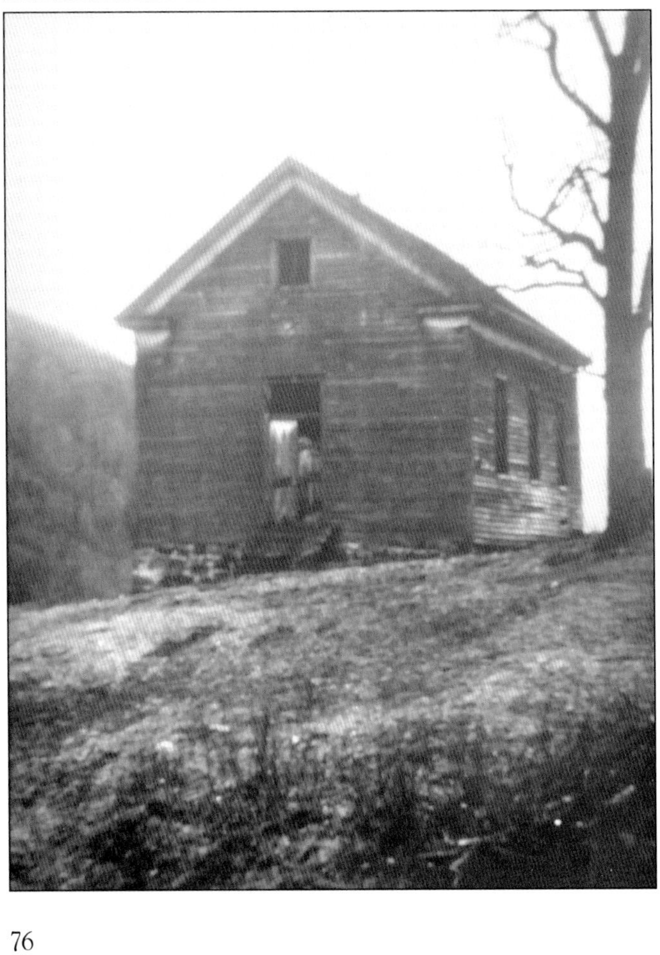

Photographed in 1911, Monterey United Methodist Church stands at the corner of the two main roads in Highland County: Routes 250 and 220. This is the second church building to be located on the site. The first was built shortly after Adam and Rachel Fleisher deeded the landed for a church. That first, smaller building was taken down in 1898. During the Civil War, the congregation represented differing opinions regarding the conflict. (Courtesy of Kent Botkin.)

Fairview Methodist Church was situated on Route 600 in the Back Creek area of the county. Back Creek is in the Blue Grass District, west of Monterey. The church was eventually closed and the land sold to Robert Harold. (Courtesy of the Highland County Historical Society.)

Victory Chapel Advent Christian Church was formed in Mustoe in September 1904. Land was donated by Mustoe Corbett, and the church was named in honor of his wife, Victory Jane Corbett. Moved back from Route 220 and placed on a new foundation in 1940, the church was given an addition of several rooms. Rev. Donald E. Rose is the current pastor. (Courtesy of the Highland County Historical Society.)

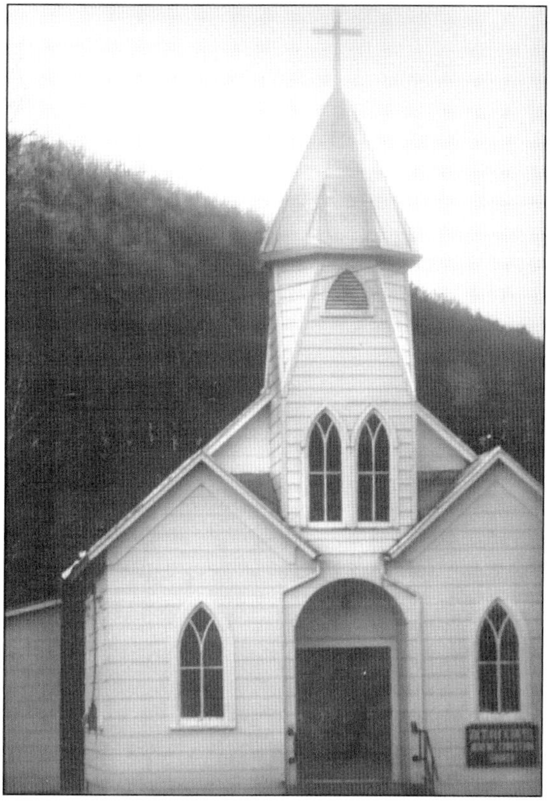

For years, White Church stood in physical contrast to all others in Highland County. It was the only two-story church of its time and was painted white, an uncommon practice then. No firm building date exists, but John Sitlington deeded land for a building in 1851. The structure was abandoned in 1903. (Courtesy of the Highland County Historical Society.)

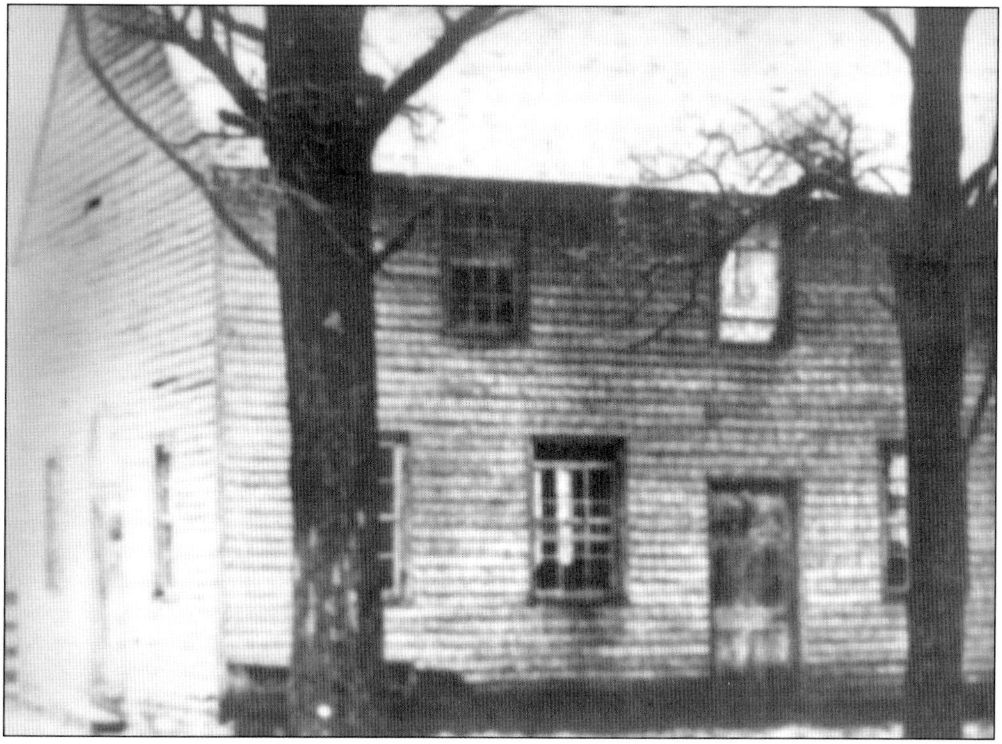

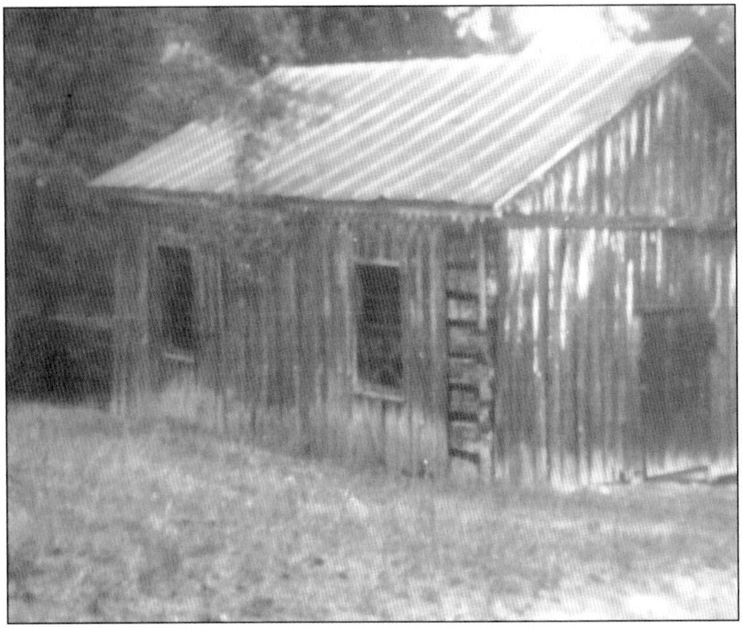

Prospect Church, located down Route 678 on land now owned by R. D. and Sandra Robinson near the Bath County line, served as a multi-denominational church for the community. It catered to both Lutheran and Brethren congregations. The building no longer stands. (Courtesy of the Highland County Historical Society.)

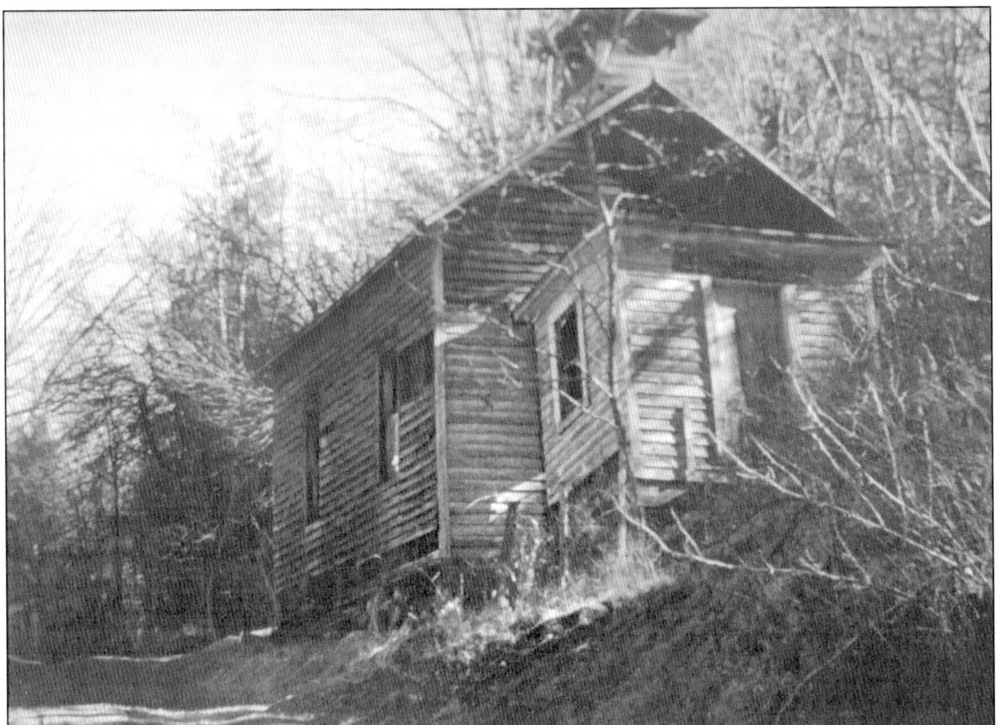

Pleasant View Church stood in the Anthony's Burg community near McDowell. A part of the African Methodist Episcopal Church, it once was a thriving, largely African American congregation. The building collapsed in the 1980s. The AME church grew out of the Free African Society established by Richard Allen, Absalom Jones, and others in Philadelphia in 1787. The biggest era of denominational development occurred during the Civil War and Reconstruction. (Courtesy of the Highland County Historical Society.)

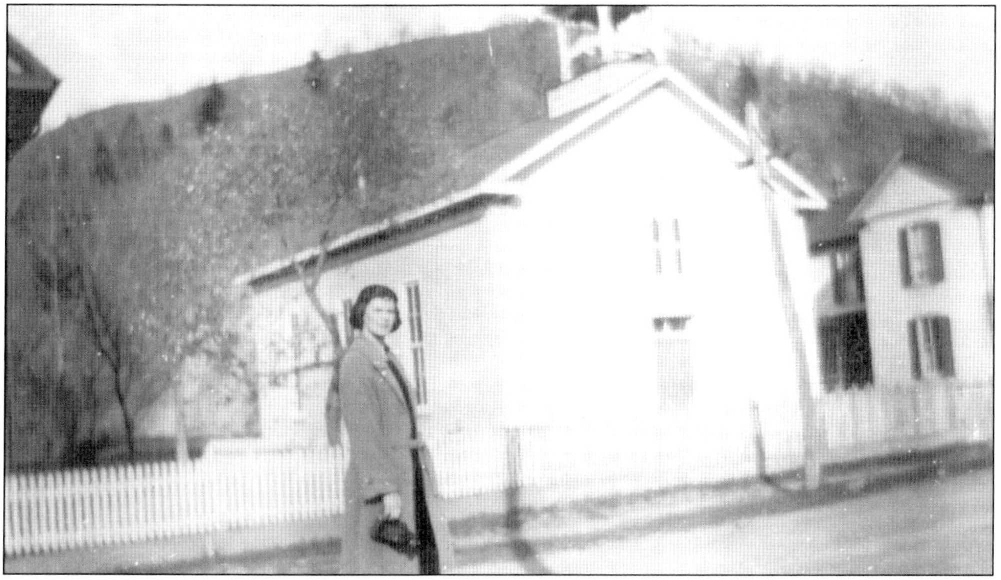

Built in 1875, McDowell United Methodist Church was originally covered in an adobe material, but in 1956, the members of the church added an educational section and covered three sides in a brick veneer. In 1961, the Statler Brothers (then known as the Kingsmen) performed at a Homecoming celebration at the church. This was just four years before their big break with "Flowers on the Wall." (Courtesy of Lyle and Georgianne Maloy Hull.)

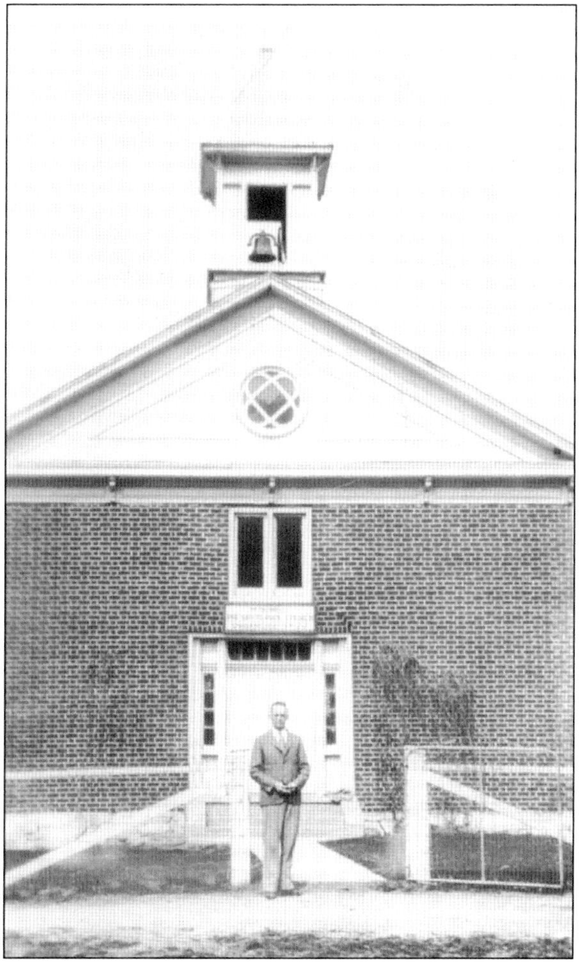

McDowell Presbyterian Church erected this building in 1856 with the addition in 1958 of a second church building on this patch of land. The congregation was organized as a union church with 19 members in 1822. The church was used as a hospital during the Battle of McDowell in May 1862, when the pews were broken up to use as firewood. Rev. Lyle Moffett, the pastor for many years, stands in front. (Courtesy of Robin and Nancy Vance.)

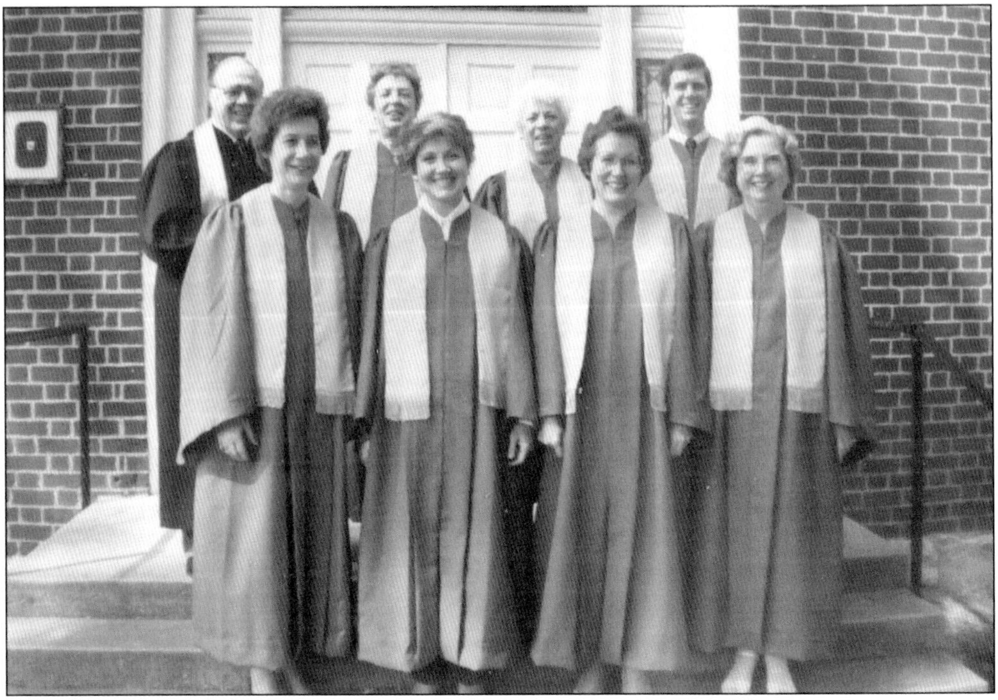

Music is an important part of any church community, and that holds true for McDowell Presbyterian Church. The choir includes the following, from left to right: (first row) Carolyn McCray, JoAnn Harkleroad, Lucille Maloy, and Sarah Samples; (second row) Rev. Les LaPrade, Betty Hogshead, Sue Robinson, and Ken Gibbs. (Courtesy of Sarah Samples.)

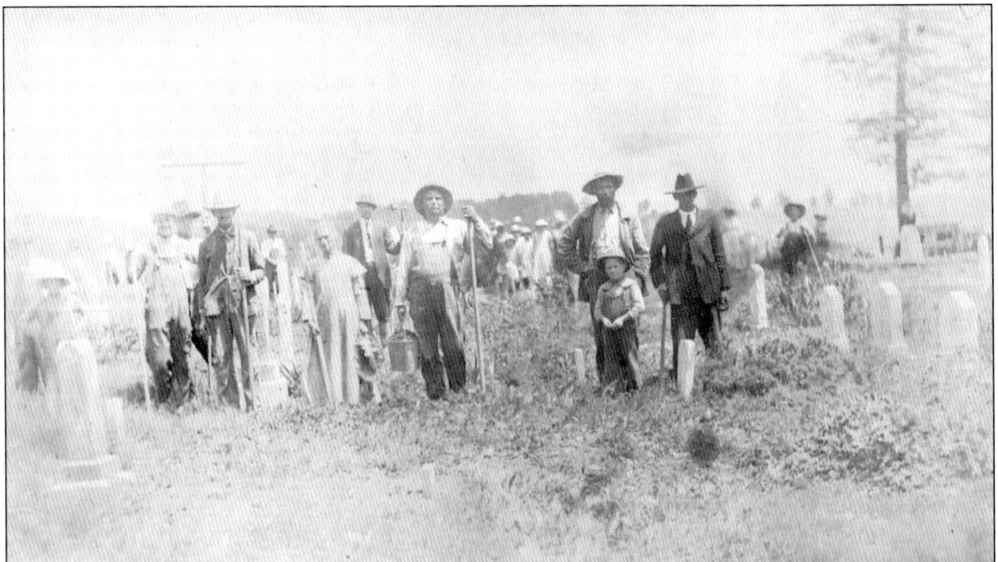

Located behind McKendree United Methodist Church on the Bull Pasture River, just north of McDowell, the McKendree Cemetery had 390 names on the tombstones as of 2006 and is still in use today. The oldest grave is that of Elizabeth Wooddell, who was born on November 22, 1813, and died on November 8, 1892. Workers pose on a day of cleaning up this well-maintained church cemetery. (Courtesy of Kent Botkin.)

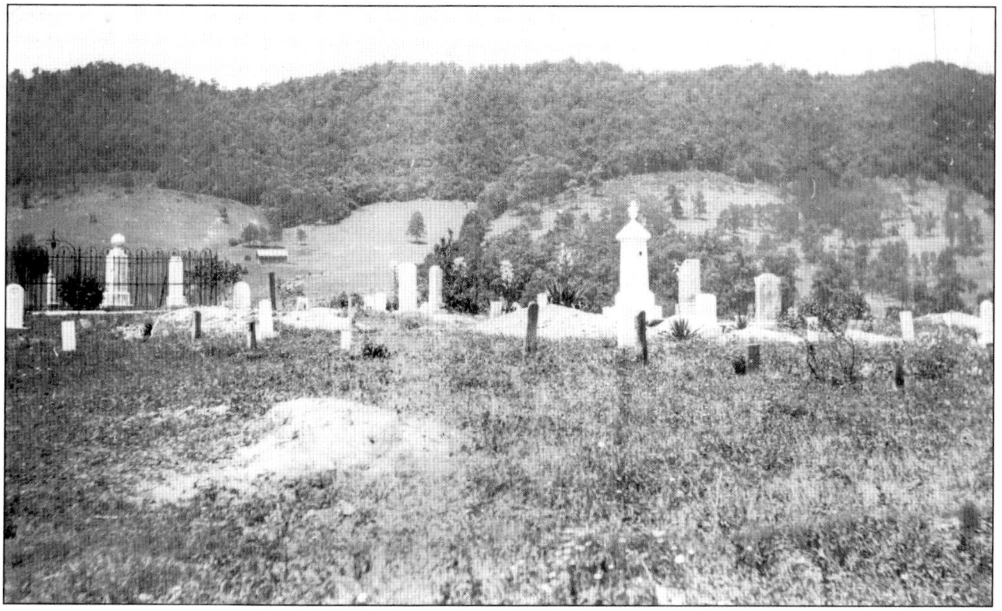

Highland County is particular about how its dead are buried. There are many cemeteries in the county—from family graveyards with only a few plots and old church cemeteries that have not been used or visited in decades, to battlefield burial grounds and cemeteries that are still in use today. This Mill Gap cemetery is the final resting place for many loved ones. (Courtesy of Libby Woods Hefner.)

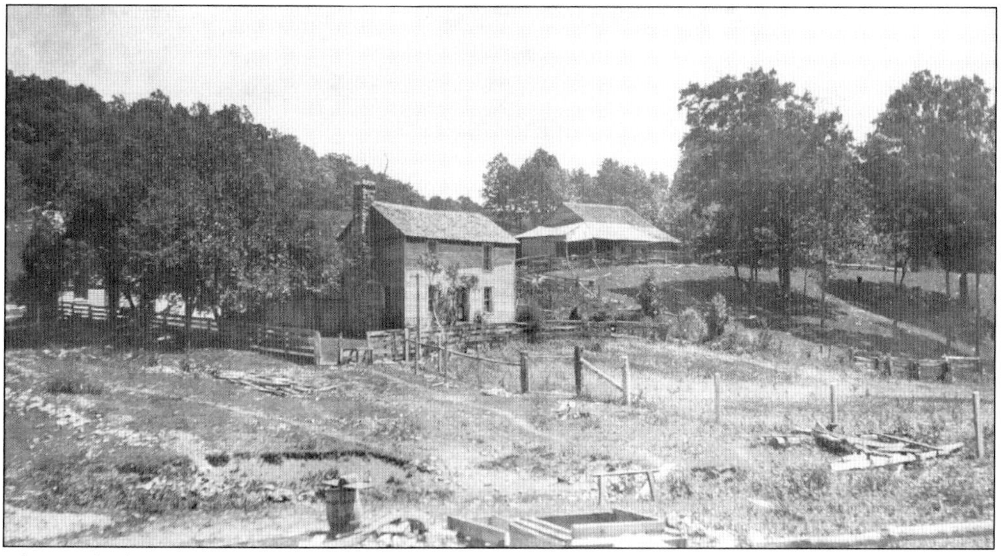

The Wade family home, photographed on July 19, 1914, in Mill Gap was used as a location for prayer meetings, Bible studies, and early meetings for the Methodist church in that end of the county. Rev. Howard Wade and his wife, Mary, lived here in the late 1800s. (Courtesy of Libby Woods Hefner.)

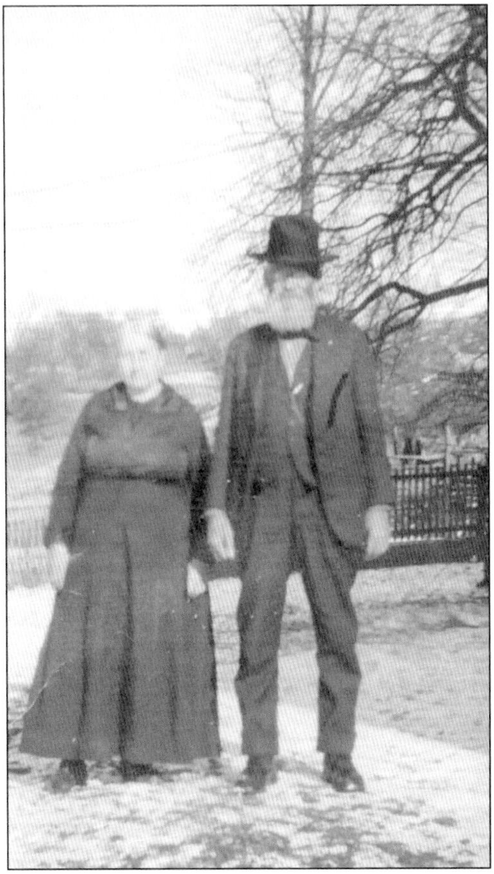

The grandson of Rev. Otho Wade, Rev. Howard Wade wed Mary in 1863. Otho was the first Methodist preacher to be raised in Highland County, though he was not born there. Howard, who became the first Methodist preacher born in the county, served in the Civil War and was captured at Smithfield. (Courtesy of Libby Woods Hefner.)

In an image marked only "Asbury Sunday School," a group of unidentified children enjoy the photographing process. Located north of Monterey in the Pines area, Asbury United Methodist Church was started in 1900 and still meets regularly. (Courtesy of the *Recorder*.)

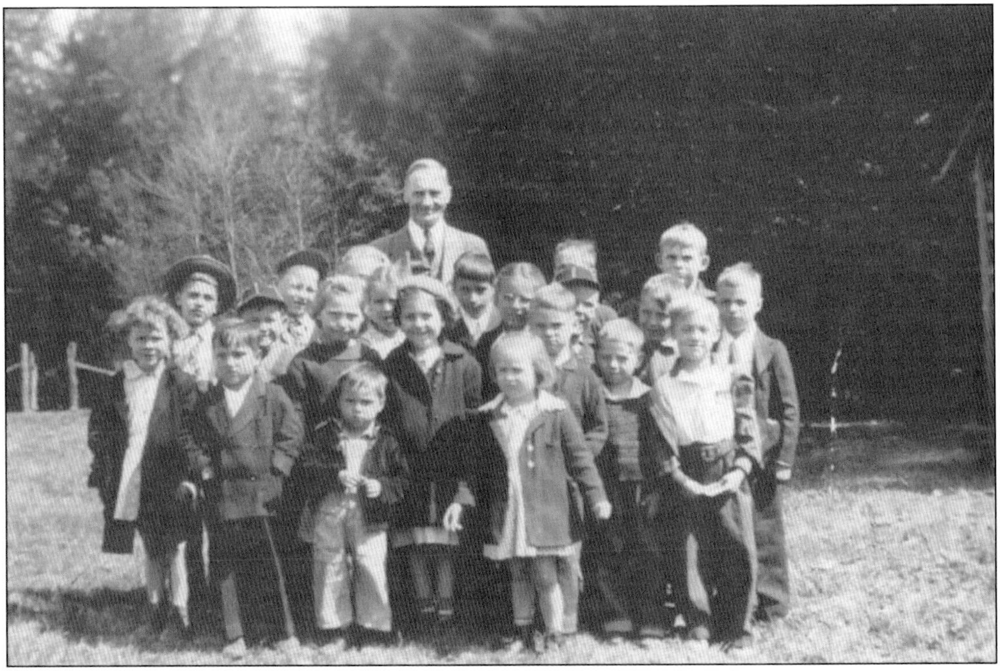

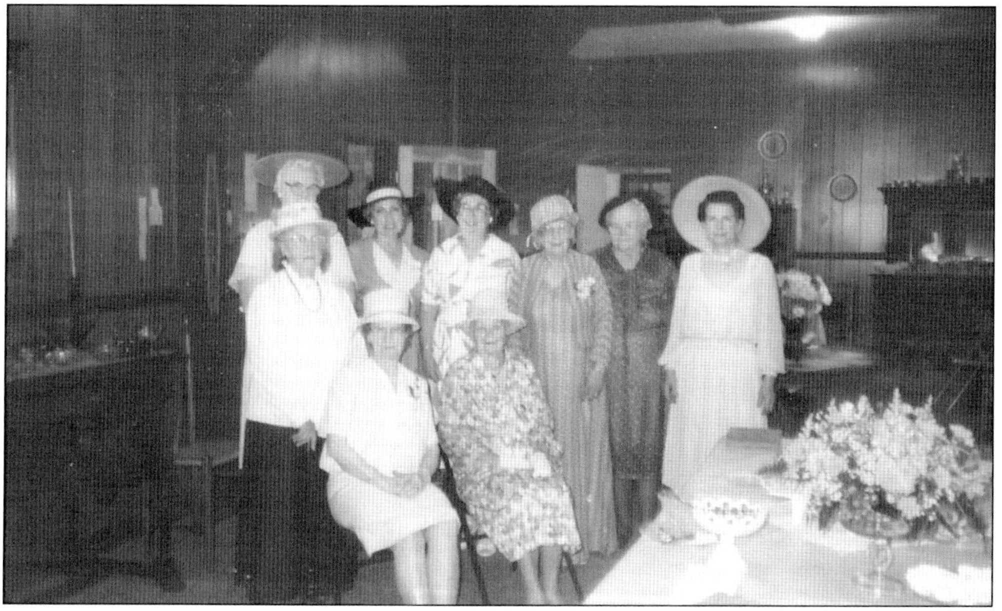

Marking the 60th anniversary of the Stonewall Women's Club, members met for a tea at the McDowell Mill in 1990 for a final meeting. The group met, in one combination or another, on the first Saturday afternoon of the month other the years. The old hats were to commemorate the event. The ladies are, from left to right, (first row) Annye Mae Simmons (standing), Ruth Wade, and Leola Maloy; (second row) Becky McClintic, JoAnn Harkleroad, Sarah Samples, Virginia Rexrode, Ann Lockridge, and Mary Lott. (Courtesy of Sarah Samples.)

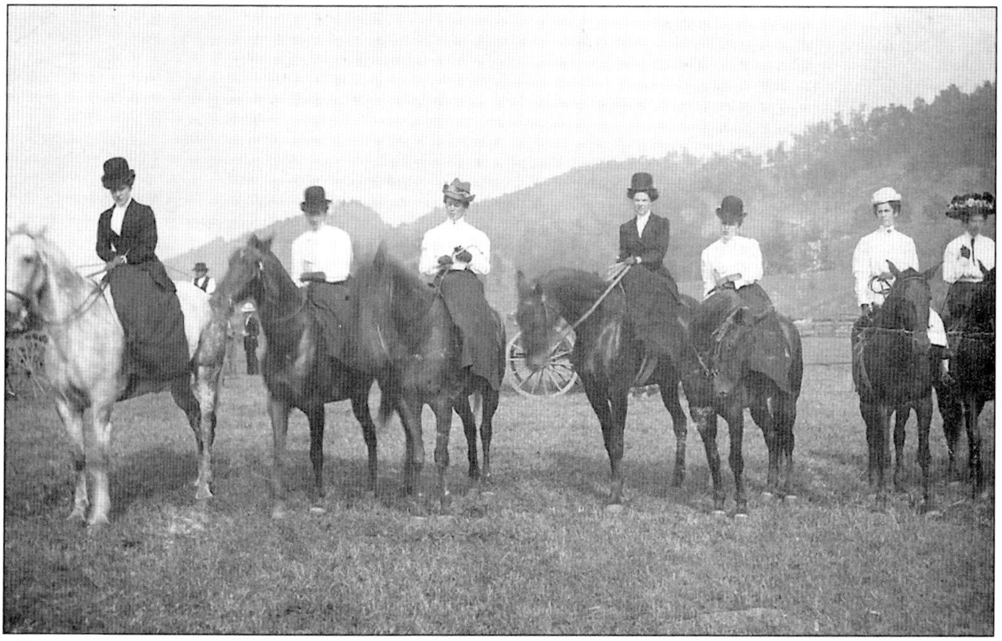

The Highland Livestock Show was a perfect opportunity for these young ladies from Highland County society to show off their horsemanship. They include Elsie Hiner Stephenson, Juana S. Sullenberger, Mrs. E. A. McNulty, Lona Fox, and Mrs. Edward Hevener. Cultured women of 1914 almost always rode sidesaddle. (Courtesy of the *Recorder*.)

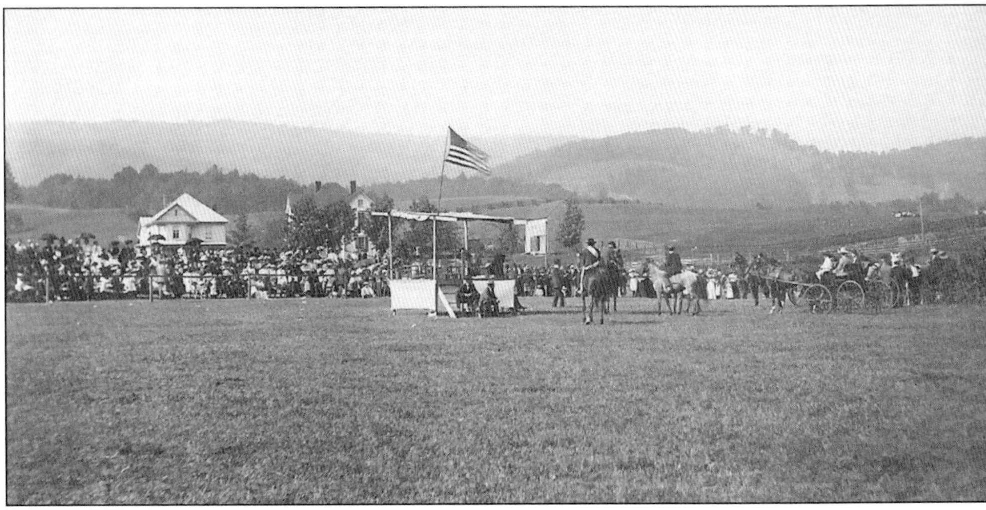

The Highland Livestock Show was held for only six years, beginning in 1910 and ending in 1916 with the escalation of World War I. The livestock show was intended to promote the selection and raising of better breeds of exhibit-type animals. The show, held on the C. T. Fleisher property along East Main Street, grew quickly. Rides were added and concession stands sprung up. Though the decision was made in 1916 to temporarily halt the show, it became a permanent break and the forerunner of the county fair ceased. On the back of one of these two photographs from the 1910 show, a note reads, "The little horse over the 'x' is Howard's [Slaven] Daisy driving. Blue ribbon in Ladies Runabout Class." (Courtesy of the *Recorder*; courtesy of the Highland County Historical Society.)

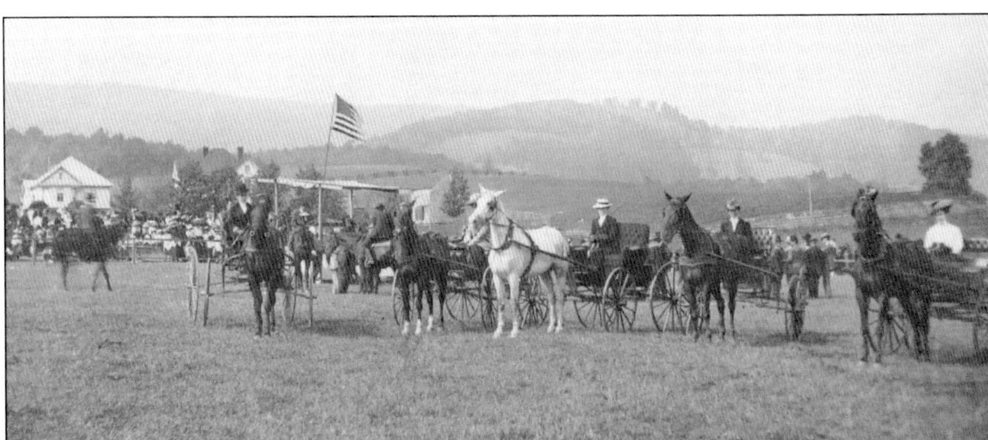

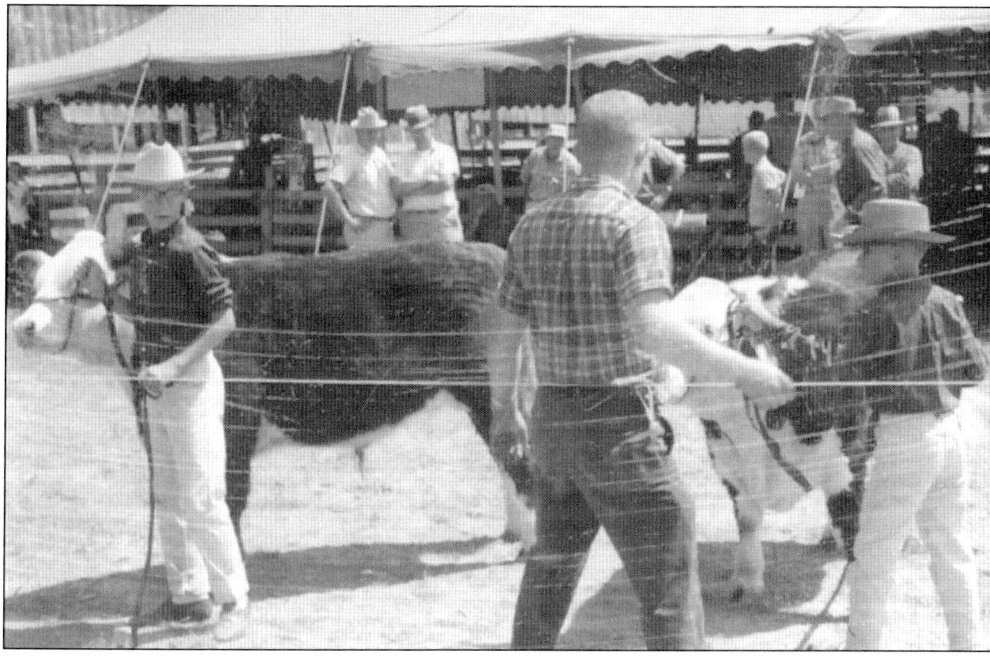

In 1951, the Highland County Fair began its streak as the longest-running county fair in Virginia. It is a classic old-time country fair with rides, cotton candy, tractor pulls, dog shows, horse competitions, and the ever-important livestock contest. As in the Highland Livestock Shows, an emphasis is placed on showing top-quality breeds and passing on skills for raising superior animals. Organized by the 4-H Club, the contest includes slots for all types of animals: poultry, rabbits, sheep, cattle, and horses. The fair is held every fall on the Highland County Fairgrounds, directly behind the public school building in Monterey, though the event was held at the Monterey Stockyard before the Fair Association purchased the current property. (Courtesy of the *Recorder.*)

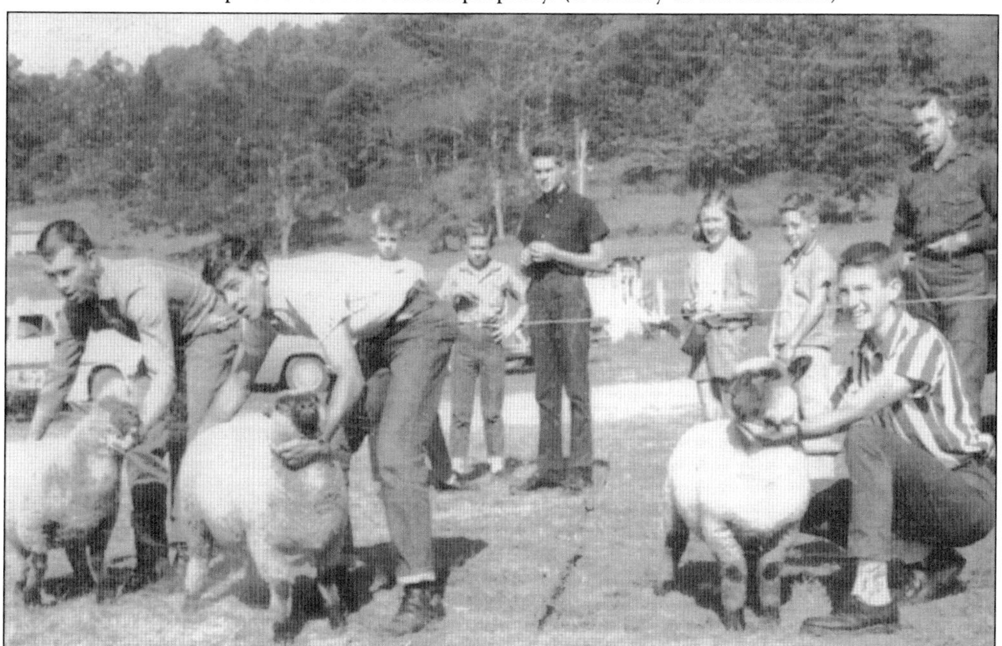

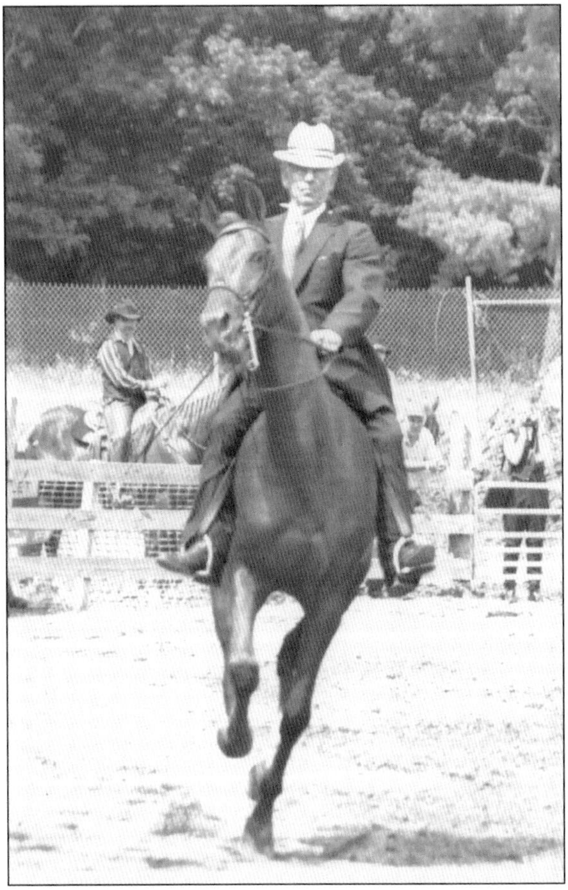

James Franklin Varner, an avid horseman, showed horses for many years and acted not only as a riding instructor but as a farrier and trainer. Varner owned and operated a breeding business, working with registered saddlebred and walking horses, and was always willing to share his knowledge of the horse business with others. Here he rides in a horse event in the fair. (Courtesy of the Highland County Historical Society.)

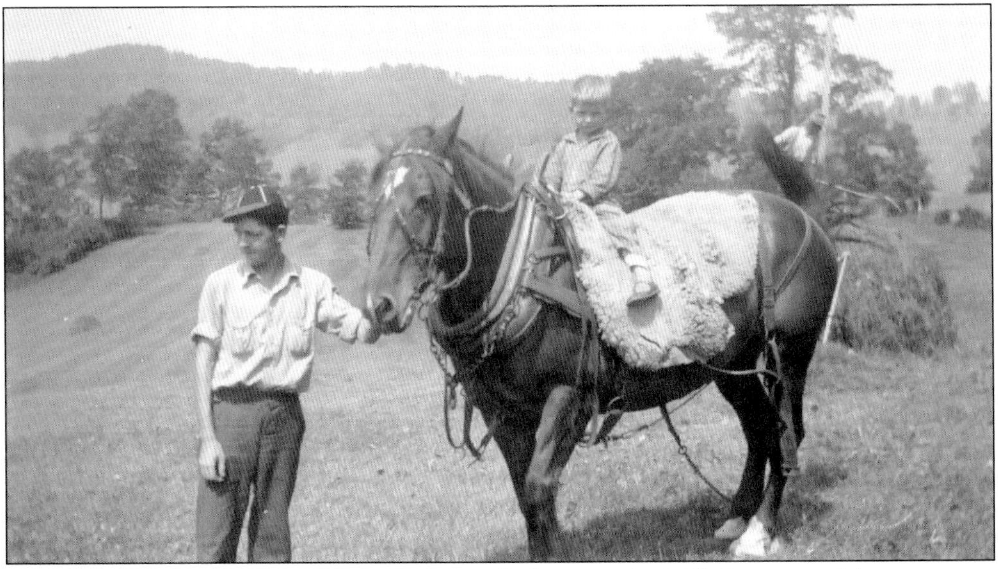

Ewell Wade leads John Henry Hiner on a friendly horse in the Mill Gap area of the county on August 8, 1946. Horses pulled double duty for both work and recreation in Highland County. (Courtesy of Libby Woods Hefner.)

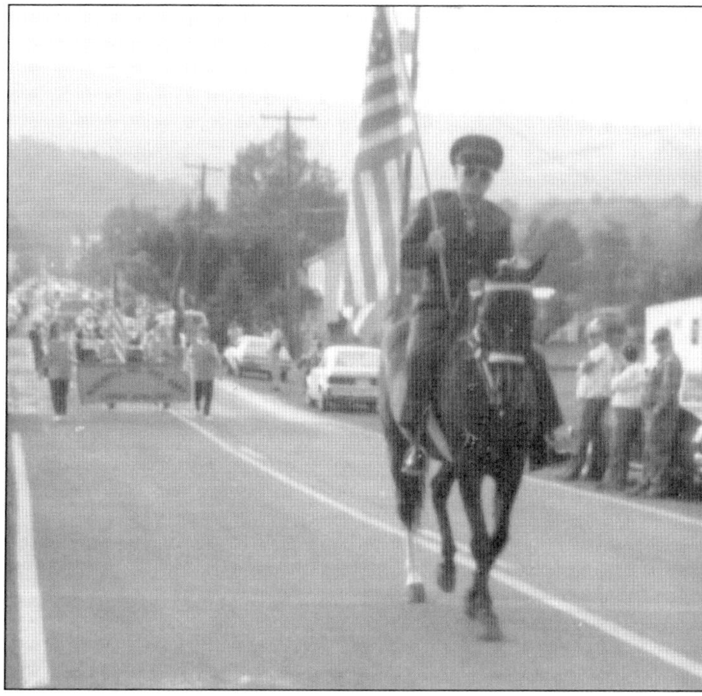

Mack Ratcliffe leads the Highland County Fair parade in 1988. The fair begins every year with this large procession though downtown. Ratcliffe was a fixture at the parade for many years. During the first parade following his death, his riderless horse walked through the parade route with Ratcliffe's boots backward in the stirrups in the classic "man lost" style, signifying that a warrior will never ride again. (Courtesy of the Highland County Historical Society.)

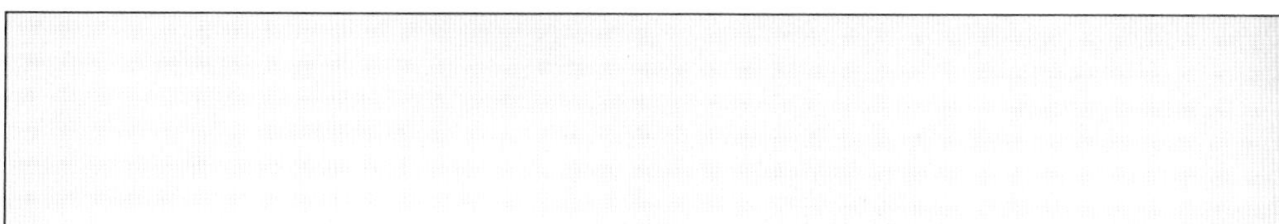

In 1970, three unidentified men help guide a horse during a horse-pulling event at the county fair. It was a common exercise to test horses in competitive settings, to see how much weight they could bear. The weight was placed on the sled, and measurements were taken of how far the horse pulled. Tractors, trucks, and pickups have also been tested in pulling ability. (Courtesy of the *Recorder*.)

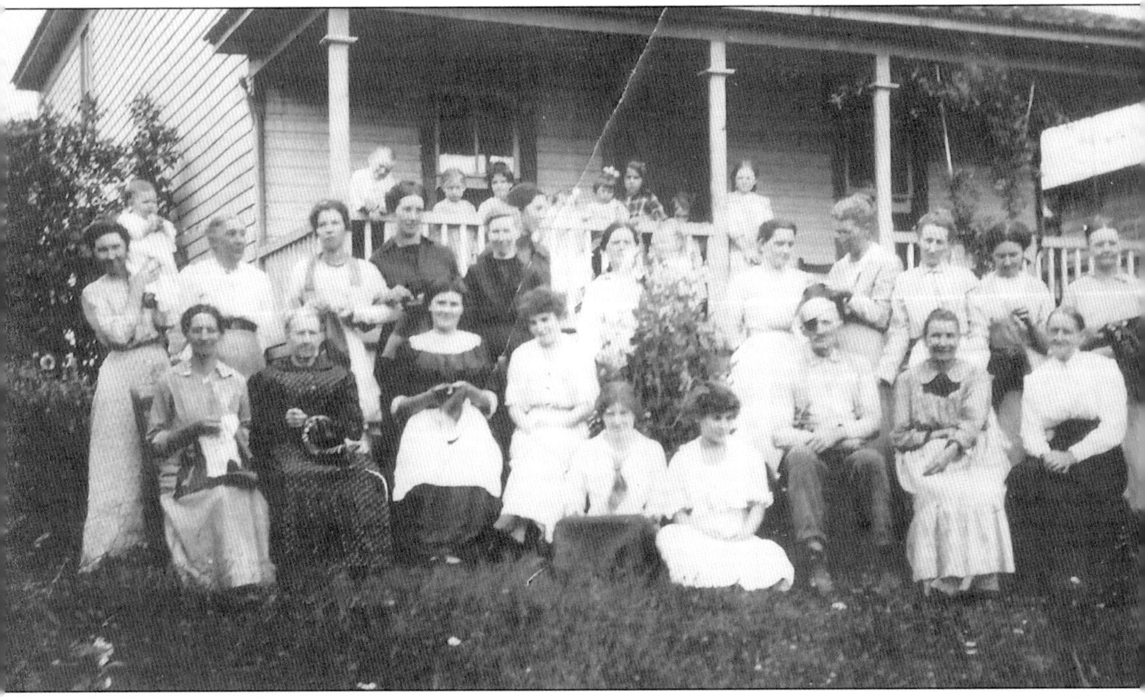

Sometimes a hobby actually helps out with a necessity. This sewing circle met regularly to talk and perform needed sewing. Their projects benefited both themselves and people outside the county. Though usually a women's group, there was one gentleman present this day. The meeting in Mill Gap included the following, from left to right: (first row) Lillie Wade, Mary Ann Wade, Mammie Clendeden, ? Bird, unidentified, ? Bird, John Wade, Laura Wade, and Nan Chestnut; (second row includes) Lizzie Woods, Kate Gumm, Doria Dumm, Lizzie Hiner, Lizzie Wiley, Lucy Hiner, Edith Chestnut, Alice Wade, Trudy Gumm, Martha Townsend, Ardenia Wade, and Evie Chestnut. The children on the porch include, from left to right, Mary Wiley, Helen Gumm, Kathleen Wade, Ressie Wade, and Mammie Wade. (Courtesy of Libby Woods Hefner.)

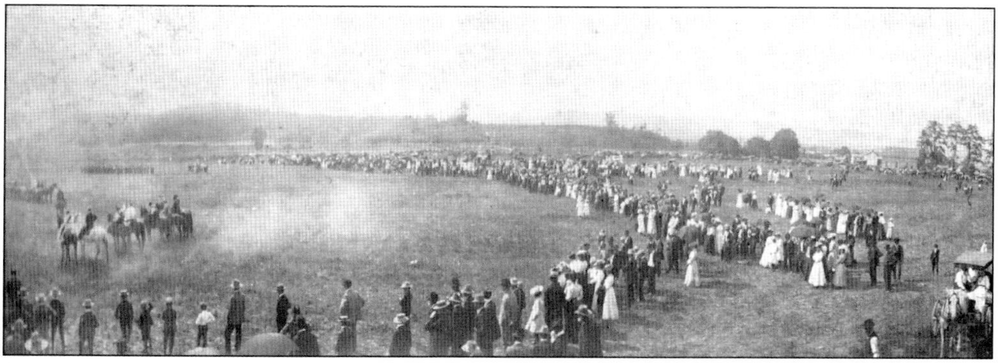

Jousting tournaments were a very popular pastime in Highland County at the start of the 20th century and for many years thereafter. In September 1902, a large tournament was held, drawing a sizable crowd to McDowell. McDowell Presbyterian Church can be seen at the far upper right of this panoramic photograph. (Courtesy of Kent Botkin.)

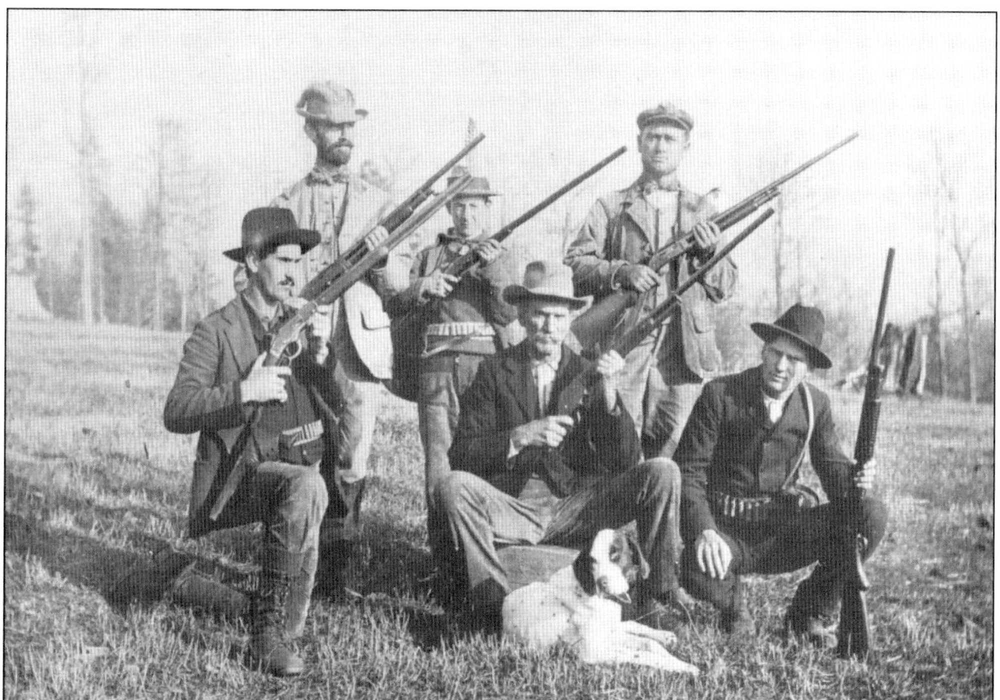

Formerly a strict necessity to keep the family fed, hunting is still an important activity for many residents, though it may not be quite as vital for food. Here men head out on a day's hunt in the Blue Grass area. In the first row are Henry Walter Mullenax (left), Henry Clay Mullenax (center), and Abraham Mullenax. (Courtesy of Janet Mullenax.)

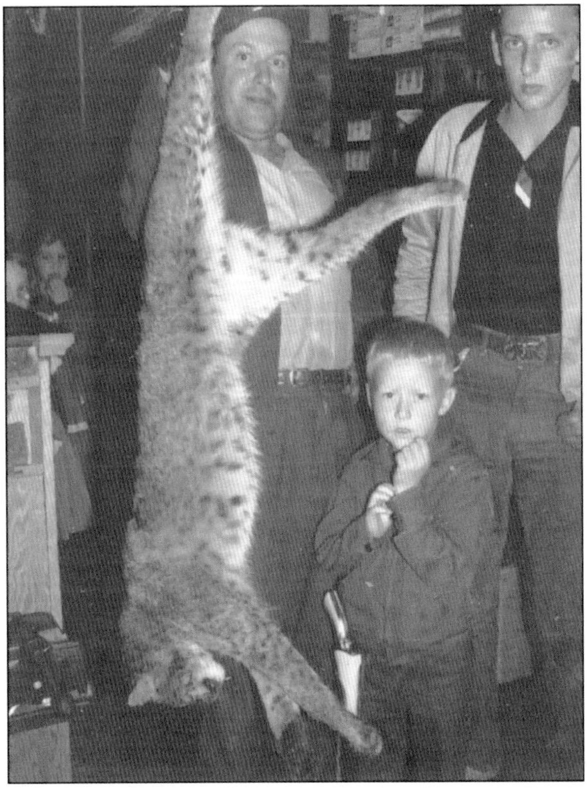

In 1962, Berlin Arbogast shot a 35-pound bobcat on his farm. According to the report, the cat was killed at 20 to 25 feet with a shotgun when Arbogast was groundhog hunting near his home. The cat approached him and made no attempt to run away. Arbogast is shown here with his son John Mark. (Courtesy of the *Recorder*.)

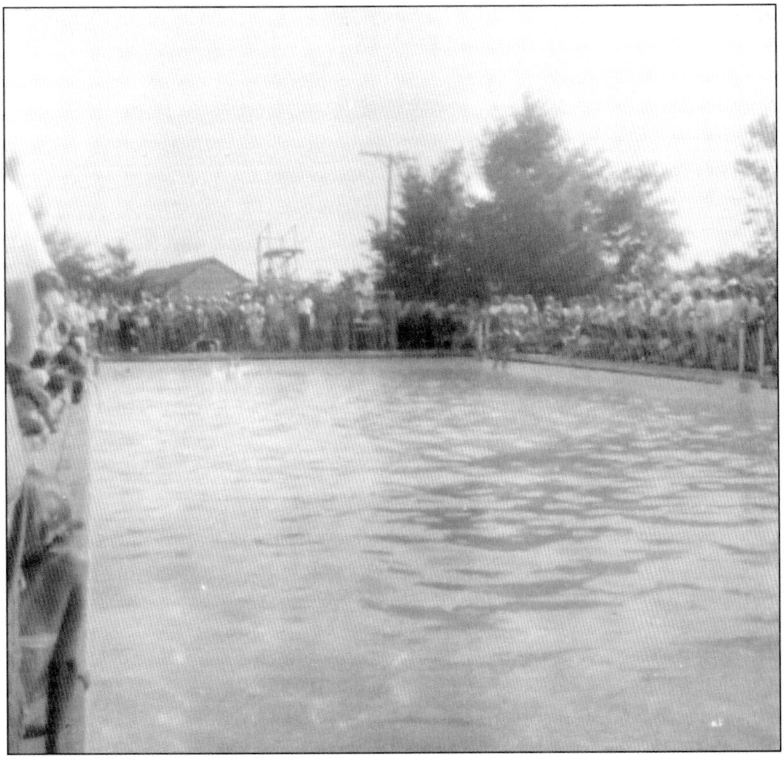

While Bolar was known for its healing mineral pools, it also had a less well-known swimming pool. One of only two public pools in the county, this was the site of many group events. (Courtesy of Mary Judy Swecker Riddick.)

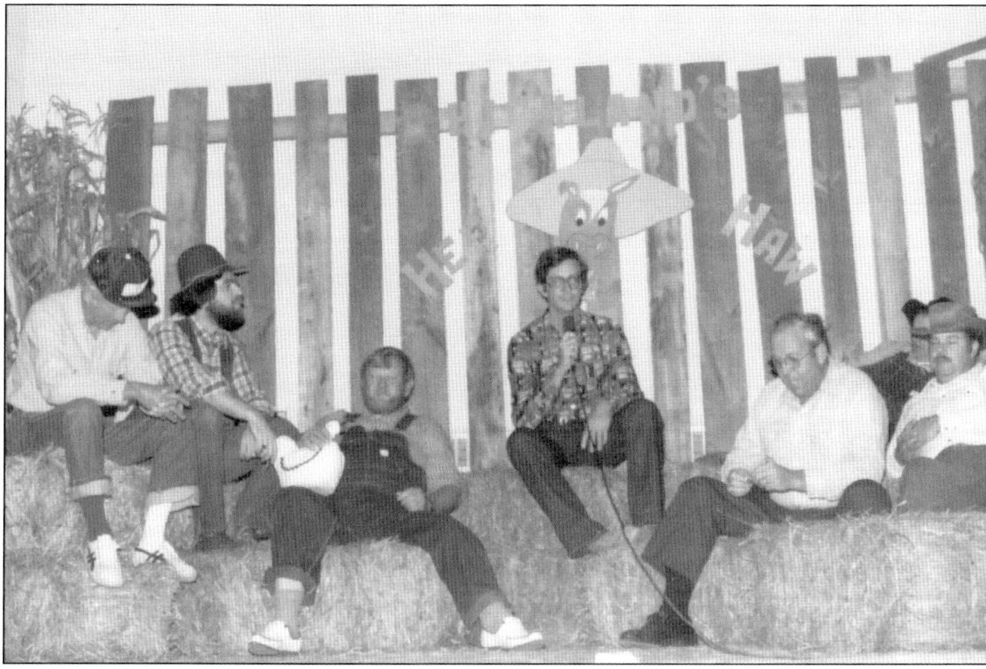

In the early 1980s, the Highland community began a series of events based on the popular television series *Hee-Haw*. Parts of the show were reenacted, songs were sung, and everything was tied back to the local area. Pictured from left to right are unidentified, Mike Bedwell, Shorty Shultz, Rev. Jerry Ginn, Jim Thompson, unidentified, and Tom Wilson. (Courtesy of the Highland County Historical Society.)

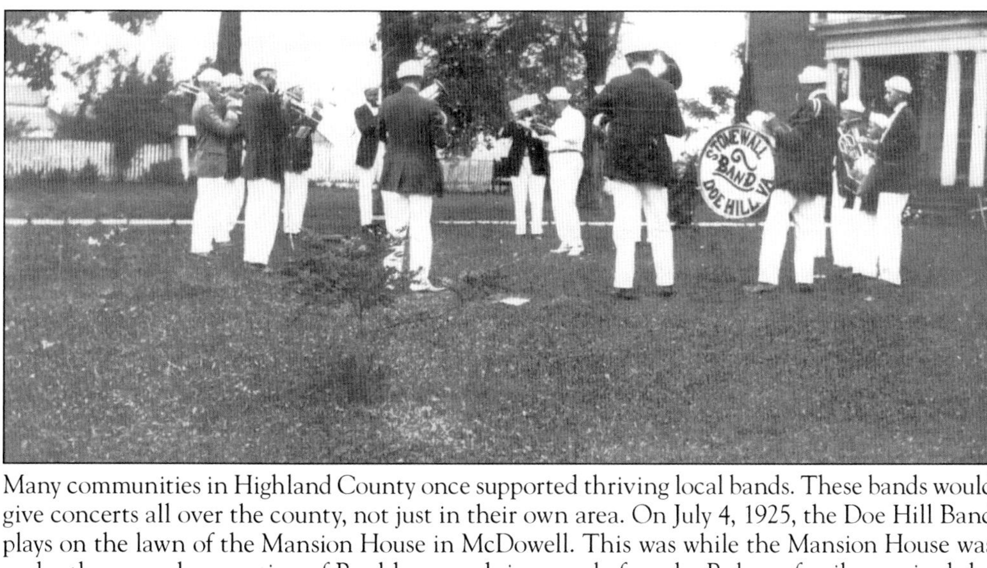

Many communities in Highland County once supported thriving local bands. These bands would give concerts all over the county, not just in their own area. On July 4, 1925, the Doe Hill Band plays on the lawn of the Mansion House in McDowell. This was while the Mansion House was under the second generation of Bradshaws and six years before the Ralston family acquired the home. (Courtesy of Lyle and Georgianne Maloy Hull.)

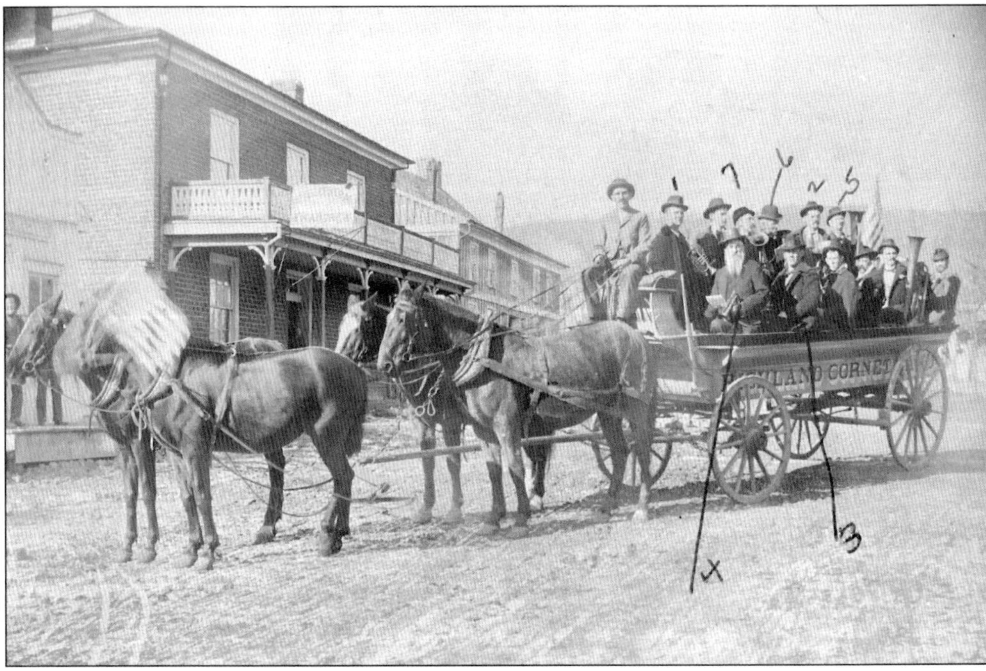

Members of the Highland Cornet Band sit in the back of a wagon, instruments and music in hand as if they are about to blow their horns. The band consists of the following: 1. Harry Slaven; 2. Hampton Matheny; 3. Thomas Slaven Jr.; 4. Capt. J. C. Matheny; 5. Jeff Jones; 6. Thomas H. Slaven; and Clifton Matheny. (Courtesy of Tate Swecker.)

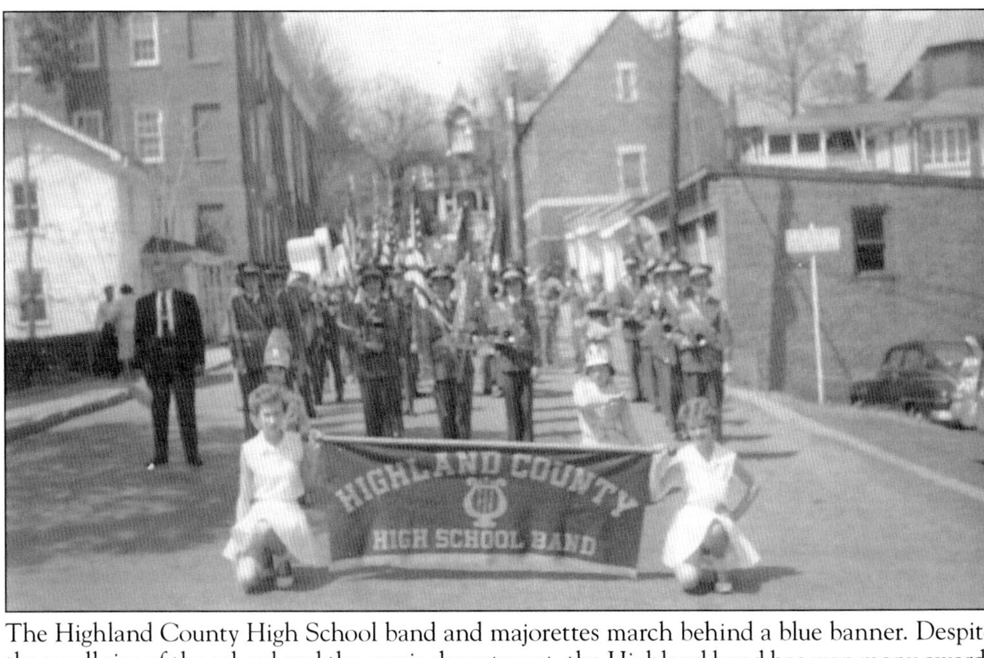

The Highland County High School band and majorettes march behind a blue banner. Despite the small size of the school and the music department, the Highland band has won many awards over the years. The same banner was used for many years through numerous band directors. (Courtesy of Mary Judy Swecker Riddick.)

In May 1947, Highland County celebrated its 100th birthday with considerable celebration, including a parade with decorated floats. In this photograph, majorettes and their accompanying band march into Monterey. Parades were a popular activity, drawing people from all over the county with the excitement of floats, bands, and other entrants. (Courtesy of the *Recorder*.)

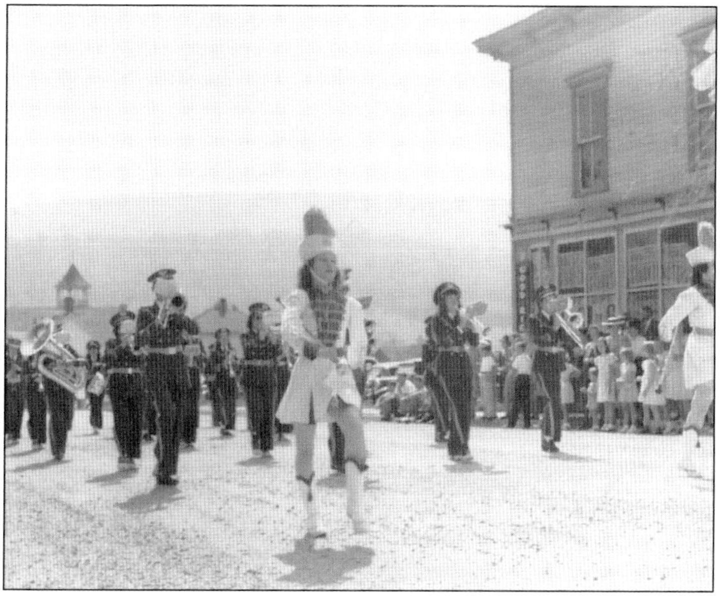

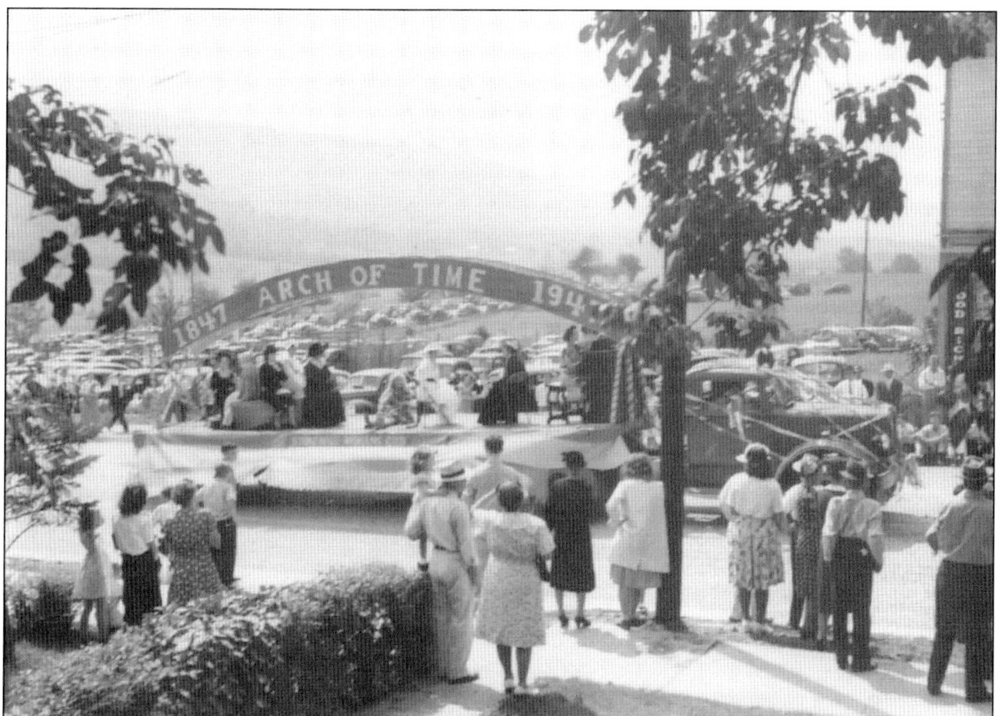

To celebrate Highland County hitting the century mark, many different organizations put together elaborate floats for the birthday parade. Here the Stonewall Women's Club created an arch to show how life has changed over the 100 years. Members of the club are dressed to represent women during the time of the county's founding. (Courtesy of the *Recorder*.)

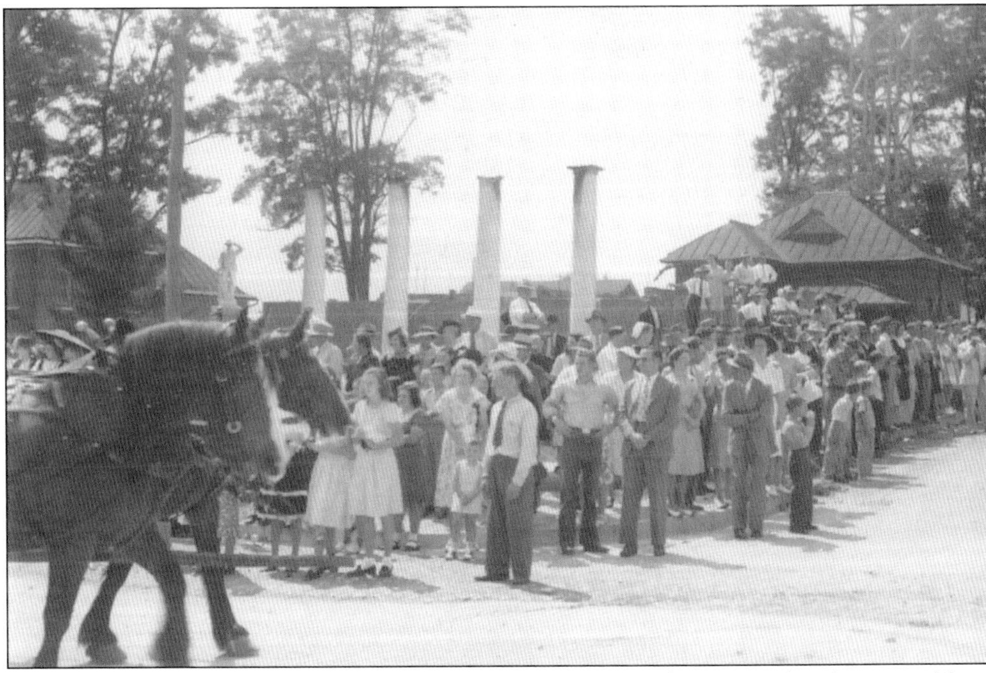

The 100th anniversary celebration parade happened just a few shorts months after several local landmarks burned to the ground. Above, the procession travels past the ruins of the Highland County Courthouse, which burned along with the Bishops Store in February 1947. As always, a parade means floats. Below, a maple syrup producer gets into the spirit of the event to demonstrate his wares and remind residents of the wonders of the liquid. (Courtesy of the *Recorder*.)

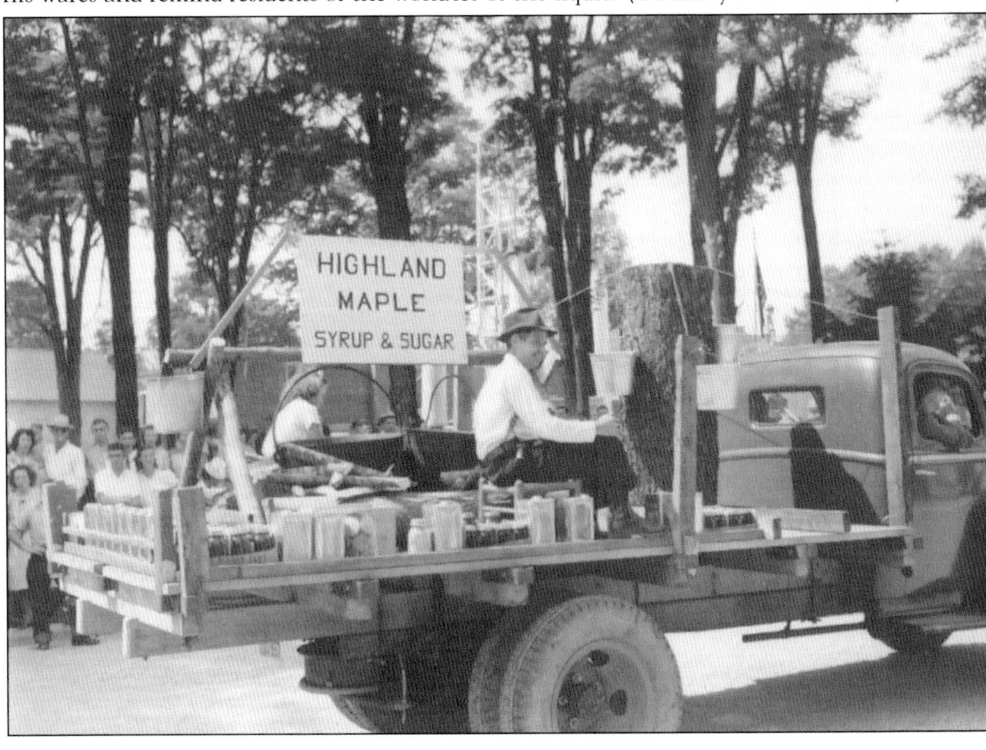

Six

PREPARING FOR THE FUTURE

SCHOOLS

Highland County is a small county. An outsider might expect that the schools would pack students in, not try very hard, and simply move the young people through the system. Nothing could be further from the truth. The county takes pride in its schools and the quality of the education provided.

In 1925, the school population included 1,351 students between the ages of 7 and 19; at the start of the 2007 school year, Highland County had 272 students enrolled in preschool through 12th grade. While there is currently only one building containing the elementary, middle, and high schools, it has not always been this way. Throughout Highland history, there have been a variety of schools and school buildings. In 1929, at least 29 schools served the eager students.

Though it was not until 1847 that the school systems were supported by a tax, an earlier law was passed to help pay for public education. Under this 1820 law, a Literacy Fund was subsidized through certain fines and penalties. In 1845, a law empowered the county to submit to the voters, if officials were presented a petition signed by a third of those voters, a question of whether or not to have a school in a certain area. In the initial scholastic experience, Methodist and Presbyterian preachers taught the classes. The school buildings were often described as 14-by-16-foot windowless log cabins.

Several standard texts predominated in the schools of Highland's early age. They included *Pike Arithmetic*, dealing with math and counting using British shillings and pounds; *Walker's Dictionary*; *Dilworth's Speller*; *Webster's Blue Back Speller*; *The English Reader*; and *Webster's Reader*. Additionally the Bible was commonly used in public schools. Students brought their lunches to school daily, as hot lunches were not provided until the 1940s.

For the 1893–1894 school year in the Blue Grass District, teacher salaries ranged from $16 to $20 a month. Three years later in Monterey, teachers were paid anywhere from $10 to $40 a month.

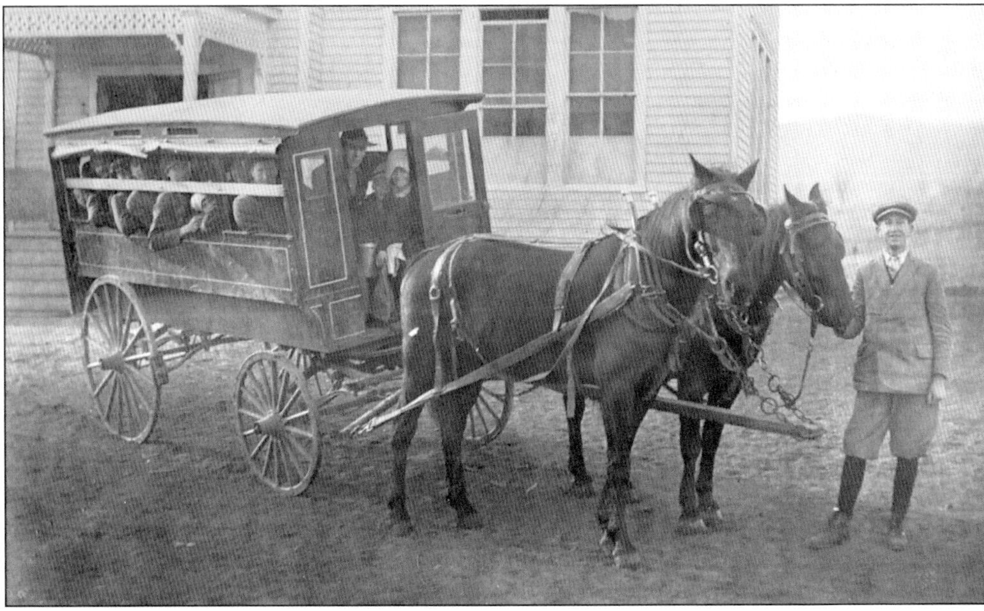

William E. Snyder drove this school hack to the Blue Grass schools. He also sold gravestone markers for Hinton Marble Works and was an agent for Stewart Iron Fence. Taken in the early 1900s, the photograph shows a leap forward in ensuring students got to school. There were rules about who could and could not ride. The school hack was reserved for students farther away from school. Students within a few miles still needed to walk. (Courtesy of Kent Botkin.)

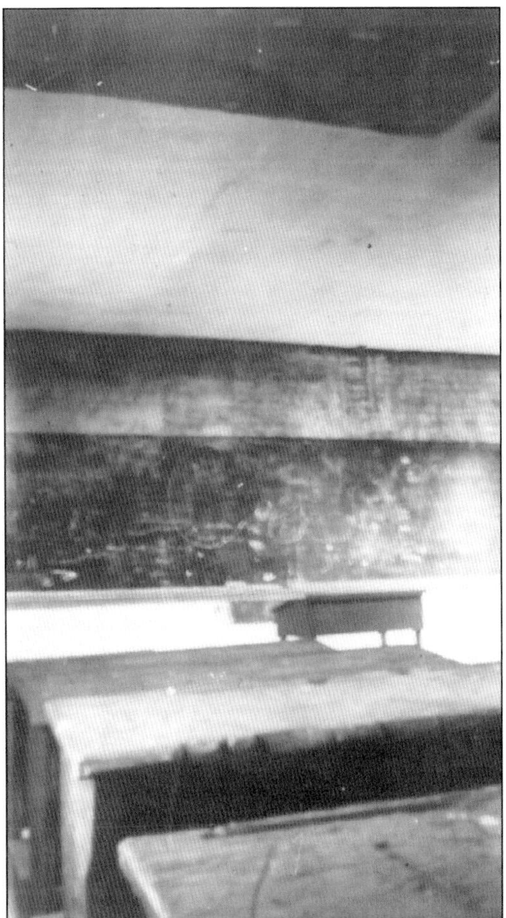

Early Highland County schools were a basic setup. Taken inside the schoolhouse at Frank's Run in the Blue Grass Valley, this photograph shows the blackboard, teacher's desk, and pupils' desks. (Courtesy of the *Recorder*.)

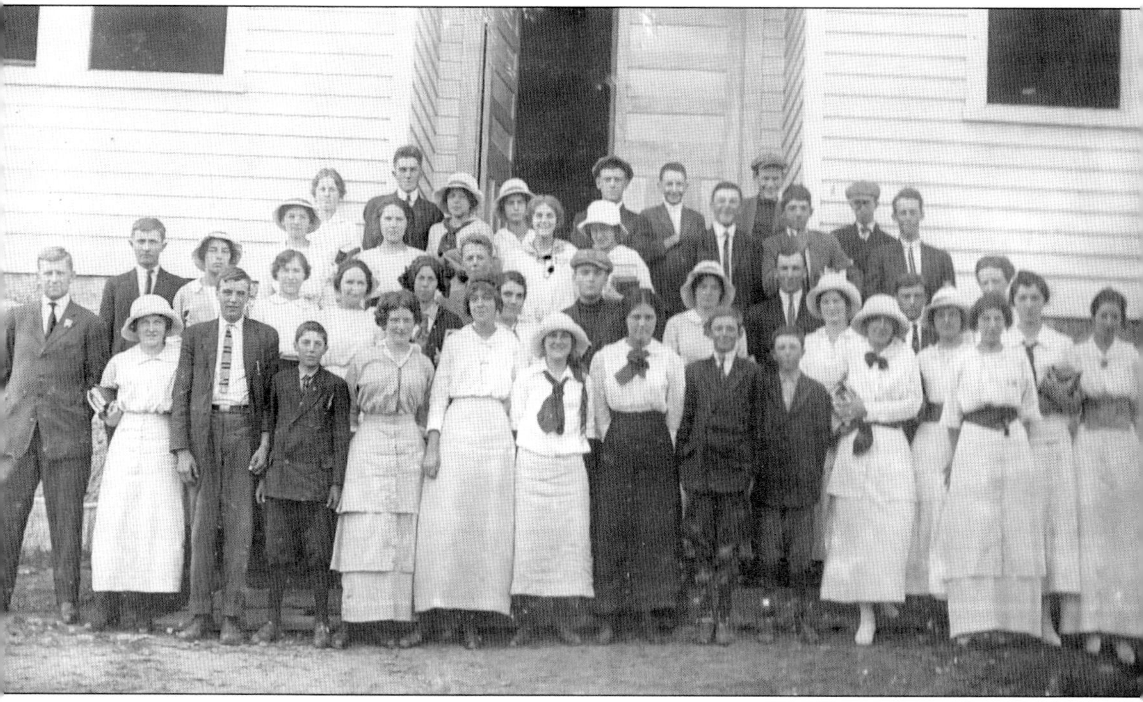

In 1914, two years after the Monterey School became an accredited four-year high school, the faculty and student body pose for a photograph. Identified people include teacher Robert Sterrett, Alice Dever, Else Terry, Rita Baldwin, Mary Hevener (Stephenson), Maude Ryder, Hubert Mackey, Lucy Grey Bird, Liza Stephenson, Adela Williamson, Ruth Doyle, Grace Gum, Paul Crouch, Hallie Herold, Alfred Eagle, Lena Seybert, J. C. Lightner, Frank Stephenson, Hoy Rexrode, Josiah Eagle, Lura Doyle, Mable Doyle, and Bobe Matheny. Mary Hevener Stephenson made the identifications in the 1970s. (Courtesy of the Highland Center.)

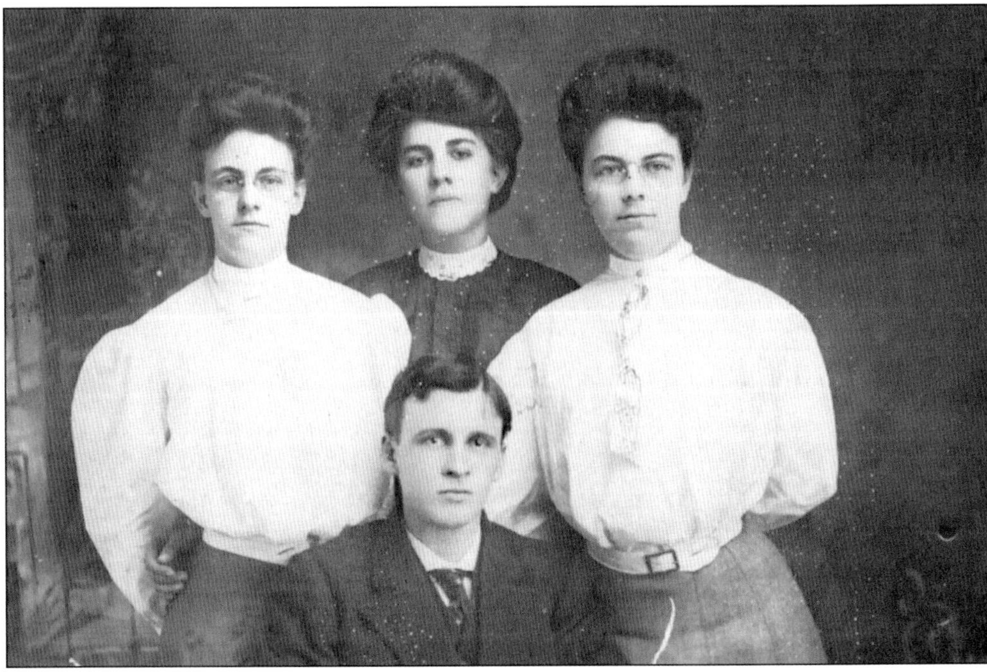

Small schools require a small faculty. This is the faculty photograph from Monterey High School in Spring 1907. As the school grew, several buildings were constructed and a larger faculty was added. (Courtesy of Kent Botkin.)

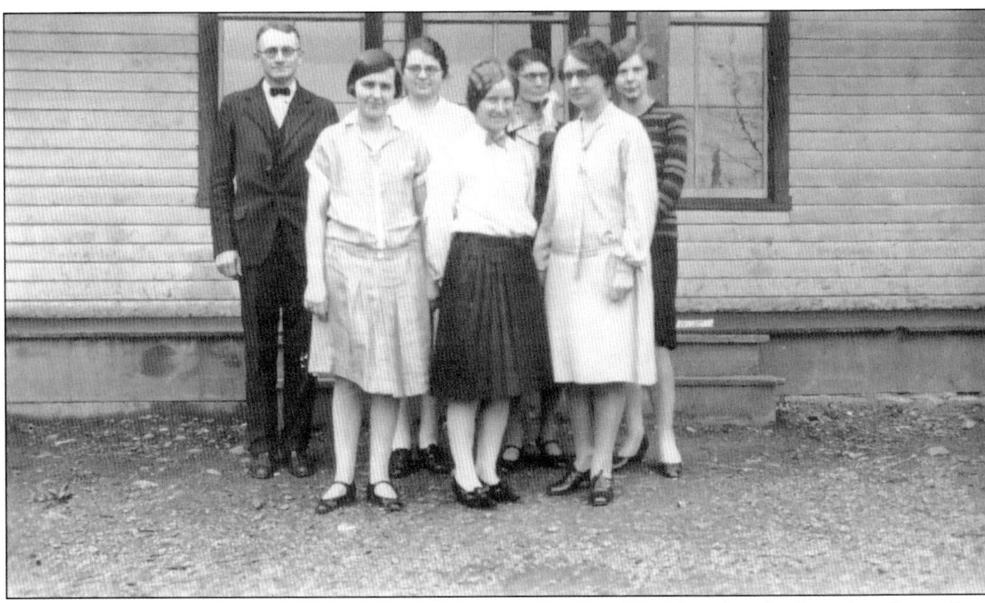

By 1939, the size of the faculty had grown, at least at McDowell High School. The school's teachers were, from let to right, Mr. and Mrs. Caleb Smith, Kathleen Shumate, Mary Maloy, Ida Quidor, Bernice Hicklin, and Clara Ervine. (Courtesy of Lyle and Georgianne Maloy Hull.)

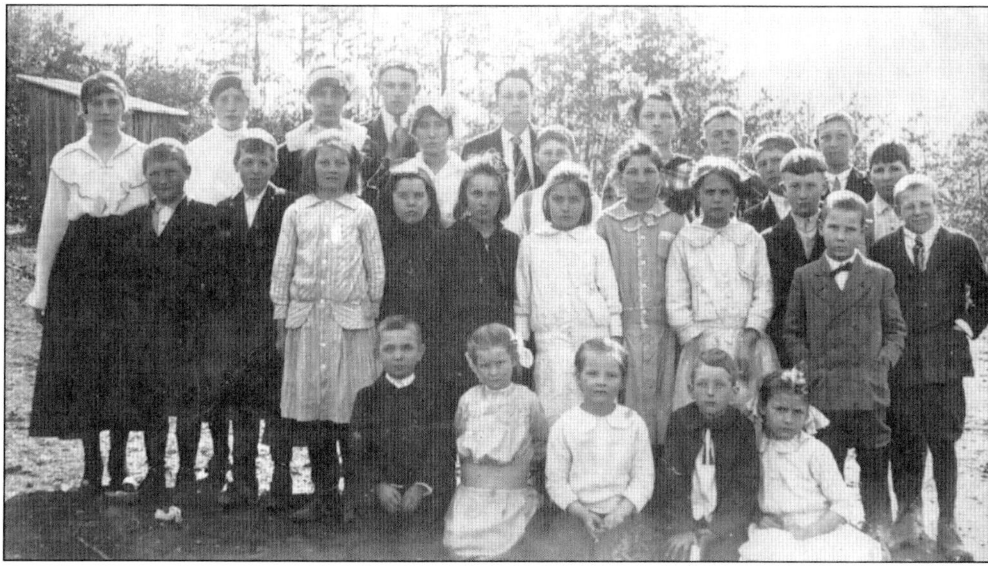

In 1916, a group of unidentified students from Headwaters School poses for a portrait. The Headwaters School was one of the last one-room schoolhouses operating in Highland County, closing in 1950. The building where these students met still exists off of Route 250 on Route 616 in Headwaters. (Courtesy of Kent Botkin.)

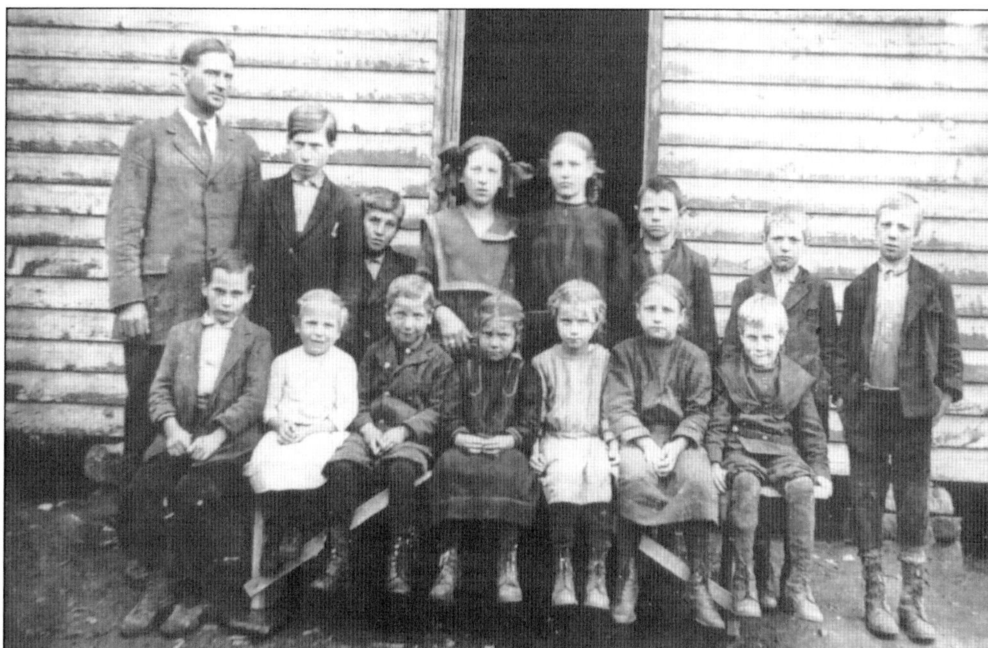

Middle Mountain School is situated between Lantz Mountain and Allegheny Mountain. Pictured from left to right are the following: (first row) Lapsley Mullenax, Sudie Barkley, Grover Barkley, Elsie Barkley, Ollie Mullenax, Ollie Barkley, and Roy Barkley; (second row) teacher Abram O. Mullenax, Richard Wimer, Fred Mullenax, Monna Mullenax, Ida Barkley, ? Simmons, Alfred Barkley, and unidentified. (Courtesy of Janet Mullenax.)

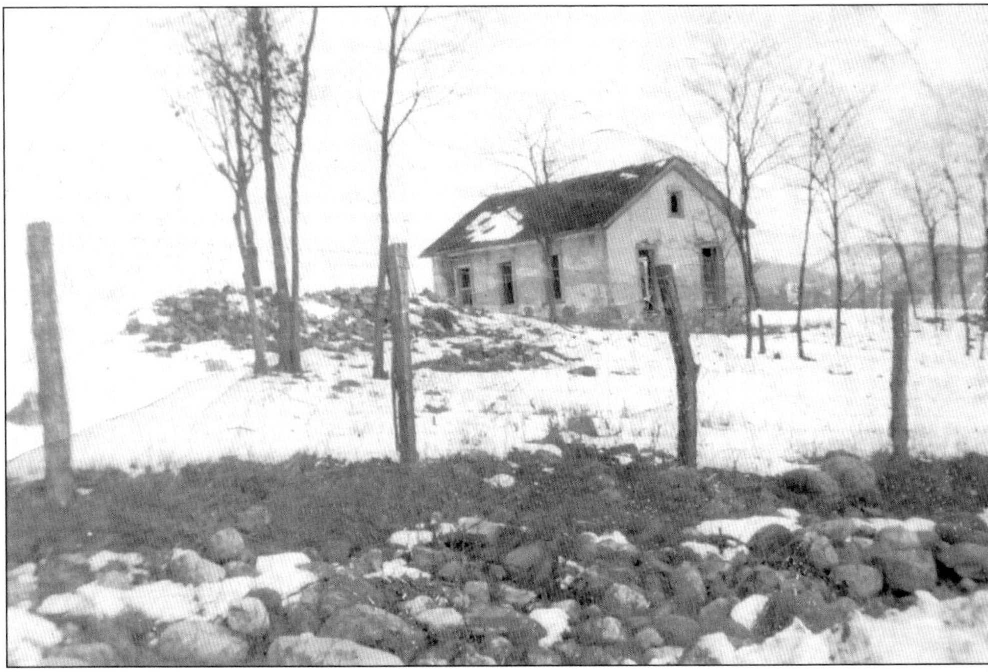

Though its exact location can no longer be pinpointed, McDowell Academy was a well-known and respected institution in McDowell. Established by Professor Sloal, with later faculty additions of Hiner Hansel and Prof. Sheffy Roller, the school taught Greek and Latin in the long, wooden building. (Courtesy of Lyle and Georgianne Maloy Hull.)

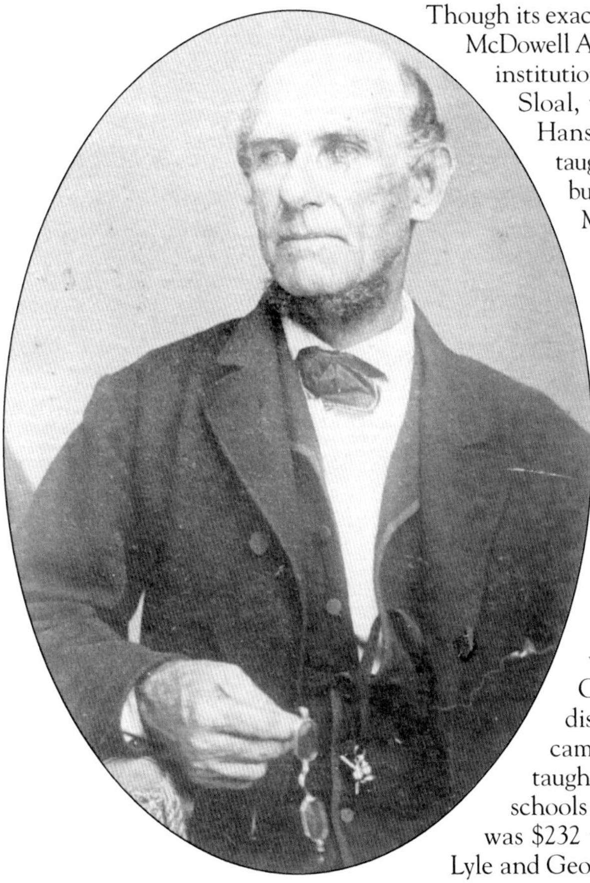

Patrick Maloy emigrated from his native Ireland in 1837. He taught school in various locations before enlisting in the Confederate army in 1861. Following his discharge due to typhoid fever in 1862, he came to Highland County to teach. Maloy taught in various settings, from small private schools to larger classrooms. His salary in 1868 was $232 for the five-month term. (Courtesy of Lyle and Georgianne Maloy Hull.)

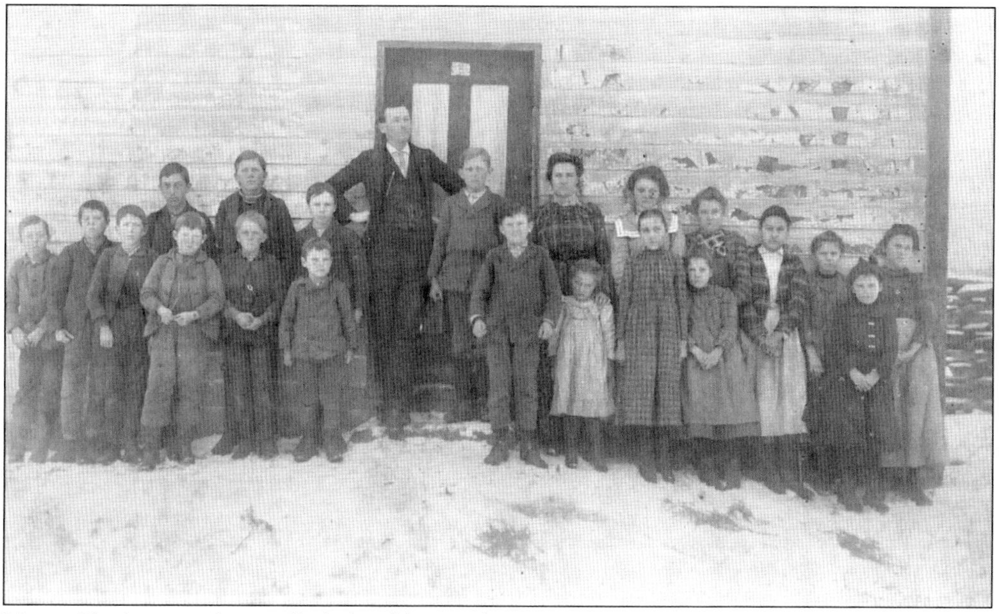

Henry Fleisher stands proudly behind his students. He taught at the Crabbottom (Blue Grass) School. This photograph was taken on February 29, 1902; the students are unidentified. (Courtesy of Kent Botkin.)

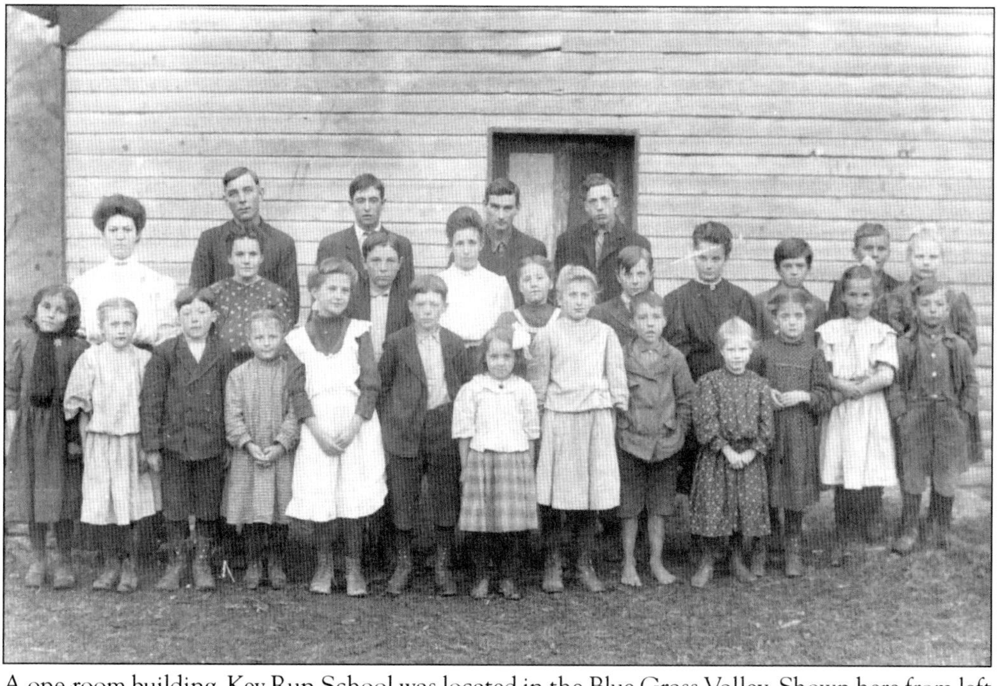

A one-room building, Key Run School was located in the Blue Grass Valley. Shown here from left to right are the following: (first row) two unidentified people, Jason Newman, two unidentified people, Ralph Newman, Geneva Will, unidentified, Owen "Dipper" Will, and four unidentified people; (second row) teacher Sudie Chew, Mary Nelson, unidentified, Ollie Mullenax, Myrtle Arbogast, unidentified, Elsie Neslon, two unidentified people, and Nellie Colaw; (third row) Ben Colaw, ? Arbogast, Foster Neslon, and Will Hildebrand. (Courtesy of Janet Mullenax.)

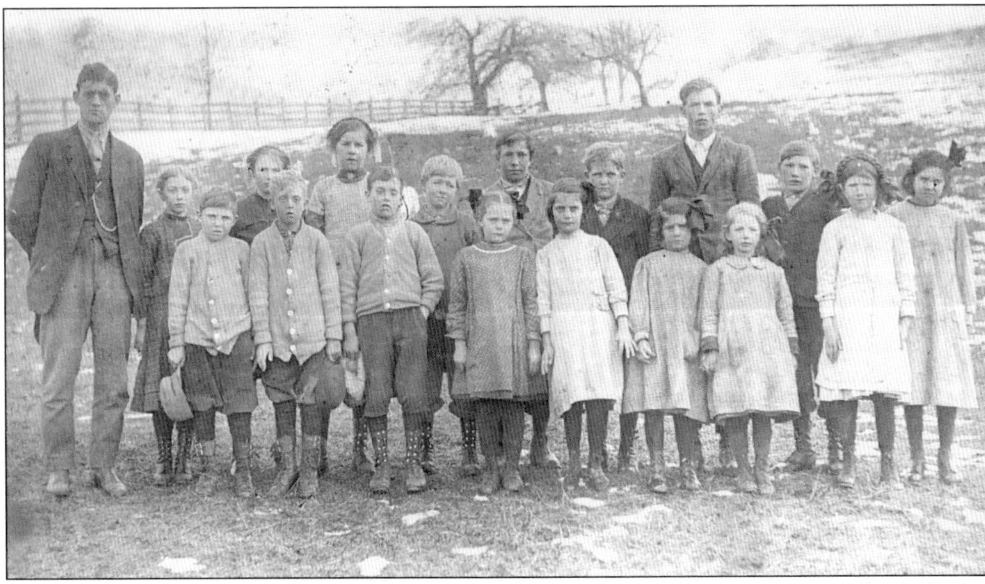

Glen Comble taught children at the Green Hill School, located on Route 84 in the Mill Gap area. The students in this photograph are unidentified. The building used for the school at Green Hill. It was later moved to Spruce Street in Monterey and placed at the entrance to the Monterey High School, where it was converted into a workshop for industrial arts classes. The building still stands in that spot. (Courtesy of Libby Woods Hefner.)

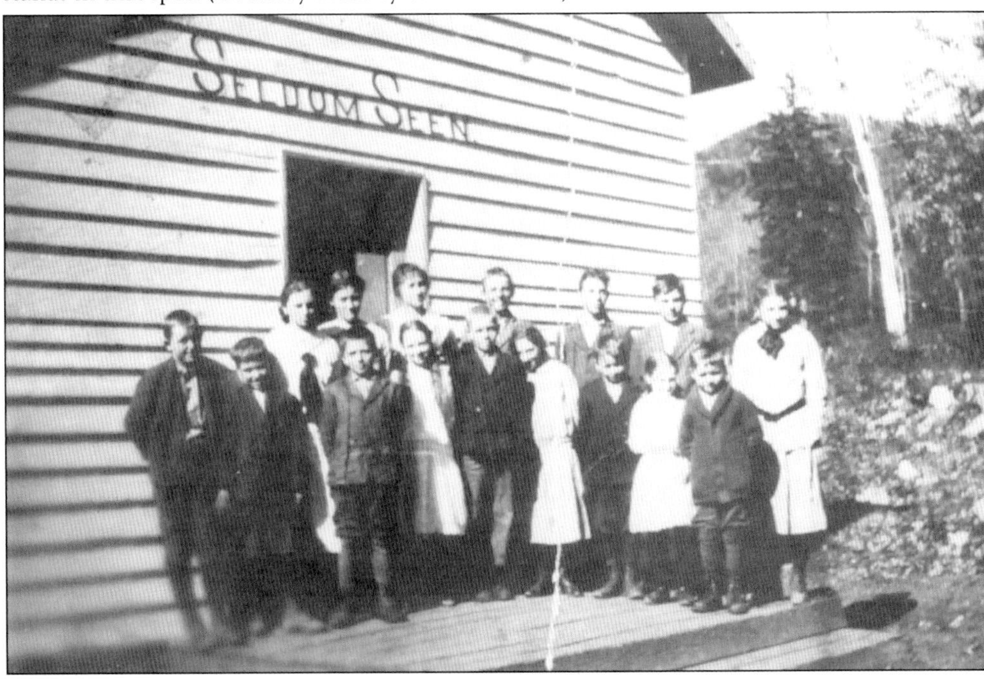

A group of unidentified school children stand in front of the Seldom Seen School. Seldom Seen was a one-room school building full of wood slab benches with hole bored in for seats for the children, and a large fireplace on the west end of the space for heat. Students remember the building as often smoke-filled, as the chimney was so large the smoke often blew back into the room. (Courtesy of Janet Mullenax.)

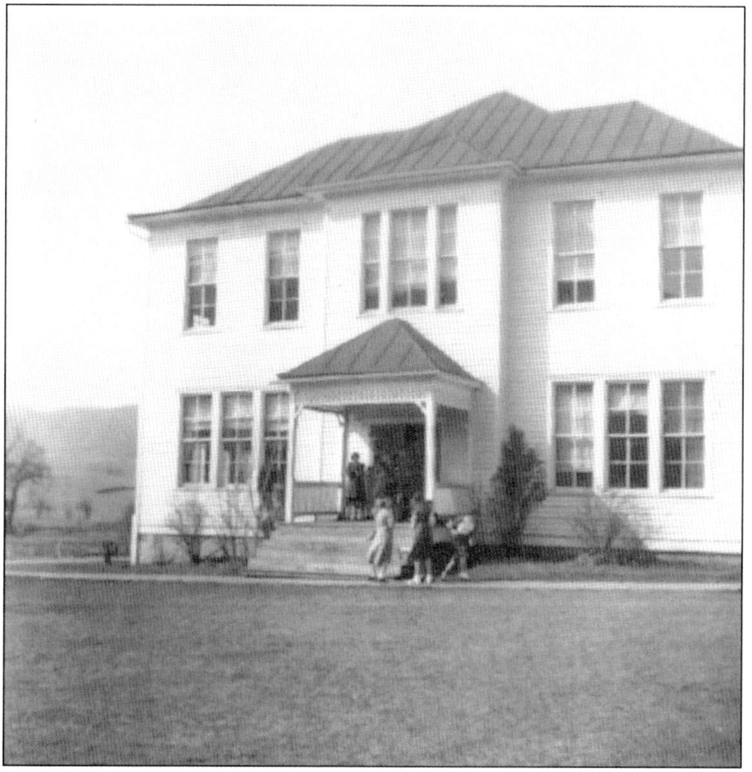

H. B. Nicholas built the Blue Grass (then Crabbottom) School for $4,036.79 in 1909. The school board's original plan was to consolidate Life School, Brick Church School, and Union Chapel School into this new high school. But parents objected, and the other schools remained open, as did the Blue Grass High School. Blue Grass earned its accreditation as a four-year high school in 1922. (Courtesy of Mary Judy Swecker Riddick.)

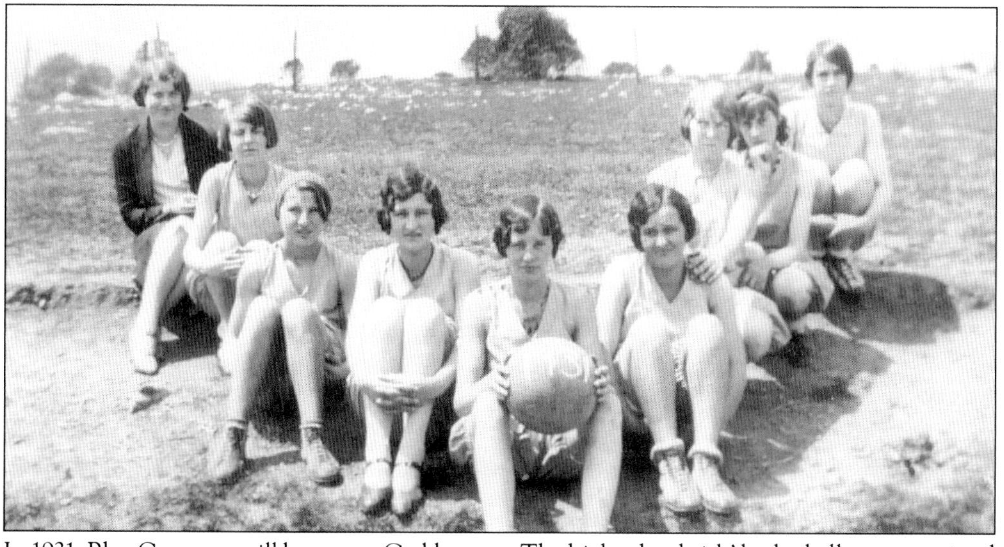

In 1931, Blue Grass was still known as Crabbottom. The high school girls' basketball team consisted of Virginia Wimer Hammer, Janet Wimer, Geneva Mullenax, Leanore Hammer, Edith Mullenax, Patty Swecker Kiser, Helen Nicholas, and Glenna Waggoner. (Courtesy of Janet Mullenax.)

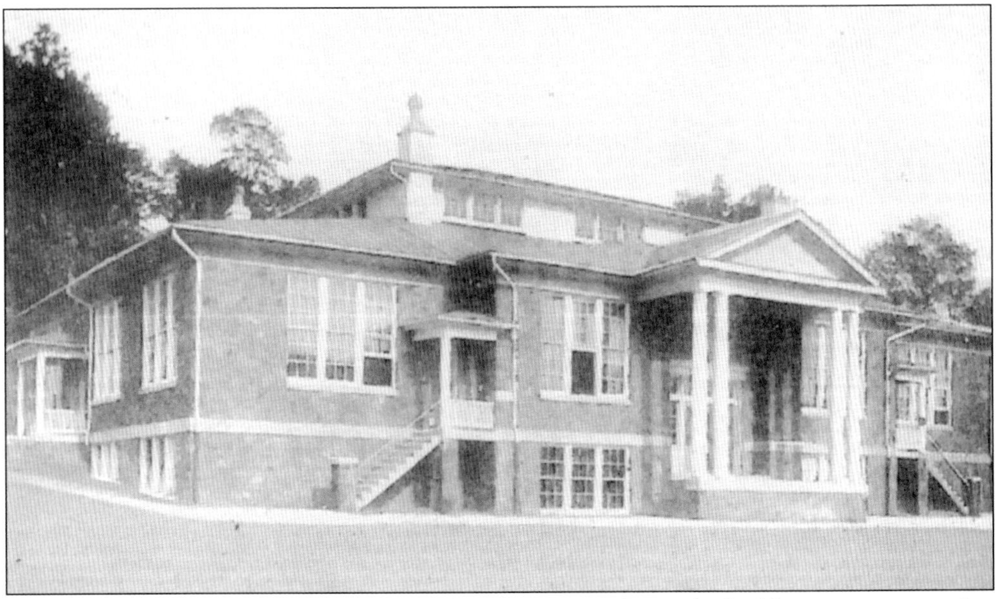

Currently the Highland Center, a business and community incubator, this building was constructed in 1922 as Monterey High School. Later serving as Highland Elementary, it was the second high school on the lot. Against state recommendations, the new building was constructed in 1921 on the same site as the old. L. W. Puffenbarger built the structure for $33,400. (Courtesy of Sarah Samples.)

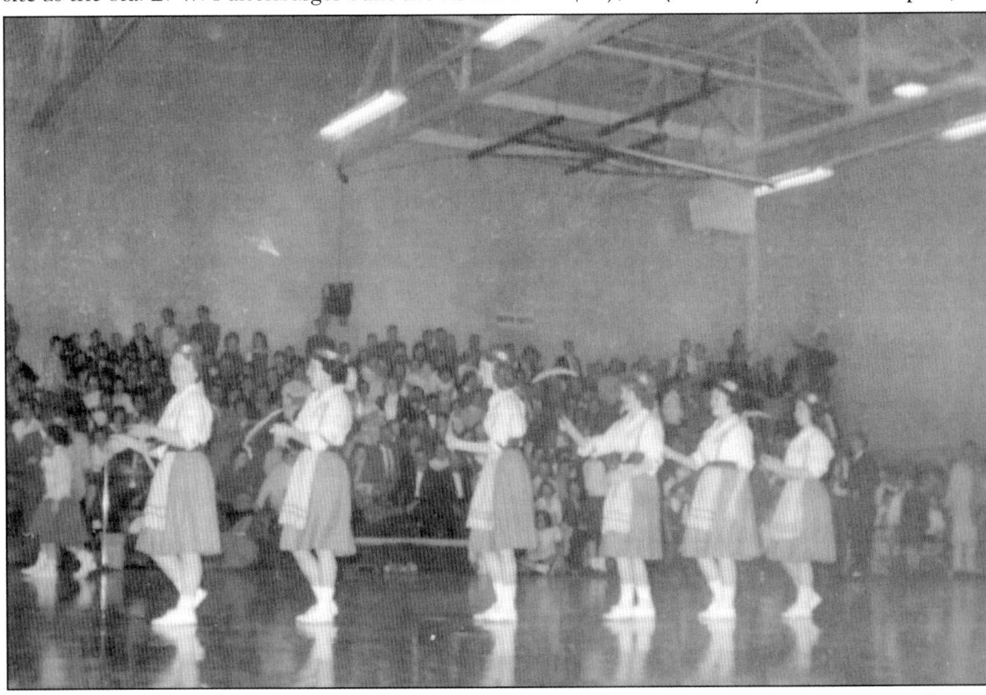

At halftime of a 1961 home basketball game, the Highland High School cheerleaders whip up school spirit. Even though both boys' and girls' basketball players wore shorts that same evening for the game, the cheerleaders wore long skirts. The cheerleaders are, from left to right, Roberta Leonard, Judy McNulty, Glenna Moyers, Bertha Terry, Beverly Malcolm, and Linda Ruckman. (Courtesy of Libby Woods Hefner.)

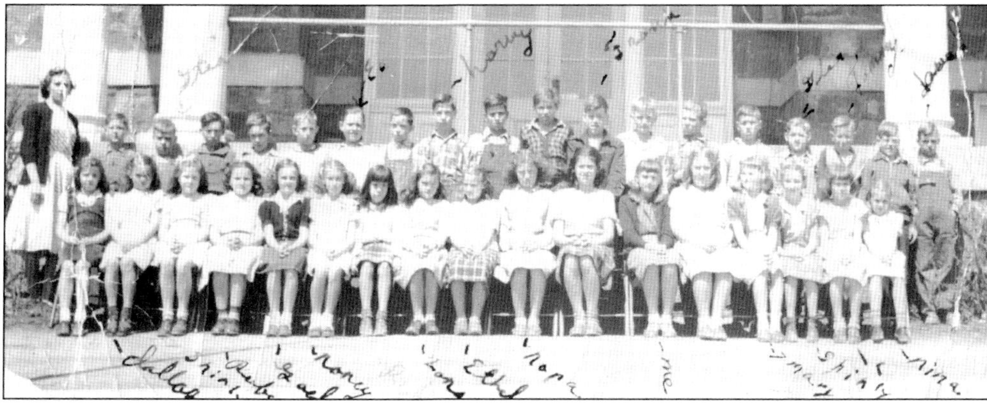

The 35 members of the fourth-grade class pose in front of Monterey High School in 1948. Their teacher, Mrs. Bennett, stands at the far left. (Courtesy of Libby Woods Hefner.)

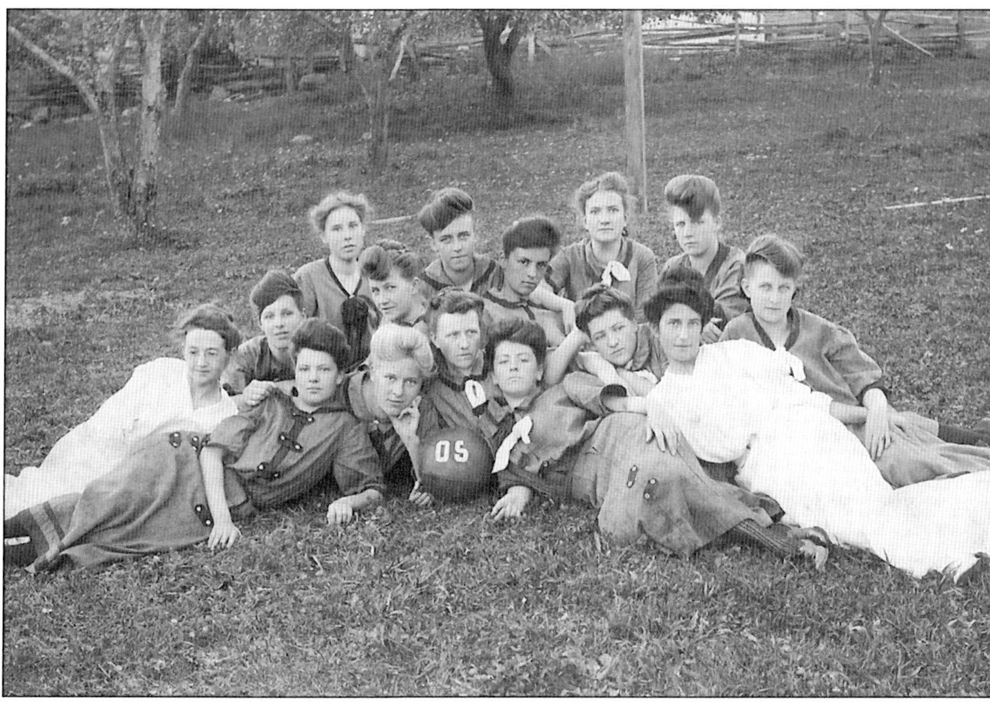

Sports have always been an important part of the school experience. Sports build community and develop relationships. These girls stare into the camera in 1905, obviously infused with confidence. The players are identified as Mrs. Cliff Matheny, Sue Hansel, Lona Fox, Bess Bishop, Kate Gibson, Janet Stephenson, Daisy Slaven, Elsie Slaven, Martha Jones, Sally Campbell, Blanche Wagner, Louie Seybert, Rachel Ogilvie, Elsie Hiner, and Jessie Campbell. (Courtesy of the *Recorder.*)

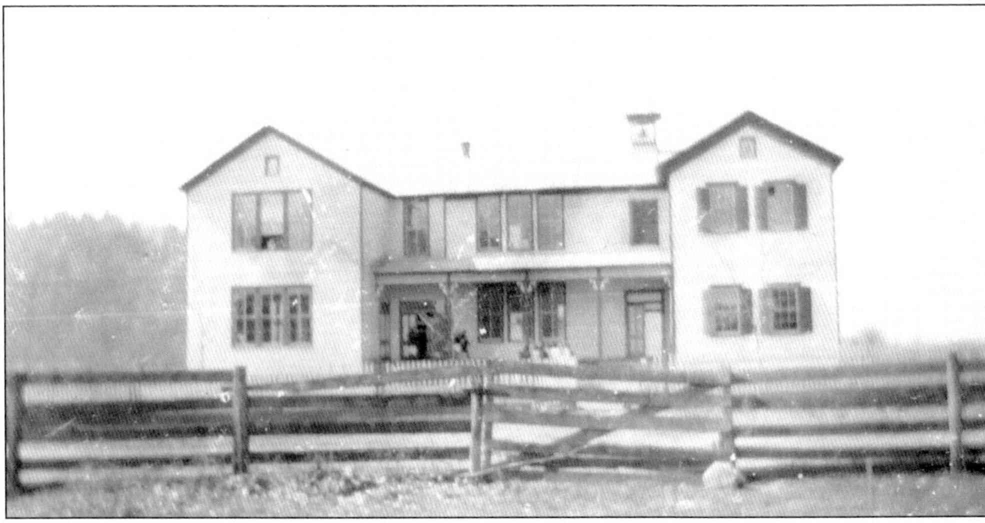

The McDowell School was accredited as a four-year high school in 1921. In 1920, an auditorium and two more classrooms were added to the building, originally a T shape, to make the fuller H shape. On Friday, May 13, 1948, this building burned to the ground. The fire flared up twice. The flames were believed to have been extinguished before they returned to become a larger fire. The school records were saved, as they were quickly retrieved and placed in the principal's car. The students were able to continue their educations, though; classes were moved to any available space in McDowell, including the Presbyterian church. After this fire, McDowell lost a high school for good. The building constructed in its place was the Stonewall Elementary School. (Courtesy of Lyle and Georgianne Maloy Hull; courtesy of Kent Botkin.)

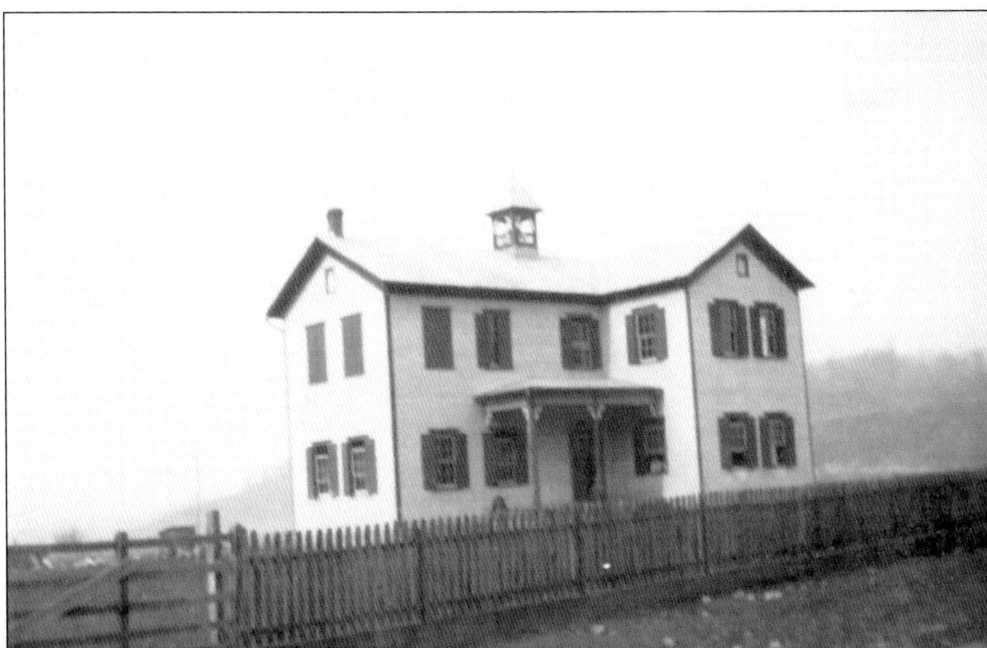

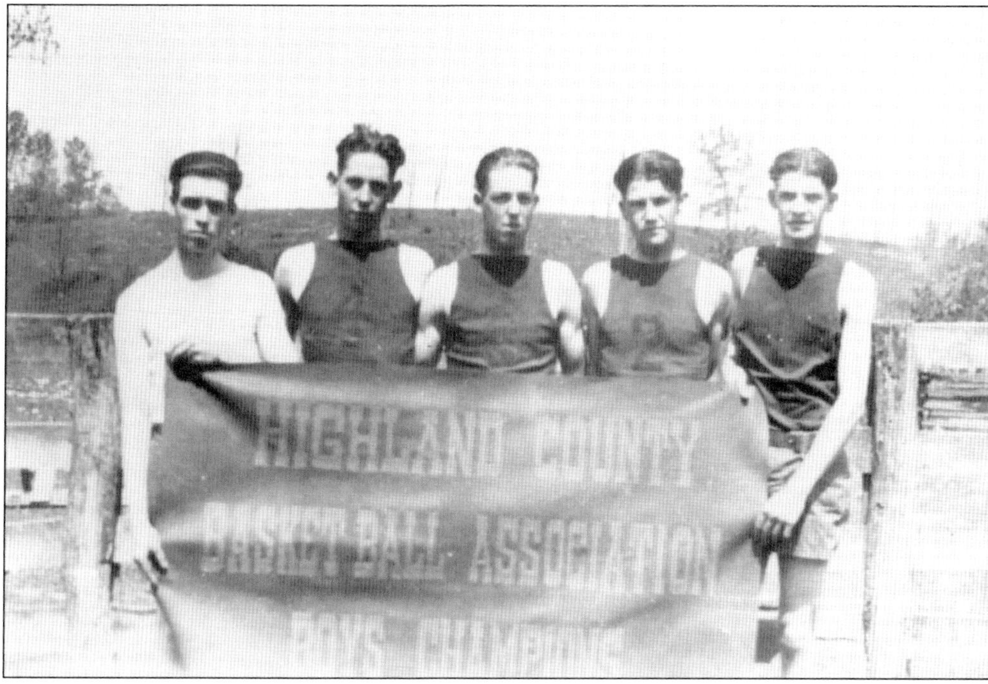

When Highland County had several high schools, rivalries were fierce. In 1926, the McDowell High School boys' basketball team won the championship. Displaying their banner are, from left to right, Melvin Ralston, Lohr Vance, Randolph Siron, Lacy Malcolm, and Stuart Lamb. (Courtesy of Lyle and Georgianne Maloy Hull.)

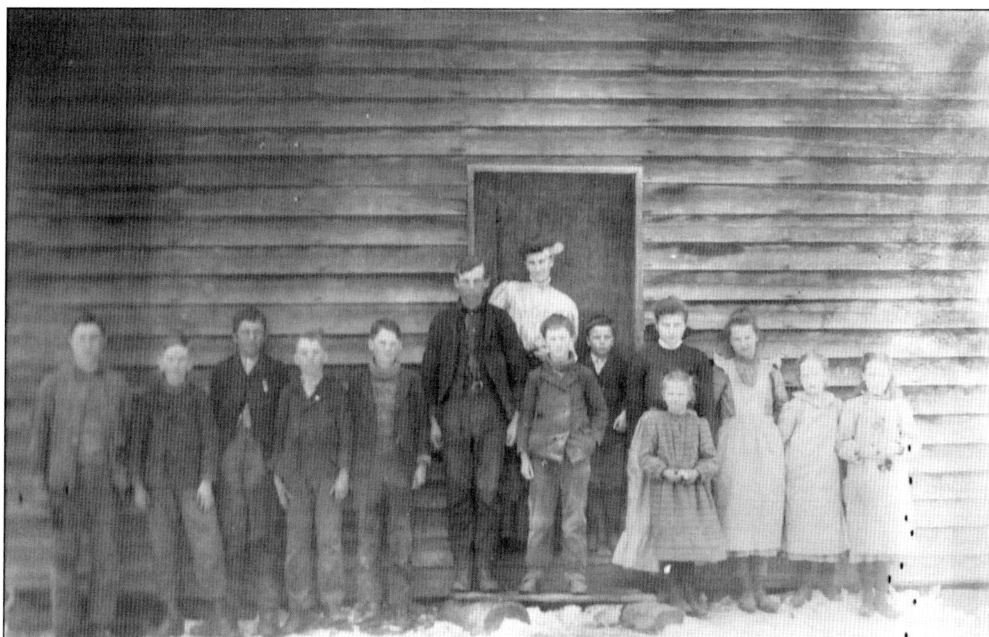

Mayme Quidor Darby poses with her students in front of the Seldom Seen School, built on land owned by Iva Woddell. Mayme was a revered educator in Highland County. (Courtesy of Kent Botkin.)

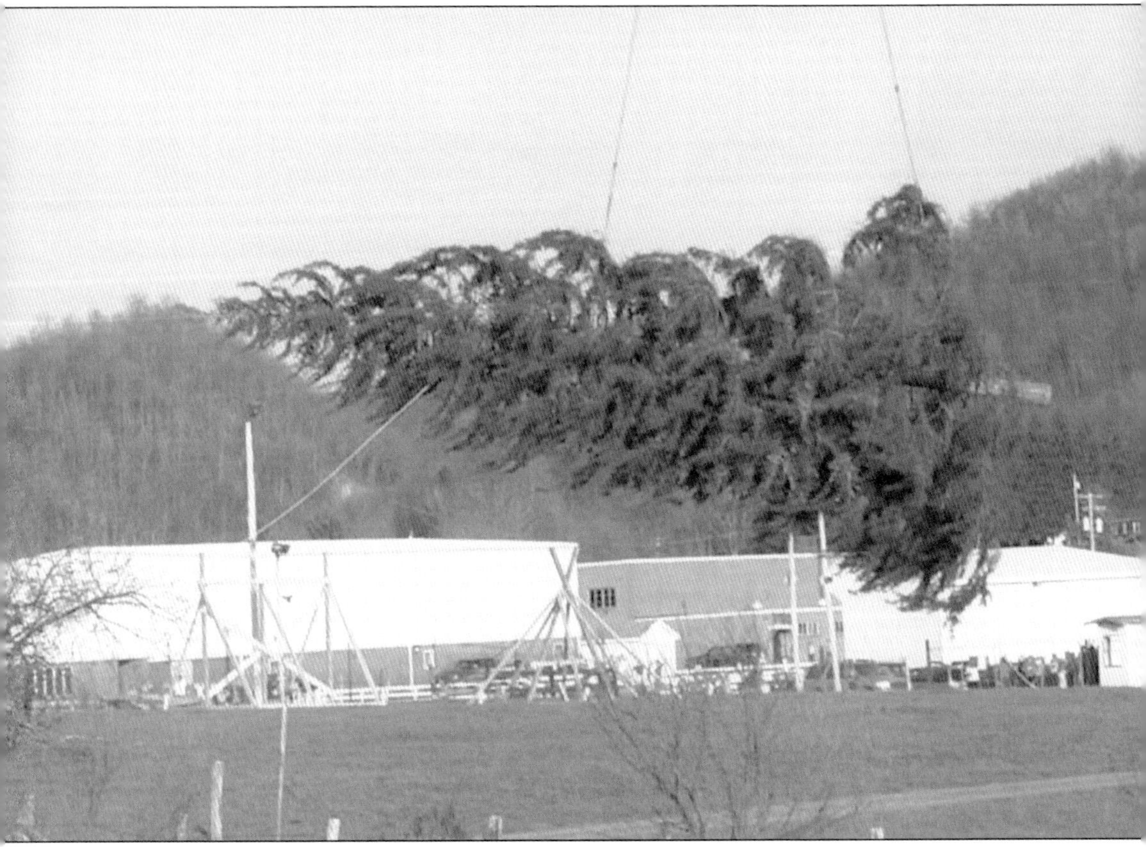

Each year, one of this country's 156 national forests provides a Christmas tree to be placed at the capitol in Washington, D.C. In 2004, the opportunity came to Highland County to donate what is known officially as the Holiday Tree and often referred to as the People's Tree. A beautiful, 65-foot red spruce, this tree is the first from Virginia to be used for this purpose. Highland County hosted a send-off celebration at the county fairgrounds with speeches, music, clogging demonstrations, and refreshments. Highland County Public School's art teacher Heather Scott oversaw school students creation of just under 1,000 large ornaments to be placed on the tree, while many community members contributed as well. In a grand illumination ceremony, Speaker of the House Dennis Hastert threw the switch to light the tree and its ornaments. (Courtesy of the *Recorder*.)

Seven

UNDERSTANDING THE PEOPLE

FACES OF HIGHLAND COUNTRY

Not all Highlanders are native to the county. In fact, like everywhere else in the nation, if traced back far enough, they are transplants from somewhere. No matter where they started, whether from a fifth-generation family or a recent newcomer, Highlanders have come together to form a community.

Highland County has a rich tradition of both rugged individualism and community spirit. Natives pride themselves on their self-sufficient way of life. Everyone is expected to take care of themselves and provide their own way; at the same time, if a neighbor needs help, the expectation is that everyone and anyone will step up. Creativity is a requirement to survive in this county, and residents are very proud of the fact that they make their own way in this world.

Many people over the years have exemplified what Highland County believes. Mary Swietzer was well known for her personality and friendliness. Osborne Wilson was a Civil War veteran and later served as a county assessor. John Paul Brown, an African American born into slavery, was later elected to serve on the Monterey Town Council.

An important, but often untold, portion of Highland County history is the story of those who came here against their will. Slavery was a part of Highland County. Not many residents owned people, but there are documented cases where, before the Civil War, slaves were owned and bought and sold in this county. This is a regretful, but real, part of the larger Southern history and to a larger degree human history in general.

The photographs included here reflect the story of Highland County. In residents' faces, both posed and candid, the pride of living shines. Most of these people are gone now, existing only in memories and photographs. They laughed, loved, married, mourned, hurt, worried, wept, and lived their lives as best they could; their stories are at once universal and unique. Their story is our story.

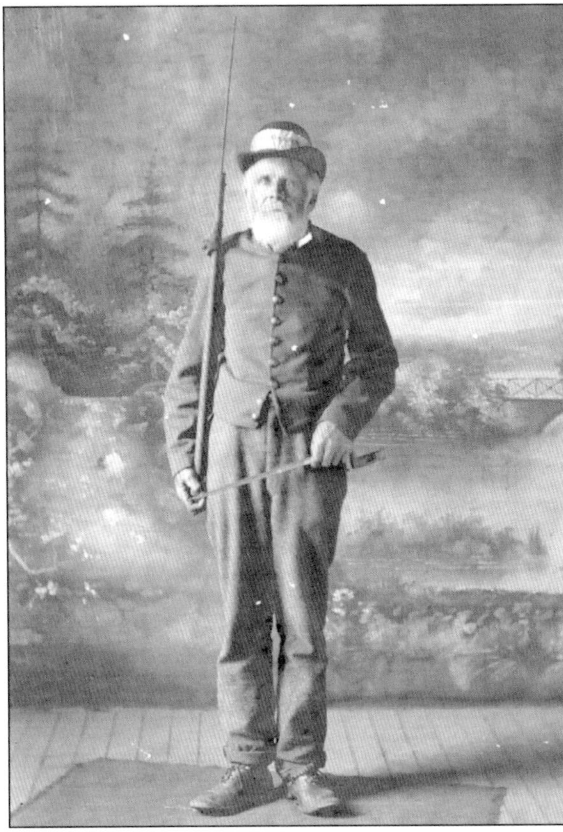

Sgt. Osborne Wilson served from 1861 to 1865 with the 31st Virginia during the Civil War. He twice worked as commissioner of revenue. As part of his duties, he assessed property values and occasionally would spend the night wherever the last call of the day happened to leave him, continuing on in the morning. His home in Monterey is known as the Osborne Wilson House. (Courtesy of Kent Botkin.)

George Colaw, born in Forks of the Water, was one of the few Highlanders to fight on behalf of the Union in the Civil War. In 1862, he enlisted in Company E of the 94th Illinois Volunteer Infantry at the age of 13. Colaw "fought many major battles" and returned home to Highland, where he married Lucy Simmons in 1884. Buried in Colaw Cemetery, he died in 1908. (Courtesy of Kent Botkin.)

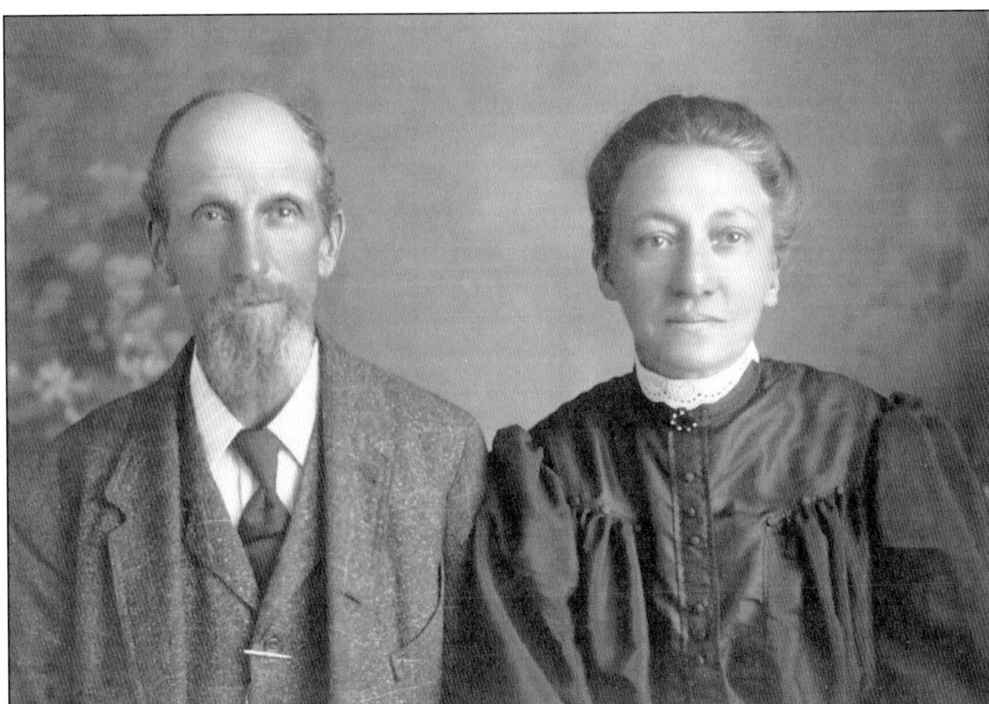

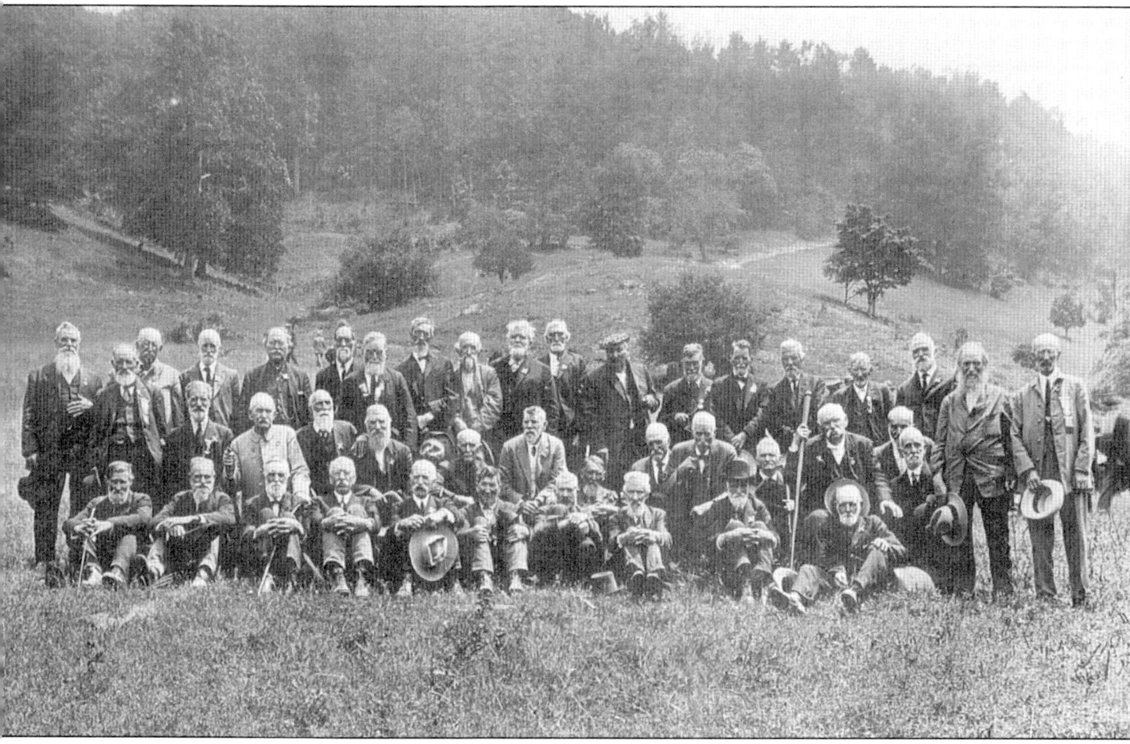

A reunion of Confederate survivors from Highland County was held on the site of the Battle of McDowell on Sitlington's Hill. This photograph was taken on July 9, 1910, about 48 years after the end of this bloody and deadly conflict. Shown from left to right are the following: (first row) John Pruitt, Jake Shumate, M. Corbett, Wes Kinkaid, ? Ross, James Wilson, Abel Siron, Frank Marshall, Silas McClung, and George Hiner; (second row) unidentified, "Bomb" Cunningham, Henry Simmons, Washington Rexrode, James Woods, Abraham Armstrong, J. B. Bradshaw, A. A. Stephenson, ? Blagg, L. McClung, Josiah Corbett, ? Blagg, and unidentified; (third row) ? Cunningham, Dr. H. H. Jones, nine unidentified men, Curtis ?, George Hocklin, Gilbert Siron, W. H. Vance, William Stuart, unidentified, Addison Rexrode, Abbott Armstrong, and unidentified. (Courtesy of the Highland County Historical Society.)

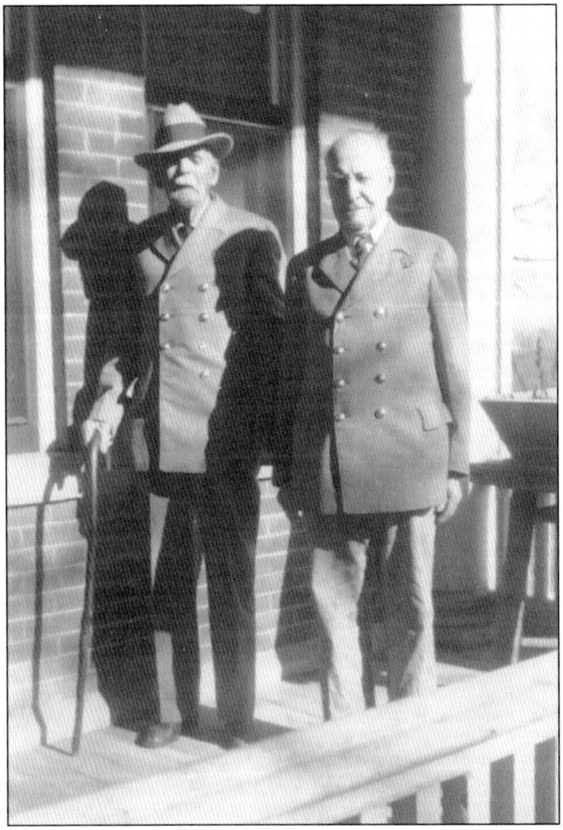

David A. Sheffer and Captain Coffee stand together on February 18, 1934, more than 70 years after they fought, along with Highland native W. H. Vance, in the Battle of McDowell. All three men were attached to Gen. Thomas "Stonewall" Jackson's brigade. (Courtesy of Robin and Nancy Vance.)

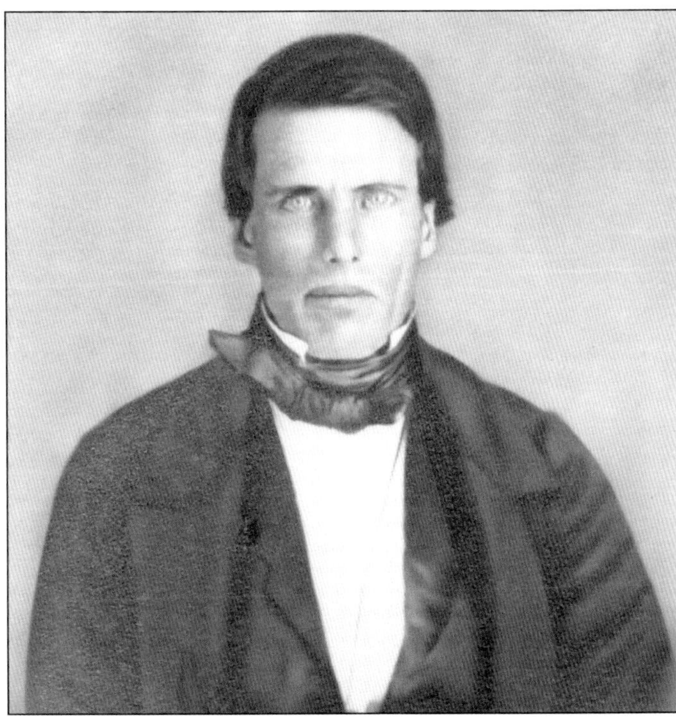

Washington Stephenson, the first elected sheriff of Highland County, served as a constable in Bath County before the creation of Highland. Serving as a deputy in Highland to appointed Sheriff Andrew H. Byrd, Stephenson was elected and served two terms as sheriff from January 2, 1853, to December 31, 1856, after the change of the Virginia constitution requiring the election of sheriff by the people for the term of two years, with a limit of two terms. (Courtesy of the Highland County Historical Society.)

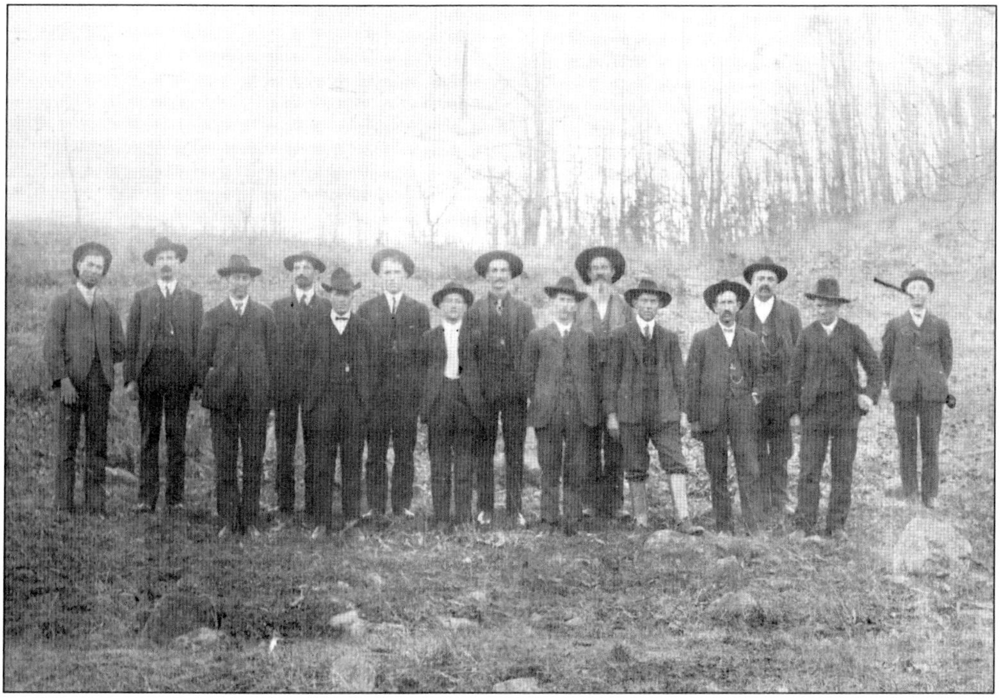

Performing their civic duty, members of the jury stand with Sheriff Ed Arbogast. As a young man, Arbogast served 12 years as sheriff of Highland County, from 1899 to 1911. The group pictured is identified only as the "Siron Jury." (Courtesy of the *Recorder*.)

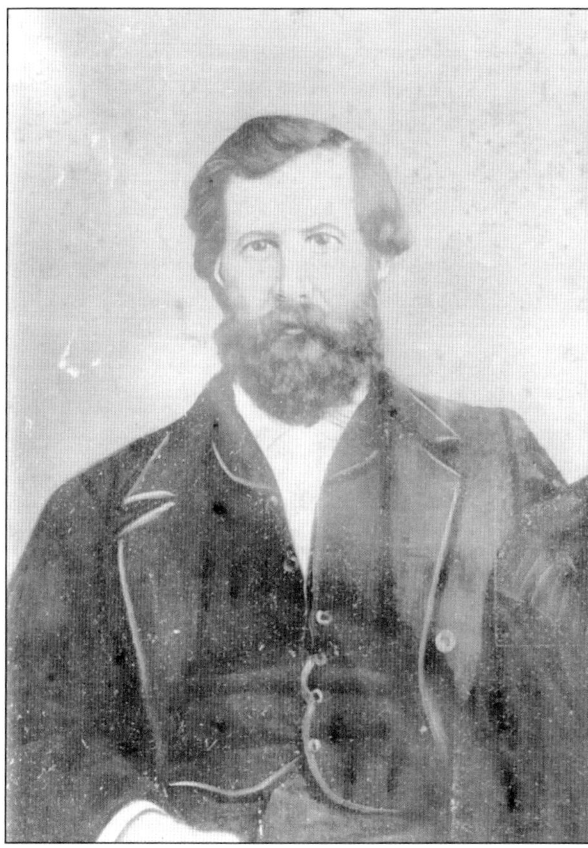

A pillar of early Highland County life, William "Squire" Hevener owned a 600-acre farm in Blue Grass. He served as a Virginia state delegate, representing both Bath and Highland Counties. Squire was able to pay the commutation fee to avoid the draft in the Civil War. Approximately 86,724 draftees paid this fee, normally $500 in the South and $300 in the North, during the war. (Courtesy of Kent Botkin.)

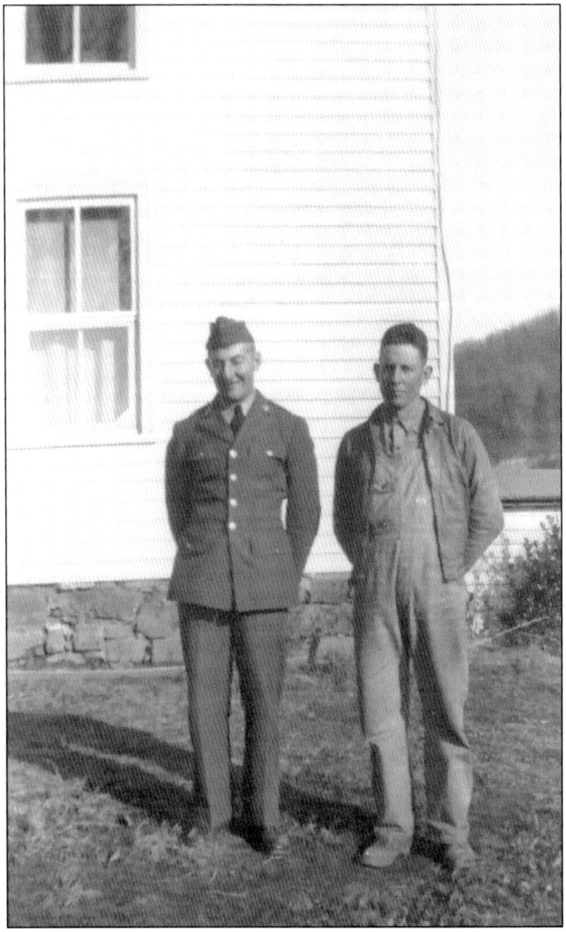

During the Christmas of 1941, Bruce Vance came home on furlough to visit with his family. Lohr Vance, while not serving in the armed services, was a member of the Civilian Airplane Spotters. It was Lohr's job to look out for suspicious planes flying overhead. In some places, spotters would spend two hours an evening each week for about eight or nine months. (Courtesy of Robin and Nancy Vance.)

The influenza epidemic of 1923 cost many lives. In some cases, entire families were decimated. This Patna family, all but destroyed in a few days, included Mary Armstrong (young girl), Albert Armstrong (baby), Mabel Virginia Armstrong (holding baby), John Wesley Armstrong (straw hat), Warwick H. Armstrong (young boy), and Mark Kinkaid (rocking chair). Warwick was the only one to live through the epidemic. (Courtesy of Kent Botkin.)

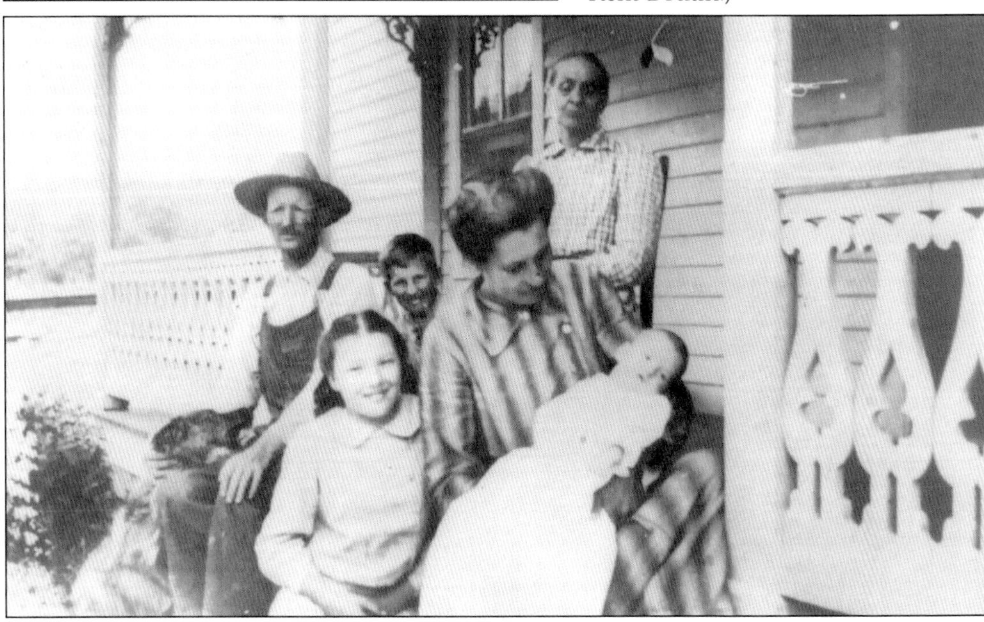

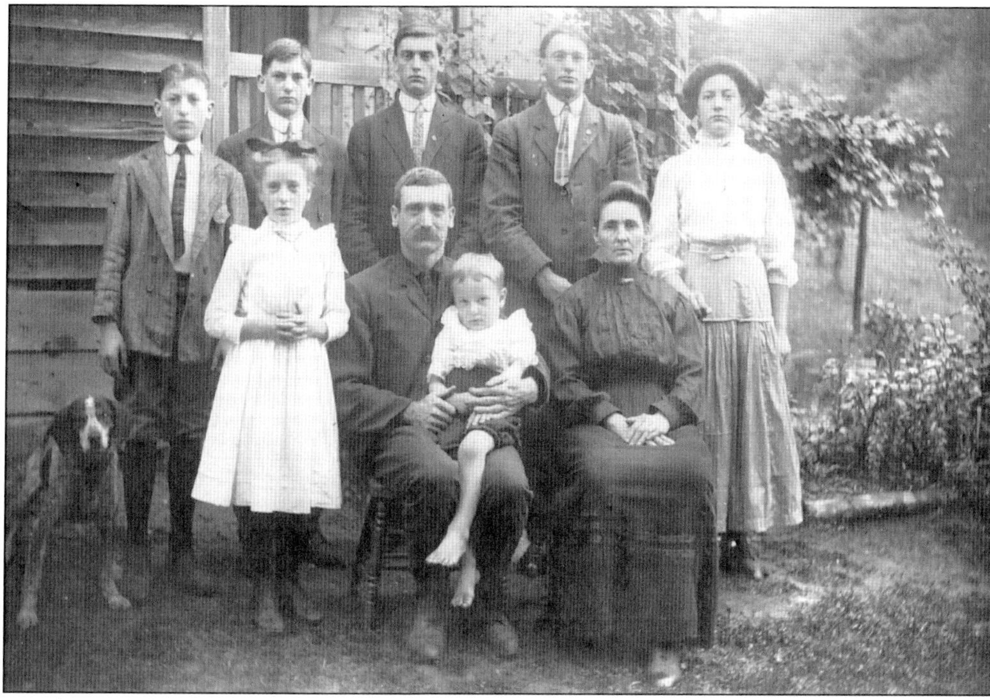

Members of the William A. Hodge family gather for a portrait in front of their home. Many stories are told about the well-known family. "Grandma" Hodge was known as a hardy mountain woman who once went after a rattlesnake with her bare hands as it attempted to curl up under her front porch. Her son Roy Hodge worked as a game warden in the Headwaters area. (Courtesy of Kent Botkin.)

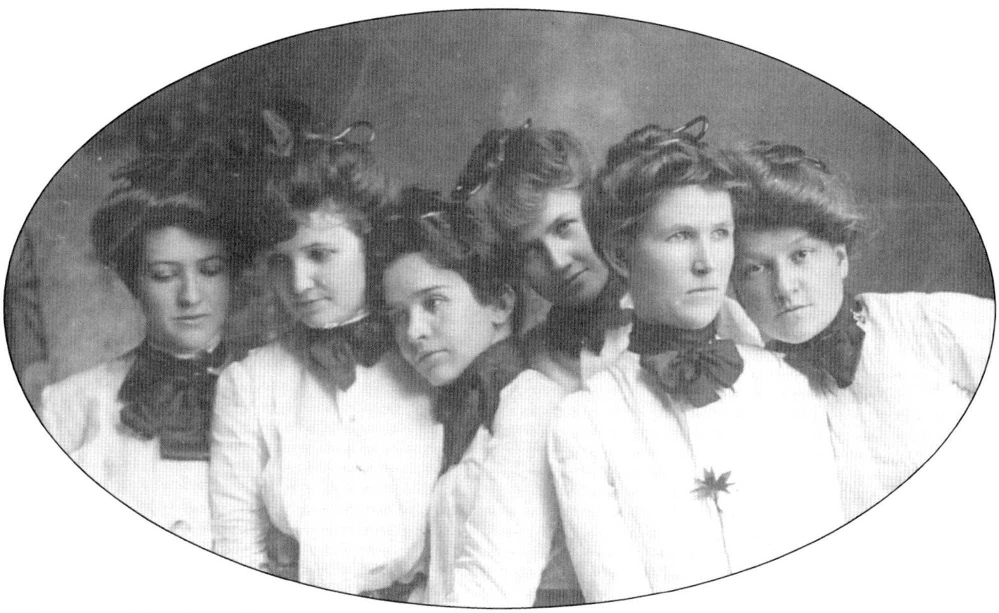

Taken at Suddarth Studios in Monterey, this photograph represents "The Only Shirt Waist Club in Monterey." Pictured from left to right are Daisy Slaven, Eva Campbell, Abbie Fleisher, Sallie Campbell, Helen Campbell, and Elizabeth Brock. (Courtesy of the *Recorder*.)

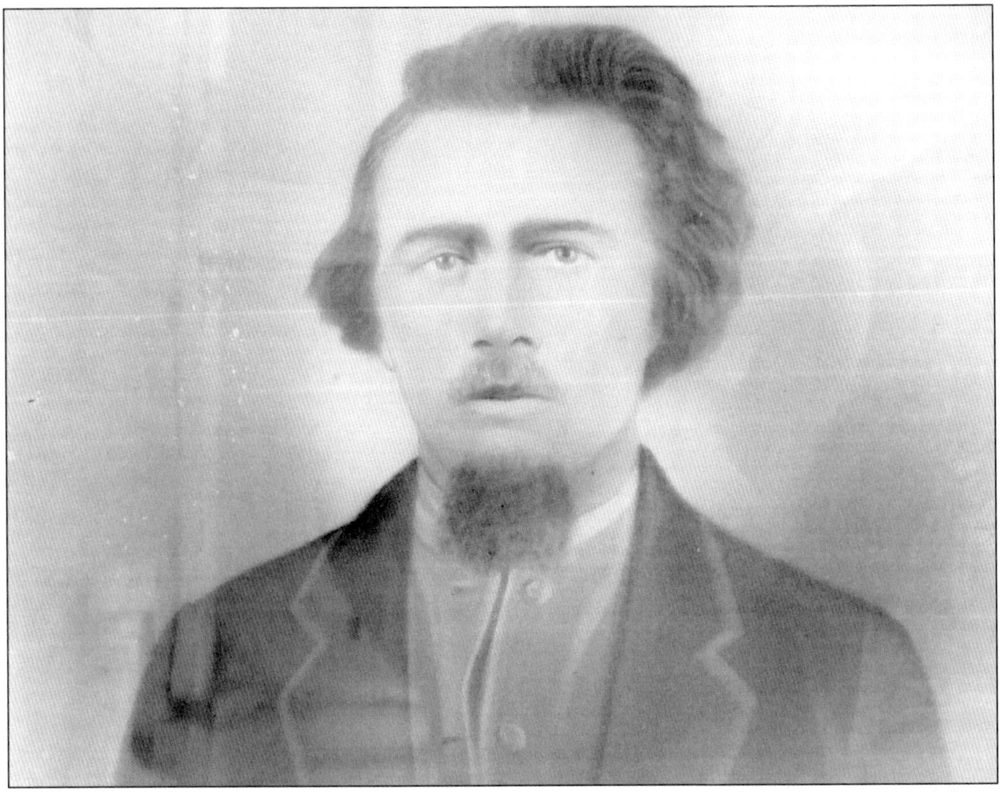

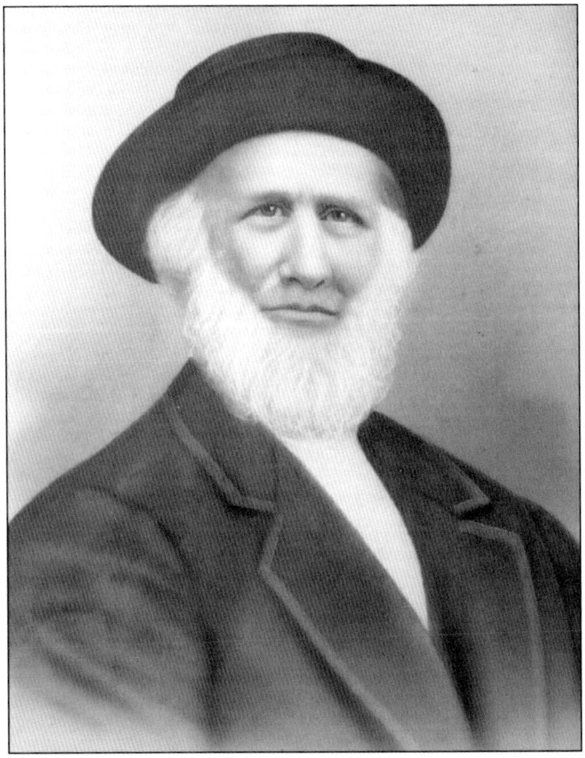

Peter Woods was a patriarch of the Woods family from the Back Creek and Mill Gap sections of the county. A Civil War veteran with the 20th Cavalry unit, he married Rachel Bird in 1868; together they raised four children. (Courtesy of Libby Woods Hefner.)

George Vance, the son of Benjamin Handel Vance, was born in Highland County in 1815 and traveled West during the Gold Rush of 1849. Married four times, he was on his way back to Highland when his wife and family died. Vance went through Panama and landed in Norfolk, arriving home the day after their burial. Vance died in 1859. (Courtesy of Robin and Nancy Vance.)

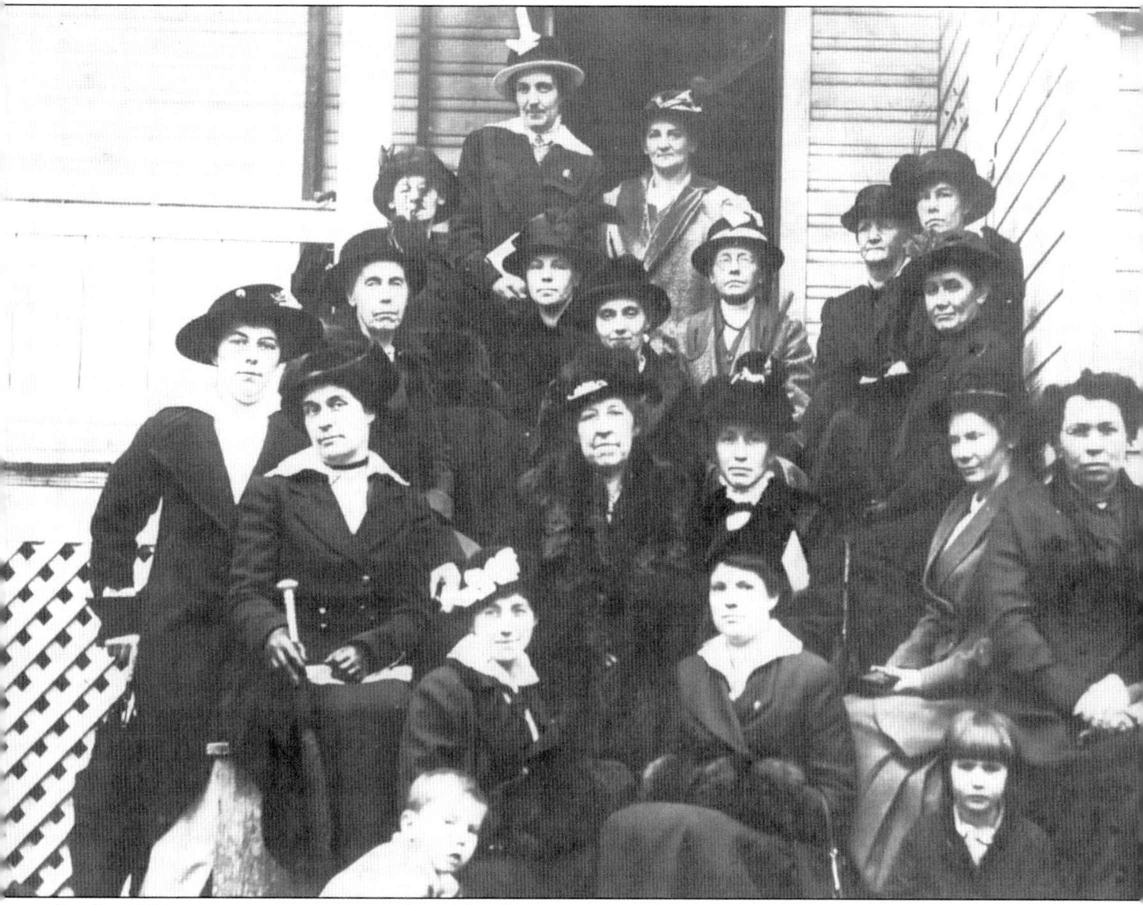

In the 1920s, prominent women of Highland County pose for a group portrait. Several of that era's leading families are represented. Shown here in descending order are Mrs. Don Sullenberger, Jessie Hicklin, Maggie Jones, Mabel Jones, Mrs. A. B. Warwick, Mrs. C. A. Bird, Hannah Simmons, Mollie Trimble, Cora Eastham, Mrs. C. W. Trimble, Mrs. Paul Slaven, Mrs. John Whitelaw, Mrs. Lloyd Sullenberger, Mrs. V. B. Bishop, Mrs. L. L. Lawrence, Mrs. Hampton Matheny, Mrs. R. C. Jones, and Mrs. C. B. Fox. The children are identified as Frank Wilson and Dot Wilson. (Courtesy of Kent Botkin.)

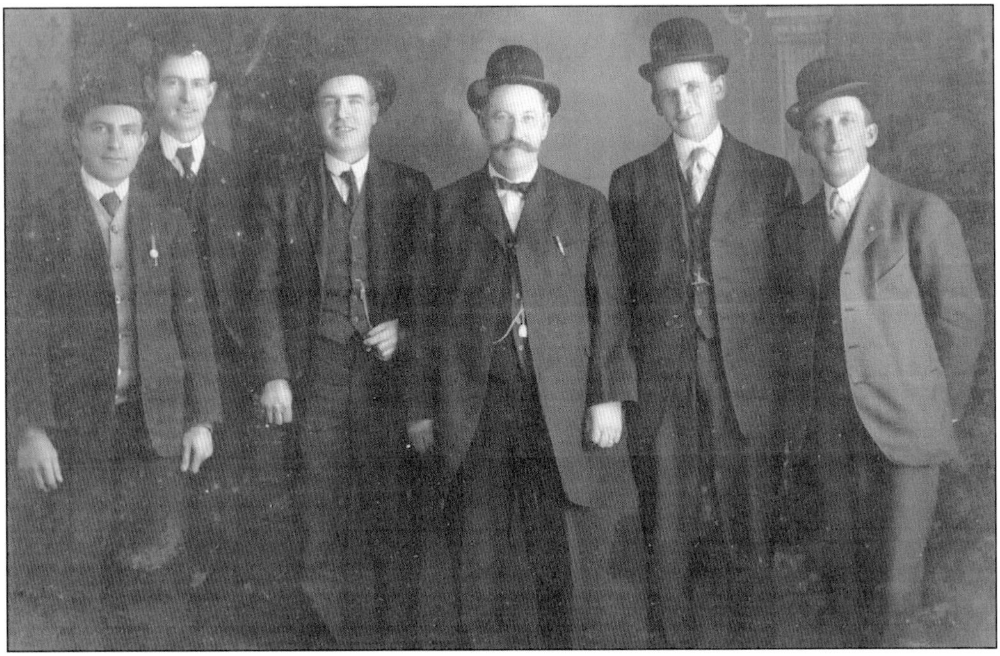

This image from the early 1900s is a virtual *Who's Who* listing for the county. The men are, from left to right, H. B. Wood, J. C. Matheny, John Whitelaw, unidentified, Clyde Hiner, and Edward Arbogast. Wood published the *Recorder* for 50 years; Whitelaw served as commissioner of revenue for 11 years; and Arbogast worked as sheriff of the county for 12 years. (Courtesy of Kent Botkin.)

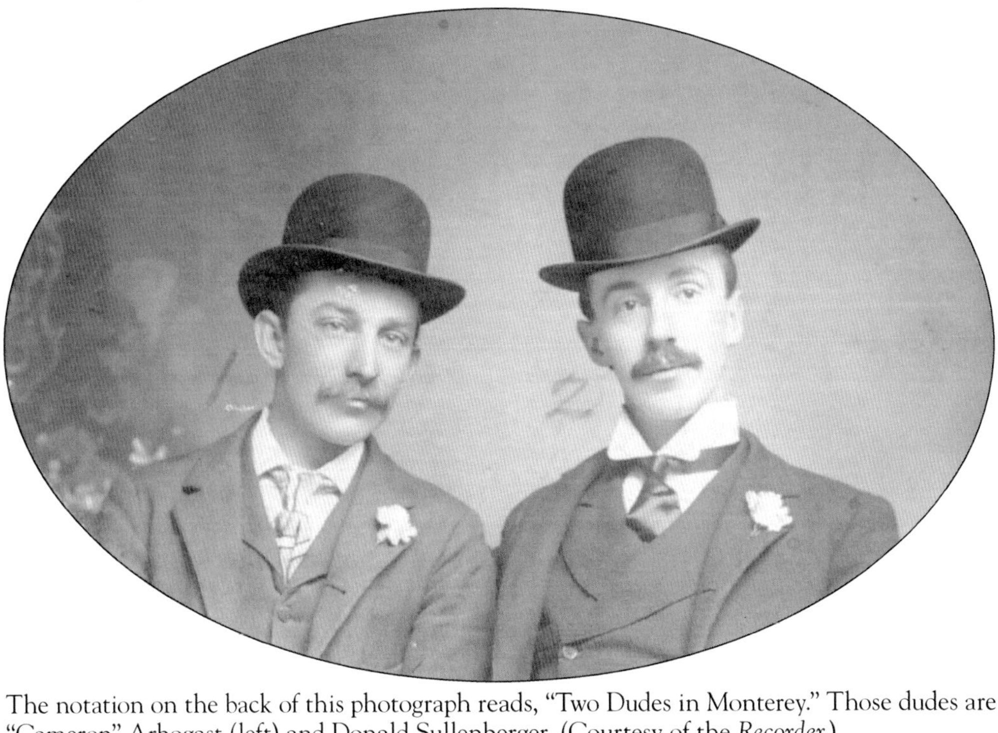

The notation on the back of this photograph reads, "Two Dudes in Monterey." Those dudes are "Cameron" Arbogast (left) and Donald Sullenberger. (Courtesy of the *Recorder*.)

Squire Wilson, standing in his front yard gazing at Route 250 in 1925, was a large landowner along the Cowpasture River. He was a squire by all measures. According to family legend, the son-in-law of the Mansion House owners, the Bradshaws, would never go out the front door without donning white gloves to signify that he did not perform manual labor. (Courtesy of the Highland County Historical Society.)

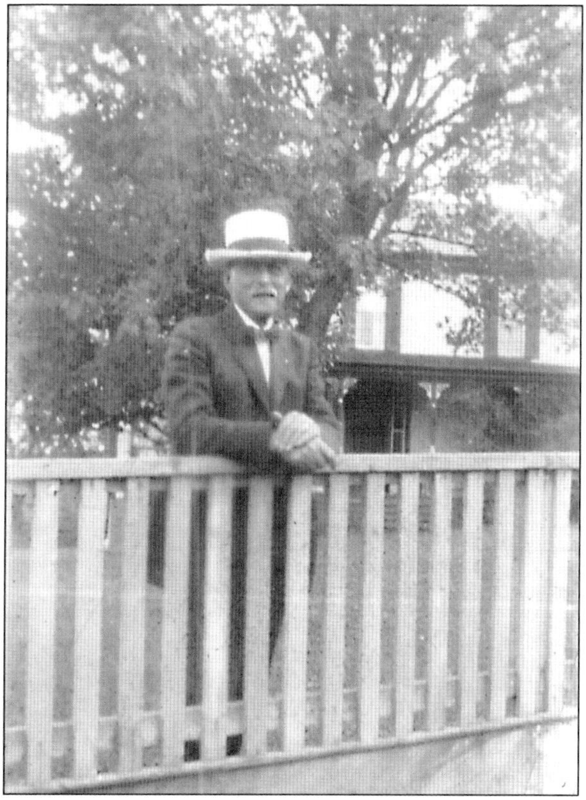

The Quidor family was well known in Highland County. Dr. Leroy Quidor was a physician based out of McDowell. After his death, his widow opened a millinery shop. Other famous members were Miss Ida and Miss Maime, who taught generations of schoolchildren, developing reputations as very stern but quality educators. (Courtesy of Kent Botkin.)

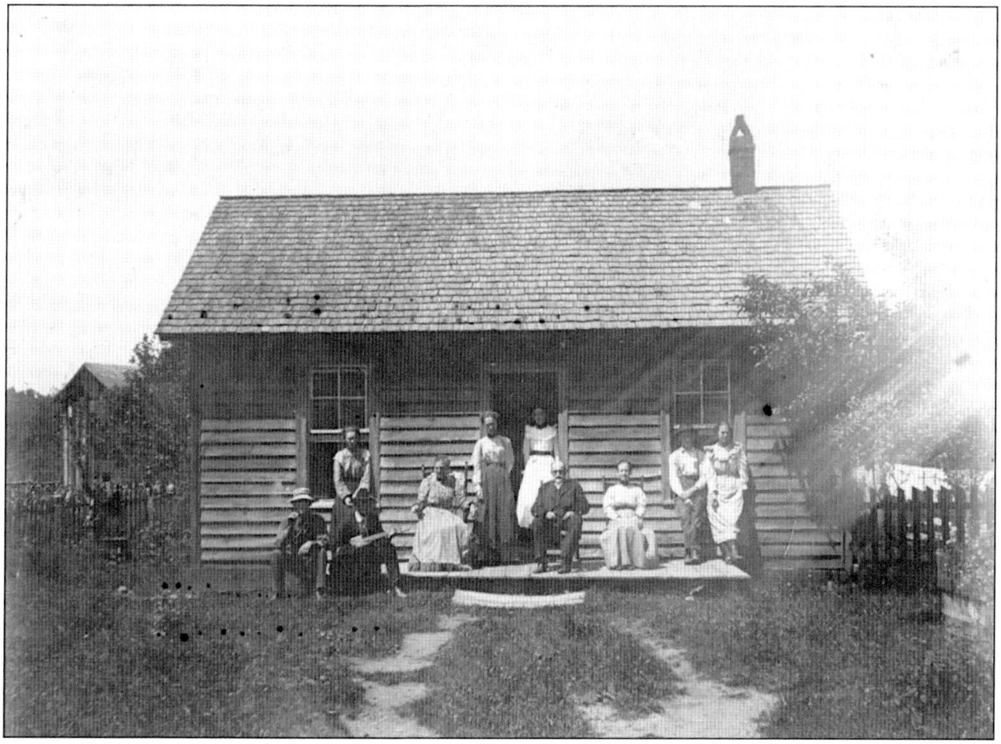

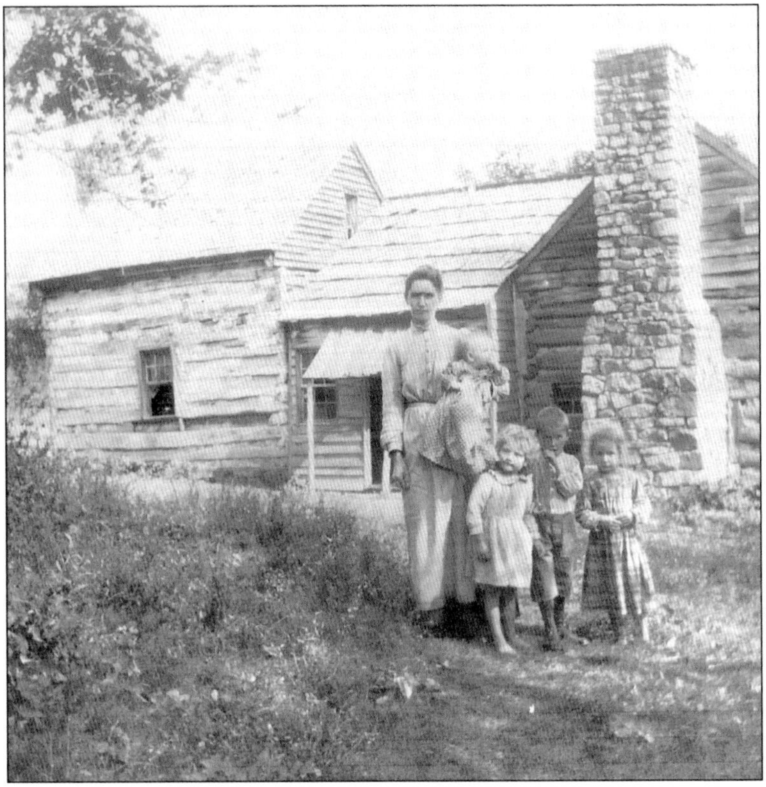

Frances M. Pullin Davis became the second wife of Andrew Salisbury Trumbo Davis on May 4, 1893. The couple had four children together: Susan Hazel in 1894, Andrew Salisbury in 1896, Martha T. in 1898, and William Robert in 1891. At their home on Davis Run in June 1902, they present the classic, hard-edged homesteading family. (Courtesy of Omar King and the Highland Historical Society.)

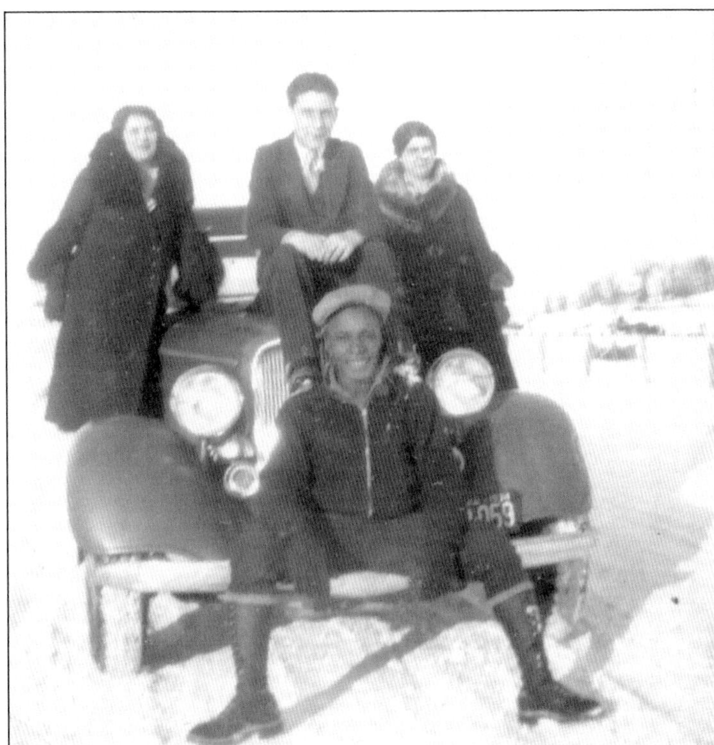

Friends pose on a car after a drive in the snow in 1934. Occupying the front is Ray Lewis. Ruby Woods (left), Dick Woods (center), and Mammie Woods sit in the back. (Courtesy of Libby Woods Hefner.)

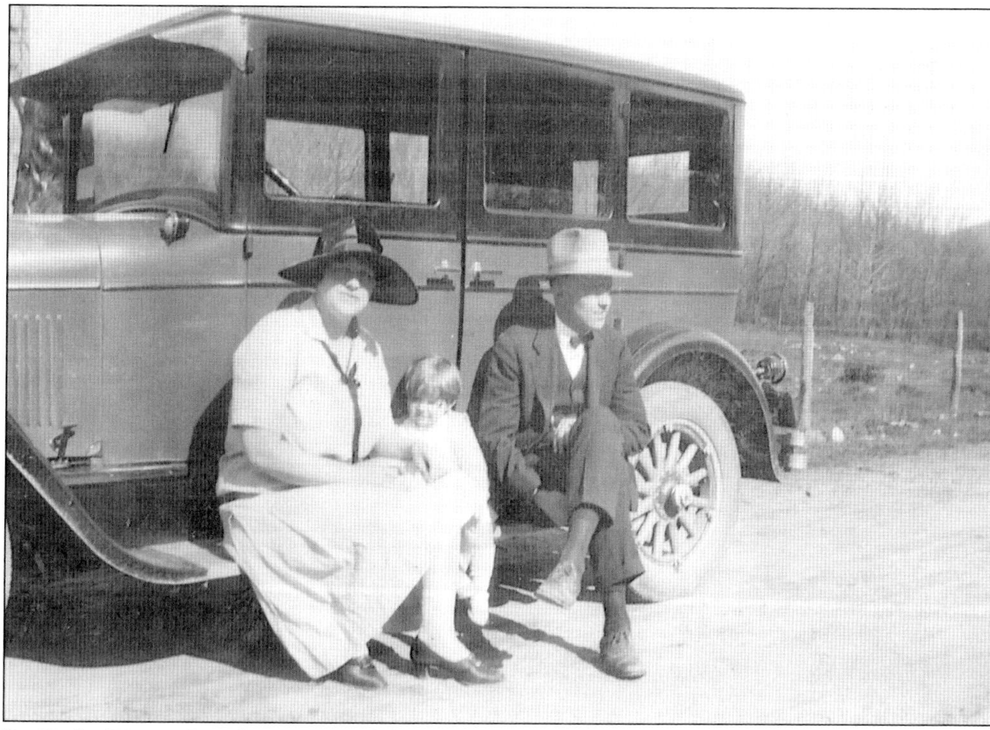

Dr. Berlie Trawic Swecker, seen with his wife, Lillian, was an extremely popular physician who practiced in the Blue Grass area. His son Ralph Hull Swecker went on to develop a dental practice in Monterey. (Courtesy of Janet Mullenax.)

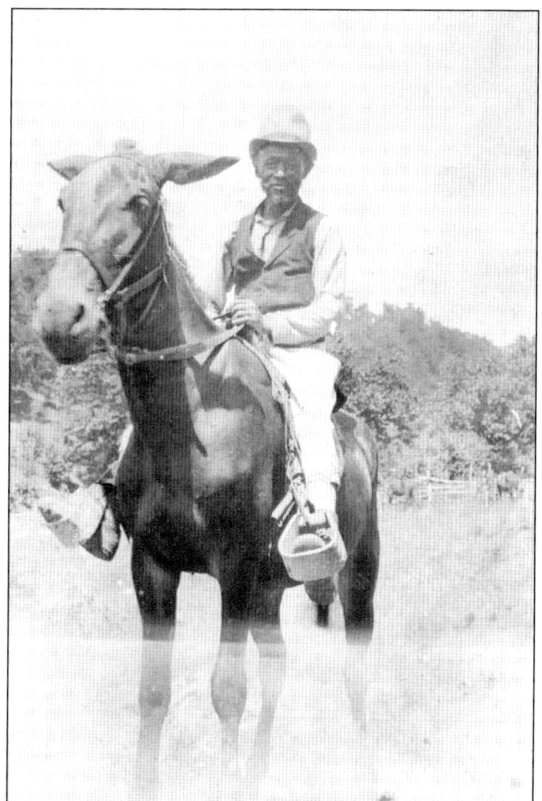

Born and raised in a log cabin, Charlie Smith lived on Bruce Vance's farm outside of McDowell. He worked on farms in the community, riding his mule up and down the roads. (Courtesy of Robin and Nancy Vance.)

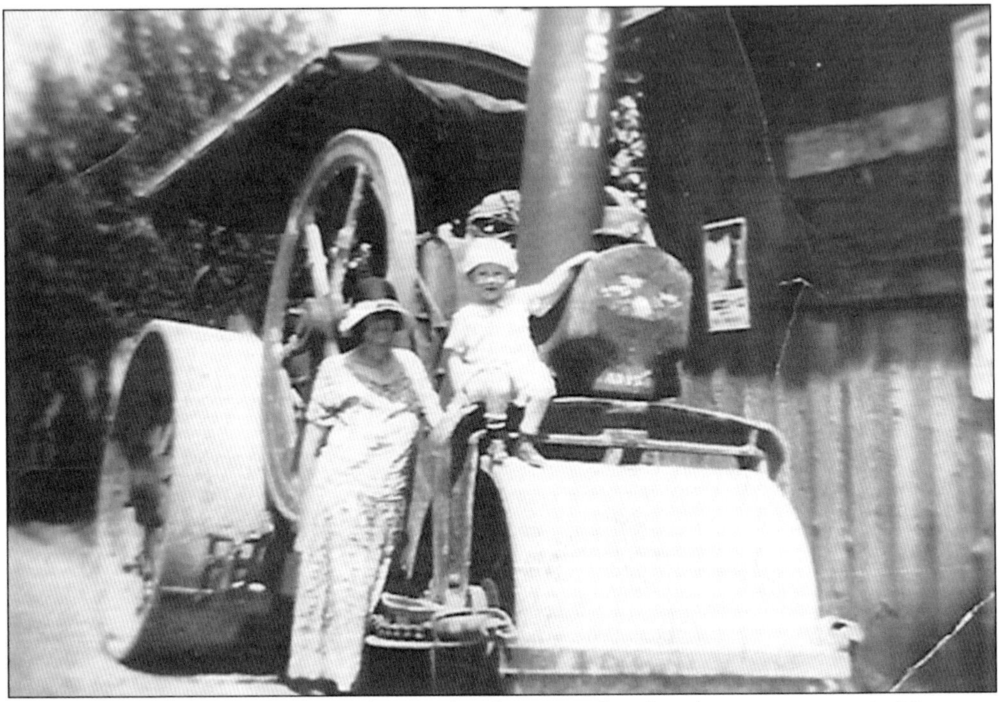

In 1925, Mary Vernon and her son John stand with a piece of road-surfacing equipment in Monterey. John entered the navy when he was 17, stationed on a hospital ship as a dental assistant in World War I. He remained in the navy and served in Korea in a field hospital. He died of ulcerated colitis in Florida at the age of 39. (Courtesy of Becky Sherwood.)

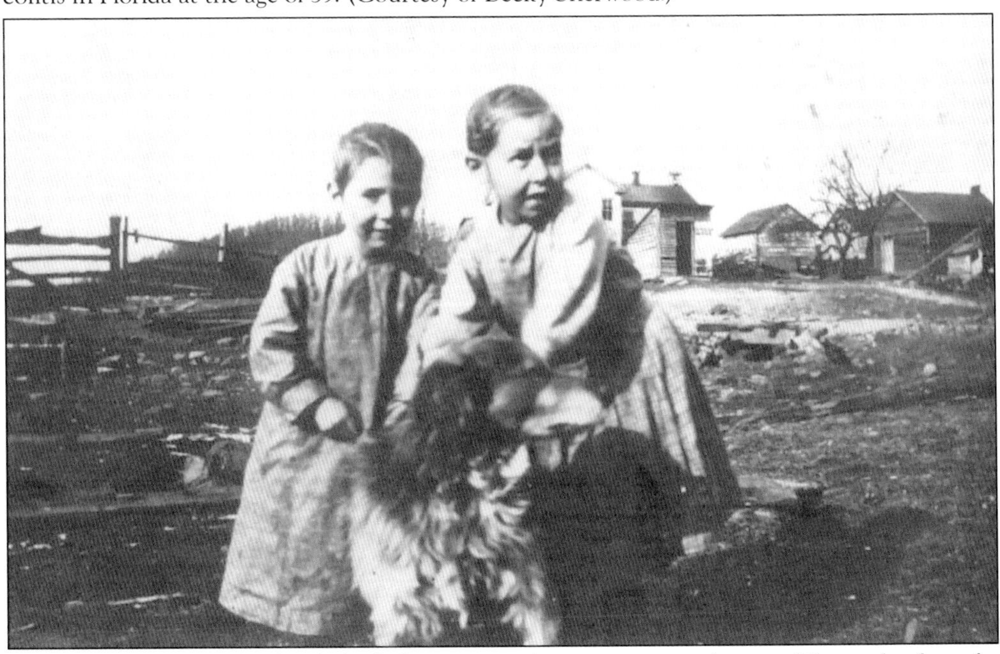

Though everyone in the family had chores to perform, no matter the age, life on the farm for children was not all work. Here Helen (left) and Josephine Vance play with their beloved pet dog. (Courtesy of Robin and Nancy Vance.)

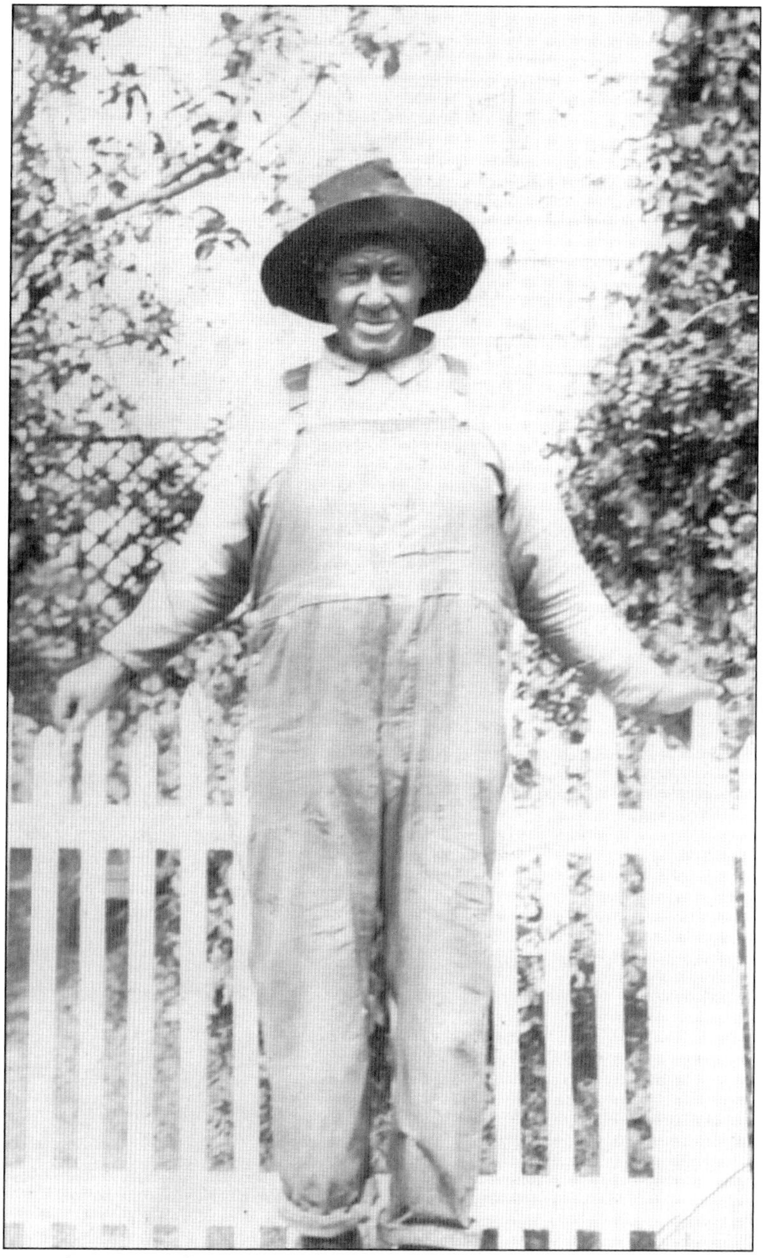

John Paul Brown, born in Hightown in 1858, carved out a life for himself that virtually confirmed the American story. He spent nearly 40 years of his life in Hightown before moving to Monterey in 1894. Prior to the move, Brown met and married Mattie Daugherty. They had four children. A blacksmith, Brown opened a shop in Monterey, where he worked daily until his death in 1937 at the age of 79. He became a pillar of the Monterey community, owning several pieces of valuable real estate over the years. One of the pieces is the lot on the corner of Routes 220 and 250, across from the Methodist church, where the post office stood for many years. During his tenure in Monterey, he was elected by the townspeople to several terms on the town council. After Brown's death, he was buried in the Thornrose Cemetery in Staunton, Virginia. (Courtesy of Kent Botkin.)

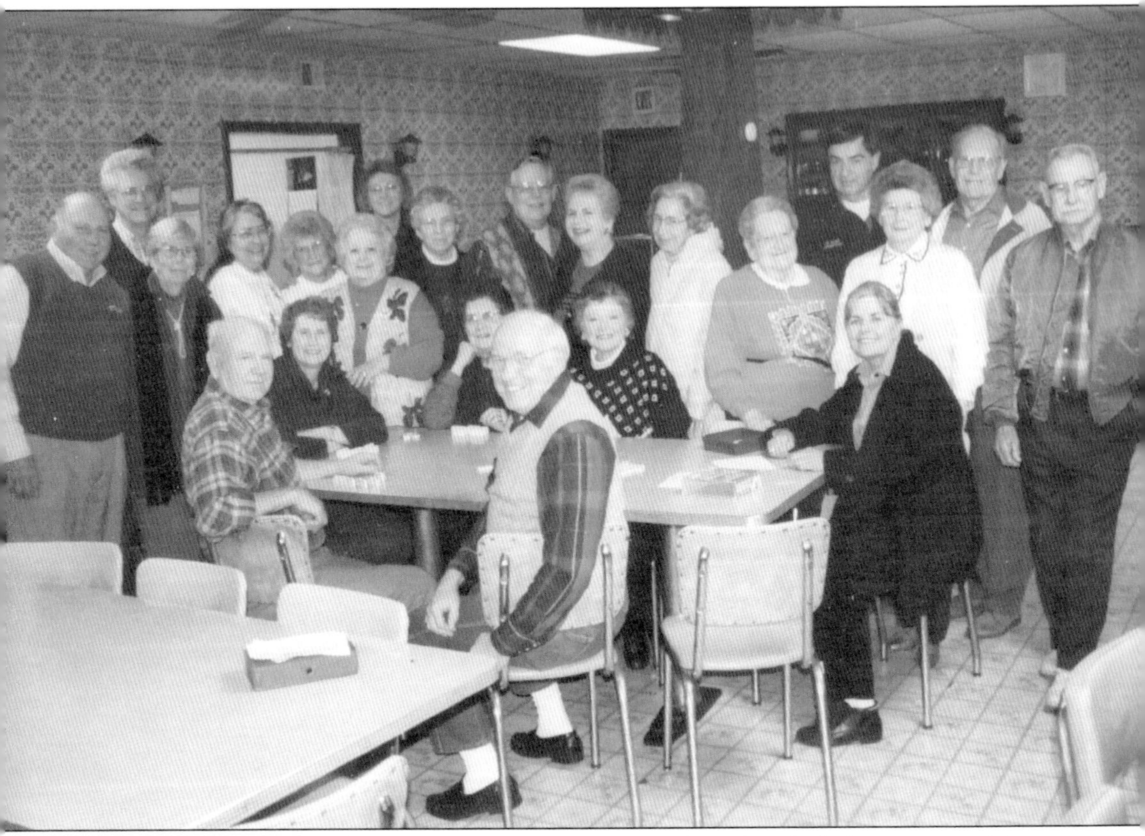

Known as the Chicken Foot Gang, this group met regularly at the Maple Restaurant in Monterey to play a domino variation called chicken foot. The Maple Restaurant was a fixture in downtown Monterey for years. One of the oldest restaurants in town, it served home-cooked meals for more than 35 years, with specialties including rainbow trout. Pictured from left to right are the following: (first row) Francis Fenn, Norma Reynolds, Jessie Lee Hiner, Pat Patterson, Anne Tesh, and Pat Adams; (second row) Ben Bocchicchio, Melvin "Bucky" Reynolds, Mary Bocchicchio, Kathy Patterson, Gaye Herold, Lillian Dever, Jackie Stephenson, Norma Jean Echard, Bill Ellenburg, Mary Ellenburg, Pat Niswander, Mary Hammer Swietzer, J. Harry Tesh, Delores Fenn, Garland Dever, and Bill Niswander. (Courtesy of the Highland County Historical Society.)

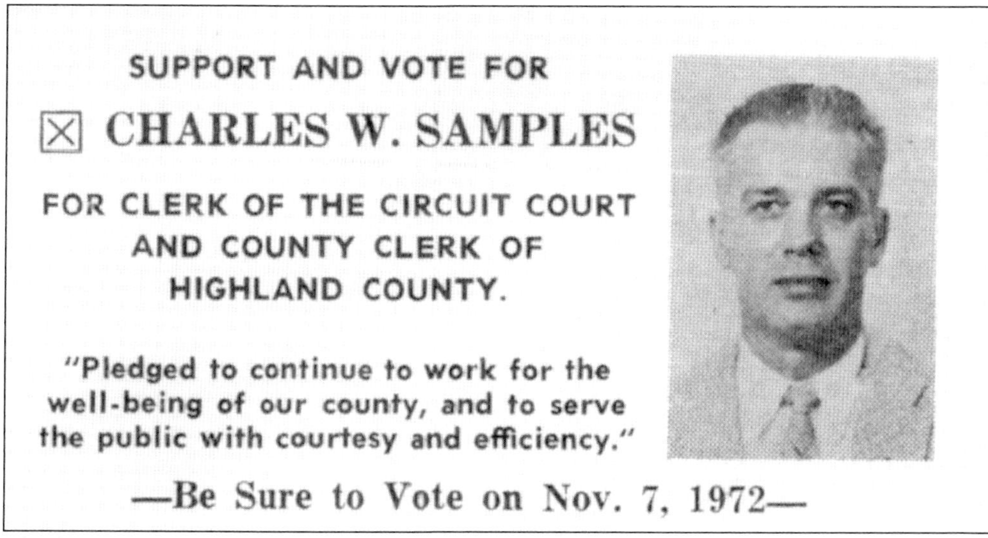

Charles W. Samples served as clerk of courts for Highland County from 1972 to 1975. He was appointed to fill an unexpired term and then needed to stand for reelection by the citizens of the county. This campaign card is from that election. He won the contest but did not run again. Previously Samples had worked as a schoolteacher. (Courtesy of Sarah Samples.)

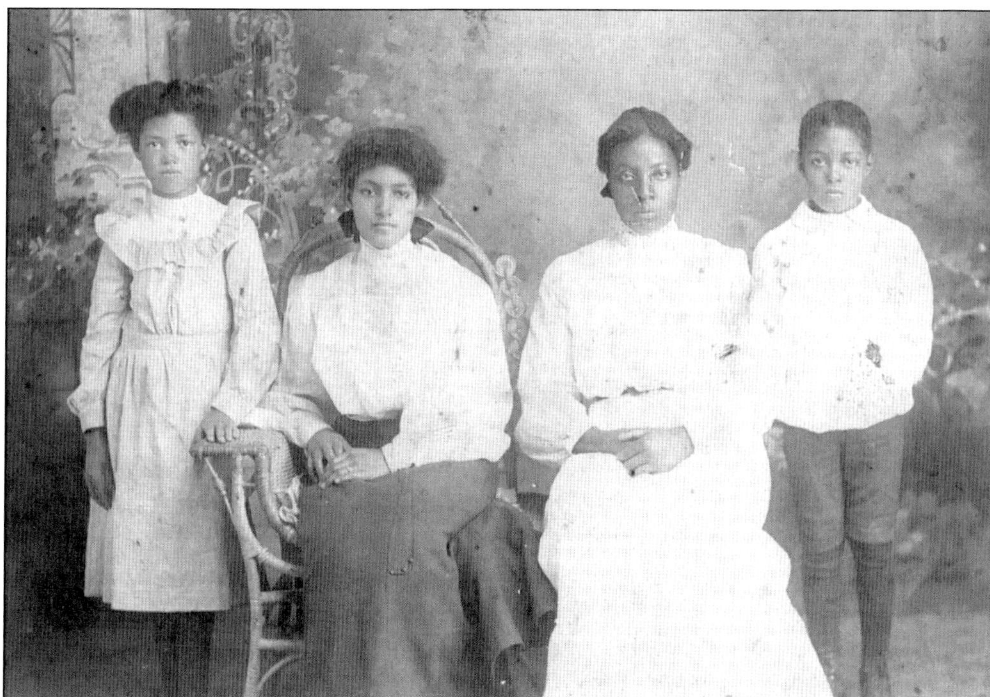

In this photograph, taken in September 1907 at Suddarth Studios, the children of John Paul and Mattie L. Brown of Monterey pose for a family portrait along with a friend. Shown here from left to right are Elsie A. Brown (age 11), Janet V. Brown, Myrtle Skuggs (age 23), and John Brown. (Courtesy of Kent Botkin.)

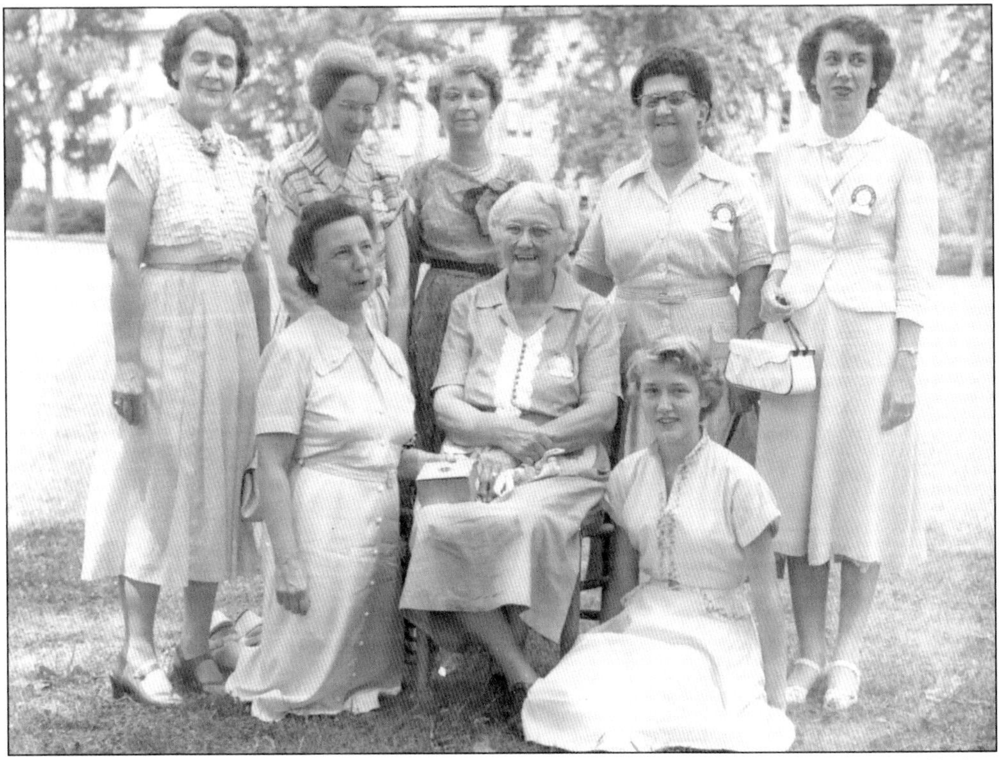

At the Rural Institute of Rural Affairs, held at Virginia Tech in Blacksburg, a group of ladies enjoys a laugh. Pictured from left to right are the following: (first row) co-extension agent Virginia Rubish, Fannie Samples, and Mary Kay Hull; (second row) Edna Jenkins, Mable Hiner, Emma Hevener, Jess Hiner, and Mary Catherine Smith. Mary Kay Hull was the 4-H winner that year. (Courtesy of the Highland County Historical Society.)

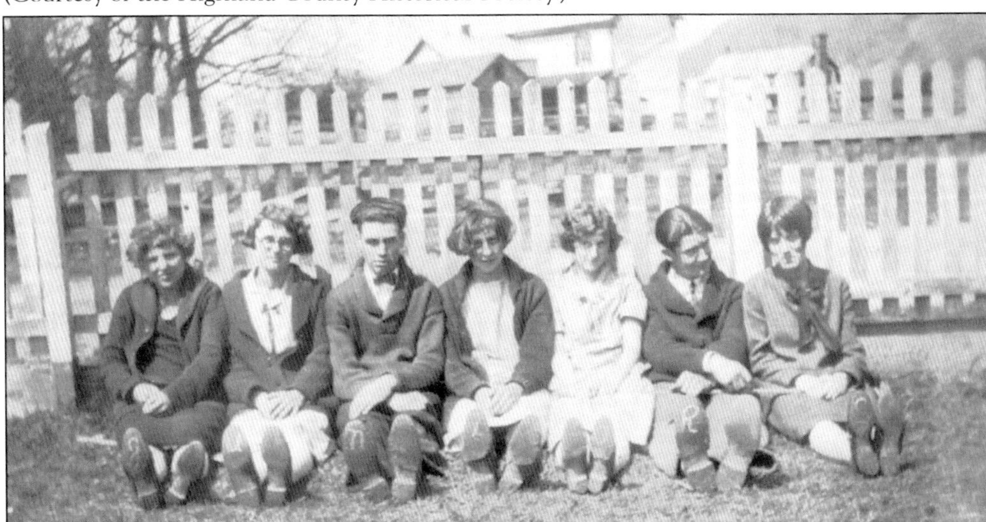

People always enjoy the company of good friends and some time in the sun. Sitting along a fence in McDowell, from left to right, are Hattie Siron, Vernon Simmons, Melvin Ralston, Josephine Vance, ? Shumate, Malcolm Lacy, and Charlotte Bradshaw. (Courtesy of Robin and Nancy Vance.)

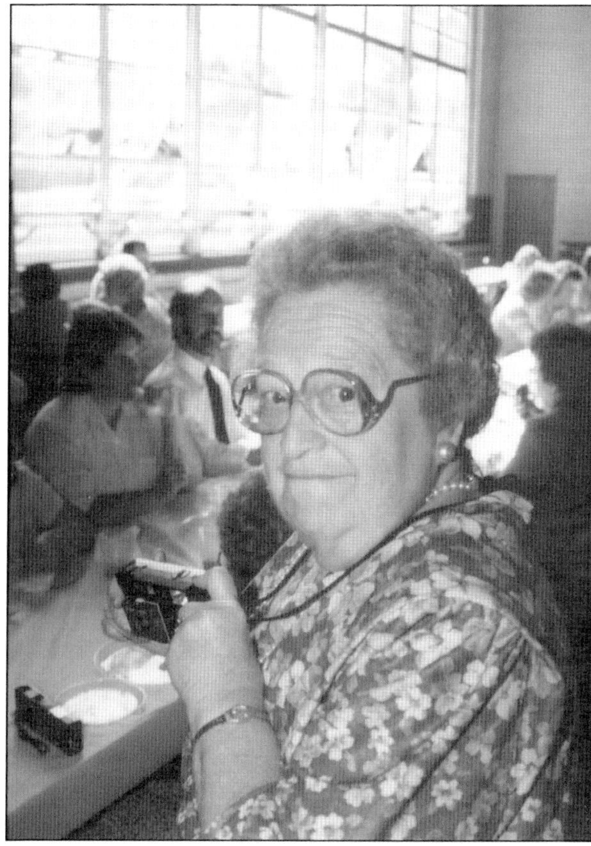

A business owner, factory manager, newspaper reporter, radio personality, and local historian, Mary Hammer Swietzer inserted herself into every aspect of Highland County life. Well known in the county, she married Ernest Taft in 1943. The couple lived in Staunton for several years before moving back to Highland in 1951. (Courtesy of the Highland County Historical Society.)

BIBLIOGRAPHY

Morton, Oren F. *History of Highland County Virginia.* Baltimore, MD: Regional Publishing Company, 1985.

The New History of Highland County, Virginia 1983. McDowell, VA: Highland Historical Society, 1983.